THE HOUSE OF THE SINGING WINDS

In the Kitchen, 1911, 24 by 20 ins.
Private Collection

THE LIFE AND WORK OF T. C. STEELE

THE HOUSE
OF THE SINGING WINDS

SELMA N. STEELE · *THEODORE L. STEELE* · *WILBUR D. PEAT*

Indianapolis
INDIANA HISTORICAL SOCIETY
1966

The paper in this book meets the guidelines for permanence and durability of the Committee on Production Guidelines for Book Longevity of the Council on Library Resources. Glatco Matte is a fully coated
alkaline paper designed for printing type and illustrations with clarity, depth, and uniformity.

Library of Congress Cataloging-in-Publication Data

Steele, Selma N. (Selma Neubacher), ca. 1870-1945.
  The house of the singing winds : the life and work of T.C. Steele / Selma N. Steele, Theodore L. Steele,
  Wilbur D. Peat.—[2nd, rev. ed.]
      p. cm.
    Includes index.
    ISBN 0-87195-053-7 (cloth)—ISBN 0-87195-055-3 (paper)
    1. Steele, Theodore Clement, 1847-1926. 2. Painters—Indiana-Biography. I. Steele, Theodore L.,
  1905-   . II. Peat, Wilbur David, 1898-1966. III. Title.
  ND237, S68S7   1990
  759.13—dc20
  [B]   90-36786
                                                                                CIP

FOREWORD TO 1990 PRINTING

THEODORE CLEMENT STEELE, one of Indiana's renowned artists, was praised for his detailed portraits and later for his impressionistic landscapes. He was pivotal in the shaping of the Brown County Art Colony and the development of Hoosier art. Today the increasing interest in American Impressionism and regional art reaffirms Steele's significance to the arts in Indiana.

The House of the Singing Winds, originally published by the Indiana Historical Society in 1966, gives a detailed account of T. C. Steele's life and work. Its seventy-six illustrations demonstrate his importance to the art world in his time and ours. The personal description of his life in the late nineteenth and early twentieth centuries is an important addition to the historical and cultural heritage of the people of Indiana.

This new printing was made necessary by the continuing demand for information about T. C. Steele. It has presented the Indiana State Museum System, under the auspices of the Indiana Historical Society, with the timely opportunity to rephotograph sixty-two of the seventy-six original paintings. Modern photographic techniques and improved painting conservation have produced museum-quality illustrations. The text is unchanged from the first printing; legends for illustrations have been updated for accuracy.

Without the generous donations of Hanus J. and Kirsten Grosz, Mrs. Erwin C. Stout, and the Indiana State Museum Society, this project would have been impossible.

The assistance of many institutions and individuals proved to be essential. First and foremost, we acknowledge the efforts of the three project coordinators: Claudia Kheel, curator of fine arts of the Indiana State Museum; Rachel Perry, assistant curator of the T. C. Steele State Historic Site; and Lisa Higbee, former education specialist of the Indiana State Museum. Their responsibilities included locating all of the paintings, coordinating the photography sessions, and raising the funds necessary to underwrite the photography. Their dedicated hard work and enthusiasm ensured the completion of this project.

Our thanks to Thomas A. Mason, director of publications; J. Kent Calder, editor; Tony Woodward, art editor; and Ray Boomhower, public relations

Foreword to 1990 Printing

coordinator, of the Indiana Historical Society for their whole-hearted support. We are indebted to Linda Badger, collections manager; Jeff Tenuth, registrar; and Melanie Maxwell, media relations specialist, of the Indiana State Museum for their patience, hard work, and encouragement. We are especially grateful to David Mannweiler, Elaine Ewing Fess, and Stephen Fess for their diligent help in tracking down paintings and to Theodore L. Steele for his unending enthusiasm and aid throughout the project.

We would like to thank the institutions who permitted the photographing of their paintings. Martin Krause, curator; Susan Bowles, coordinator of photo services; Stephen Kovacik, photographer; and Debbie Scott, assistant registrar, of the Indianapolis Museum of Art were particularly helpful. We appreciate the cooperation of Edward Quick, director of the Sheldon Swope Art Museum; Alaine Joyaux, director of the Ball State University Art Gallery; Pamela Bennett, director of the Indiana Historical Bureau; Sue Small, director of the Benjamin Harrison Home; Terry Phillips, vice president for business affairs, and President and Mrs. Russell Nichols of Hanover College; Lou DeBruicker, foundations secretary of the Columbia Club; Anita Martin, archivist at Eli Lilly and Company; Bonnie Hill, university curator of Indiana University; Sharon Theobold, executive director of the Greater Lafayette Museum of Art; Gary Yarrington, curator of the Lyndon Baines Johnson Library; and Mary Ann Eckhart, secretary of the Butler University Library.

We are also grateful to Format Incorporated, particularly Jeff Fewell, photographer, and Vice President Wayne Williams for handling most of the photographic work and remaining cheerful throughout the hectic scheduling. We offer very special thanks to the many individuals who allowed us to borrow priceless works of art from their homes to be photographed and to the entire Steele family for their kind support. And finally, we thank the many enthusiasts who have visited the T. C. Steele State Historic Site (formerly the T. C. Steele Memorial) in Brown County and shared in T. C. and Selma's vision of "the sanctuary of the future." Their encouragement was a constant source of motivation.

RICHARD A. GANTZ
Executive Director
Indiana State Museum and Historic Sites

FOREWORD

IN THE FALL OF 1964 Professor R. Carlyle Buley, of Indiana University, handed Mr. Eli Lilly a manuscript copy of "The House of the Singing Winds," by Selma N. Steele, wife of the painter Theodore Clement Steele. Mr. and Mrs. Lilly read with much pleasure Mrs. Steele's reminiscences which cover the "Brown County period" of Mr. Steele's life and work, extending from 1907 until his death in 1926, and Mr. Lilly suggested that the Indiana Historical Society consider publication of the manuscript. From this suggestion the present volume has evolved.

Professor Donald F. Carmony, of Indiana University, who held publication right to Mrs. Steele's manuscript, generously relinquished it to the Society. Theodore L. Steele, grandson of the artist, agreed to write a biographical sketch of his grandfather, concentrating on his life down to 1907, the year of his marriage to Selma Neubacher. Theodore L. is the son of Brandt T. Steele, the elder son of Theodore C. Steele by his first marriage. Wilbur D. Peat, director emeritus of the John Herron Art Museum in Indianapolis, was asked to assist in the selection of the paintings to be reproduced for illustrations and to prepare a critique of the artist's work.

The original manuscript of Mrs. Steele's work is in the Lilly Library at Indiana University. It is reproduced herein, with minor editorial changes, in its entirety except for a few pages in the third section which are irrelevant to the theme of this volume. There is also some rearrangement of the material at the end of this same section.

The biographical sketch by Theodore L. Steele is based largely on papers collected by Brandt T. Steele, which include T. C. Steele's journals, notebooks, sketchbooks, and family correspondence.

The Society wishes to express its thanks to those individuals and institutions whose paintings are reproduced in this volume.

Many people have been called upon for assistance and information. Our thanks for aid in obtaining photographs are due to Ronald Buksbaum of the Lafayette Art Center, Garret J. Boone, Jr., of De Pauw University, Thomas L. Gordon of Hanover College, Harold K. McDonald of Wabash College,

Foreword

Milo Nadler of Indiana University, and William E. Story of Ball State University. Robert D. Starrett, director, and Charles Raney, custodian, Indiana State Museum, and Mr. and Mrs. Fabius Gwin, custodians of the T. C. Steele Memorial, were unfailingly co-operative. The help of the following individuals is also gratefully acknowledged: Wilmer H. Baatz and Mrs. Mary Craig, Indiana University Library; Eleanore Cammack, De Pauw University archivist; Mary E. Charlton and Dorothy Lower, Fort Wayne Public Library; Cecilia Chin, reference assistant, Art Institute of Chicago; Mrs. Erna F. Grimm, Waveland Public Library; Mrs. Alice P. Hook, librarian, Cincinnati Art Museum; Lee Hubbard, University of Missouri Library; Elfrieda Lang, Lilly Library, Indiana University; Anne I. Ni Castro, reference assistant, Cleveland Museum of Art; Jens Nyholm, librarian, Northwestern University; B. Joseph O'Neil, Boston Public Library; Mrs. Martha Scharff, St. Louis Public Library; Harold Teitelbaum, Chicago Public Library; Don Thompson, librarian, Wabash College; and Velma E. Weist, Huntington Public Library.

Special thanks are extended to members of the staff of the Indiana State Library, particularly to Mrs. Hazel Hopper, head of the Indiana Division, Mrs. Frances Macdonald, manuscripts librarian, Thomas C. Krasean, field representative, and Mrs. Carolynne Wendel Miller, head of the Genealogy Division, and to Miss Caroline Dunn, librarian of the Indiana Historical Society.

Dorothy Riker, editor of the Indiana Historical Bureau, has been helpful in all phases of the project.

The grant from Lilly Endowment, Inc., in support of this publication is gratefully acknowledged by the Indiana Historical Society.

GAYLE THORNBROUGH
Editor

CONTENTS

ILLUSTRATIONS

PLATES

FIGURES

Illustrations

THE LIFE

THE LIFE

BY THEODORE L. STEELE

1

THE YEAR WAS 1847. The warm dry breeze of an Indiana autumn rustled through the ripening corn and moved softly across the fields and through the patches of woodland bordering the ravines and the streams of Owen County; cloud shadows moved slowly over the rolling hills; cicadas filled the air with their vibrant, pulsing drone.

Occasionally from the farmhouse came the faint sounds of a baby crying fretfully for a moment. He had been born on September 11—Theodore Clement Steele they named him—the first child of Samuel and Harriett Steele.

Here in the rolling hills he spent his childhood, scuffled through dewy meadows fragrant with pennyroyal, roamed through shadowed woodlands; here he learned of the joys and sorrows of life in the birth of his brother Charles and of his sister Hester Ann who lived not quite a year; here he saw pleasure taken in labor and skillful workmanship. Here he grew through a childhood that still glowed in his memory, when, late in life, he wrote: "As we moved away when I was only four years old my memory of this early home is very meager. The little log house in an orchard where it seems to me it was always morning and the sun always shining, the spring and my grandfather's brick house a mile away are about all the memories I have of this early home."

This child would grow to manhood and return again and again to the hills and streams of southern and western Indiana for inspiration. He would become a painter of renown who would build a home in the hills of Brown County where each day he would stand reverently before the beauty of nature he saw around him. And he would leave an inestimable legacy of that beauty in his paintings to give pleasure and peace and solace to the souls of men for generations.

He came from a hardy breed of men, men who spearheaded western mi-

3

gration and who with their sweat, and even their blood at times, conquered the frontier. They were men like his great grandfather Ninian Steel,[1] born on the family plantation of Thunder Hill in Chester County, Pennsylvania, who with axe and plow and Bible not only wrested a home from the wilderness but brought the Presbyterian church to the frontier in Indiana Territory. They were men like his great grandfathers Andrew Evans and Captain Samuel Newell, who fought the Cherokees and distinguished themselves at the Battle of King's Mountain on the Carolina frontier—a battle considered by many to be the turning point in the Revolution; men who later took part in the governments of Tennessee, Kentucky, and Indiana. And there was Mary Armstrong, his thrice great-grandmother, who at the age of over seventy crossed the mountains from North Carolina with her family, and reestablished herself as a "yeoman," a farmer, near Harrod's Fort in Kentucky.

The descendants of these pioneer families were numerous in the prospering farms north and northwest of Gosport when Theodore Steele was a child. Harriett Steele handed down many of the characteristics of her people to her sons. She herself was apparently like them in many ways; tall and slender; calm, courageous, and dauntless in adversity; and judging from her letters late in life from Oregon—where the family's western migration finally terminated—she was also sensitive and responsive to nature.

Samuel Steele, too, carried on the traits of his family. Like his parents, he was a staunch and active supporter of the Methodist church. He was a craftsman, a saddlemaker, as well as a farmer, and his saddle shop was on the north side of the square in Gosport, four or five miles east of the farm on which he lived.

In 1852 he moved his family to Waveland in southwestern Montgomery County, about fifty miles to the north. And at nearly the same time his parents, James Armstrong and Anna Johnston Steele, and his younger brother Armstrong T., who was studying at Asbury College in Greencastle not far away, also settled in Waveland. Within a few years Harriett's parents, Jesse and Hester Evans, as well as two of her sisters and two brothers and their families had joined them. This brought together a large family connection of Steeles, Evanses, Richardses, and Couchmans who lived near each other and worked, played, and went to school together.

Exactly what influenced these families to settle in Waveland is not known,

---

[1] Ninian Steel spelled his last name without the final "e".

but undoubtedly the high character of the little town, particularly its schools, was a major consideration in their decision to do so. They themselves had good educations—as good as the frontier schools provided—and wanted their children to have them as well.

Waveland Academy, which stood on the high bank of Little Raccoon Creek at the northeast edge of the little town, was one of the best of the numerous schools established in the late forties as interest in education revived. Though the original purpose of the Crawfordsville Presbytery in establishing it was to train youth for the ministry, the curriculum was changed and broadened in 1859, and the school was renamed the Waveland Collegiate Institute. It still prepared students for entering the junior year in college but also provided a three-year scientific course covering most of the subjects taught in the scientific curriculum in college. It drew an able and interesting group of teachers to the community.

Soon after settling in Waveland the Steeles became associated with the teachers at the Academy and those who were active in the affairs of the community. They lived near the edge of Waveland—down the hill, south of Main Street. There, on the north side of Cross Street, they owned a small plot of ground and just east of it was the land of Harriett's father. Samuel did well in his business and dealt in land occasionally. His saddle shop, it appears, and the store of his brother-in-law were in the center of the town, at the northeast corner of Cross and Howard streets.

Three sons were born to the Steeles after they moved to Waveland: William Jesse, Altice Howe, and Samuel Ninian. But their daughters born in that period died in infancy: Ida Bell, before reaching her second birthday, and Mary Hattie, when she was less than two months old.

Long afterward T. C. Steele wrote about these Waveland years: "It is with pleasure and thankfulness that I recall this little town, a village of five or six hundred inhabitants, where my childhood and youth were spent. It had the usual village stores and blacksmith's and wagon and carriage shops typical of the period, but it was a community of more than ordinary intelligence and situated in a charming and pleasant country of prosperous farms."

It was typical of him to bring to mind and speak of the good aspects of those years and not dwell upon sad memories—but there were many. In the decade of the fifties two of the family group other than the three little girls had died, Harriett's mother in 1854, and Samuel's father in 1855. But the greatest tragedy of all to the family was the death of Samuel Steele himself

5

on August 16, 1861, at the age of thirty-eight. Harriett, only thirty-eight herself, was left with their five sons, the youngest, Samuel, one month old, and Theodore, the eldest, not quite fourteen. Before long, she and the children would bear one more sorrow, the death of her husband's mother in October, 1862.

When Samuel Steele's estate was finally settled three years after his death, there was little or nothing left for his family. Fortunately, Harriett's father and sisters lived nearby and helped them through the difficult years that followed.

In the fall of 1859, two years before his father's death, Theodore Steele entered the Waveland Collegiate Institute. The curriculum for the first-year students in the Preparatory Department in which he was enrolled was this: "Spelling, Fourth Reader, Spencerian Penmanship, Object lessons on Forms and Colors; Elements of Numbers; Drawing on Slates; Oral Geography; Composition & Vocal Music."

Though he had taught himself to draw long before that time and by then was far advanced, it was probably in the classes at the Institute that he received his first formal training in drawing. His interest and ability must have been apparent to his teachers, because the next year, when he was only thirteen, he himself was teaching drawing to his fellow students. And in 1865, when he was eighteen and a student in the collegiate department, the catalogue for the school listed him, T. C. Steele, as the teacher of Drawing and Painting in the preparatory department. Three years later, in 1868, he was graduated.

During his student days young Steele painted a number of portraits, some from life, apparently, and others from photographs. He began painting in oil as early as 1863 when he was sixteen and from then to 1870, as recorded in his journal, he completed at least forty portraits. Many were of his family and friends in Waveland, but an equal number were of people in other towns, principally in Lafayette and Rushville, but also one or two in Peru, Rensselaer, Delphi, Attica, and Greencastle. One was of himself and another was of his fellow student Libbie Lakin. Mary Elizabeth was her name, but everyone called her Libbie or Bess.

It was probably in 1867 that Libbie and Theodore met. She was seventeen on the 22d of February that year, a slender girl with attractive delicate features despite her slightly aquiline nose. She was a little taller—five feet four inches it is said—than her Indian pony that she rode at a gallop over the neighboring roads and meadows—her large dark brown eyes flashing joyously and her black hair flying in the wind.

All in nature was a delight to her and she enjoyed the sciences as much as music and poetry. Among her classmates who shared these interests were Stanley and John Coulter; and it was John whom she accompanied one summer in making a botanical survey in the region around Sugar Creek, north of Waveland. She shared her interests, too, with the quiet young teacher of art—tall and handsome, with dark brown hair—whose gray eyes seemed to be seeing everything about him with uncommon insight and pleasure.

She and Theodore walked and read together—Keats was a favorite poet. They enjoyed music and often sang as she played the piano. With her contralto voice and Theodore's baritone, they joined her older sister Laura and Theodore's cousin Joseph Richards—a soprano and tenor—in a quartet that was good enough to be asked to Crawfordsville and the neighboring towns to sing. Under these circumstances it was not long before they fell in love.

Libbie Lakin was born on February 22, 1850, near Rushville, Indiana. She was the second daughter of Adam Simmons Lakin and his wife Mary Cloud Matson, both of whom came from families of strong Methodist tradition. Among her people were men whose names are prominent in the annals of the church. There was her mother's grandfather, Philip Gatch, one of the first native American preachers to serve a circuit, who after retiring, broken in health by the rigors of his ministry, became a member of the first Constitutional Convention of Ohio and a county judge for twenty-two years. And there were her great grandfather, Joseph Lakin, a minister in Ohio, and his brother Benjamin Lakin of the Salt River and Shelby Circuit of Kentucky, who is said to have been the first to preach Methodism in Indiana Territory, in Clark's Grant across the Ohio River. The spiritual traits of these dedicated men appeared again in Libbie Lakin.

Adam Lakin and his family had moved to Greencastle from Rushville in the middle 1850's. There Mary Lakin died in November, 1862—when Libbie was twelve years old—soon after learning of her son Matson's death from wounds received in the battle of Richmond, Kentucky, in the Civil War. After the war Adam Lakin established a sawmill on the Neosha River in Kansas where he spent much of his time. While he was there his children, Laura and Libbie and their younger brother Charles and sister Minnie, lived and went to school in Waveland. All of them attended the Institute except Minnie who was too young at the time.

7

After completing her schooling in the early summer of 1869, Libbie went to live with her aunt and uncle, Kate and James Lakin, on the family farm just east of Rushville. In the fall Theodore visited her to make plans for their marriage. Since Libbie's sister Laura and Theodore's cousin Joseph Richards were to be married, too, they decided to have a double wedding. It took place in the Lakin home near Rushville on February 14, 1870.

Libbie and Theodore were the only members of their immediate families, except Adam Lakin, to remain in Indiana; and even they were to be away for several years. Adam Lakin returned to Rushville where his father Thomas Lakin and other relatives lived, and there he died in 1875. After their marriage Laura and Joseph Richards went to Kansas where many of the Evans and Richards families had gone upon leaving Indiana, and eventually Laura's brother Charles and sister Minnie followed them. About the time Theodore was married his mother and four brothers left Waveland and settled in Kansas with their relatives. Only his brother Charles remained there, however; William, Altice, and Samuel moved on west to Oregon a few years later, and by the early 1890's their mother had joined them. There on the West Coast she lived with her sons and their families until her death in 1908.

Just when Theodore Steele received his first portrait commission is not known, but it was probably in 1868 or 1869 after his graduation from the Collegiate Institute. It was at that time, too, that he studied painting briefly in Chicago and Cincinnati. At any rate, by 1870 he was earning his living as a portrait painter and his journal reveals that in January of that year he was doing work in Lafayette and Bainbridge, and during the month of February in Rushville.

Theodore and Libbie remained in Rushville for a few weeks after their wedding, and before they left for Battle Creek, Michigan, early in March, four more portraits had been painted. Orders for portraits apparently took the young couple to Battle Creek. They were hardly settled there when the first two, those of Mr. and Mrs. George Peters, were begun. These were followed immediately by one of another member of the Peters family. Gradually portraits were commissioned by other Battle Creek citizens, and to augment his earnings Steele also started a class in drawing. When there were no portraits to be done or classes taught, he painted studies of an ideal nature, did a "fruit piece," portraits of himself and Libbie, and a few landscapes.

Although he kept busy he must have been discouraged at times. There was little interest in art, and in spite of a vogue for portraiture, the demand for paintings was very limited. But he clung steadfastly to his decision to be a painter and was determined to be a successful one. He was aware of his ability and knew that nothing else would give him the joy he experienced from painting.

But there was more to it than that. Now there was Libbie to share his thoughts and hopes and fortunes, to inspire him, and to clear his vision with her deeply poetic and responsive spirit. He felt he could devote a lifetime of work to the search for beauty in nature and its interpretation in works of art. As memories of the last few years of teaching, painting, and dreaming passed through his mind, he felt that he should set down his thoughts about his work which he could "read over and over again at my pleasure," and in June, 1870, he wrote in his journal:

. . . with the review of the past come admonishments of the passage of time, of the flight of the days in which are folded, as the trees within the seeds, the issues of life. And then in my heart rises a grand purpose to make the present year richer in unfolding the grand things of life than the year that is passed and **gone** from my reach.

To do this requires a systematic devotion to the one object of my life, the bending of all things to the one. And this presupposes a clear understanding of the main object or purpose, so clear that there will be no mistaking it for a moment.

And now on this beautiful Sabbath of June, when the soft winds of heaven "run along the summits of the trees in music" and the sky hazy and filled with cloud shapes seems palpitant with beauty, when the whole earth wears a coronal of beauty, I feel the universal spirit breathing upon mine and am moved to re-dedicate myself to art, to art, the echo of the beautiful, and that my work may be more enlightened and successful, I will write in this my art journal such observations and suggestions whose record may be of benefit and satisfaction to me.

The first entry after this was:

The two great qualities that an artist must possess and that are essentially necessary to all who pass the point of mediocrity, are first an innate and deep love of the beautiful. Secondly mechanical skill. The first to conceive, the second to embody. And in his development, his efforts must be first to cultivate and refine his powers of conception and appreciation of the beautiful and second to train his hand until it instinctively, as it were, interprets in a material way, the products of the brain.

Such reflections naturally led to a yearning for a more congenial art environment than any middle western town offered, or even an eastern city, and for disciplined training under great masters. "Whatever advantages our eastern cities may possess for the study of art," he wrote,

9

they do not possess those of Paris or Rome or some of the German cities. The progress of American art in the last twenty years is indeed remarkable but it will be long years before any academy or gallery of art can possess the immense stores of valuable pictures that are contained in the Vatican or the Louvre. And then the American school of art is essentially landscape, few historical paintings of great merit and not an abundance of genre pictures. In genre and religious painting I think the field will widen. Taste is being cultivated and attention turned in that direction. However, the great body of the work that will be done in our country in the next twenty-five years other than landscape will be in the way of portraits. And artists though possessed with talent and inclination for better things, will have to content themselves with this, venturing into the field of genre and the historical as time and means will permit.

But I am straying from the point that prompted this discourse. It is now a settled plan of mine to visit Europe at the earliest possible period, and to spend two years in study there.

I am aware that difficulties are in my way that are great, but others possessing no more talent than I have, conquered them. And it is our part and portion here upon the earth to battle forever with difficulties. Especially is it so with him who adopts as his vocation a profession that ministers to the taste of man rather than his appetite, to his feeling for the beautiful rather than that for utility. So let me put it down as a fixed determination to visit Europe the coming summer.

Despite his determination it would be ten more years before a period of foreign study would be possible for him. But during that time it was never far out of his thoughts.

The Steeles stayed in Battle Creek until early in 1873. Two of their children were born while they were there. The first, a son, was born on November 16, 1870, and with high aspirations and romantic dreams they named him Rembrandt Theodore, but he soon was known as Brandt. The second child was a daughter, born July 7, 1872. She was named Margaret, but before long she, too, had another name. Daisy they called this little girl with her mother's dark brown eyes.

On their return to Indiana Steele painted several portraits in Rushville, including one or more of Libbie's grandfather Thomas Lakin (Fig. 1). By the end of the year they had come to Indianapolis and were living on Linden Street a few blocks north of Pleasant Run, and near the open country to the south. Steele opened a studio at No. 14 McDonald and Butler's Block located on the west side of Pennsylvania Street north of Washington.

Steele's cousin Major William J. Richards, seven years his senior and a veteran of the Civil War, had come to Indianapolis the year before from Lafayette where he had been associate editor of the Lafayette *Journal*. Now he was on the staff of the Indianapolis *Journal*. He eventually joined the staff of the Indianapolis *News* where he advanced rapidly, becoming business manager and for several years part owner of the paper. Richards and Steele held each other in high regard, and it is certain that Will did everything he could to help his cousin Theo establish himself in the city.

Another who showed an interest in young Steele when he first came to Indianapolis was Herman Lieber. Born in Düsseldorf in 1832, Lieber came to America in 1852 and to Indianapolis the following year. From a modest stationery and bookbinding business he developed a large art-related enterprise which included artists' materials, pictures, and the manufacture and sale of frames and moldings. It is not known when the two men became friends. Steele probably had purchased art supplies from Lieber's store long before he settled in the city. Now the H. Lieber & Company Art Emporium, located on the north side of Washington Street east of Pennsylvania, was less than a block from his studio, and no doubt Steele dropped in frequently for supplies and to chat with Mr. Lieber and his partner, Charles Koehne.

The Steeles were hardly settled in Indianapolis when the Panic of 1873 began to affect business, and it was not until 1879 that recovery from the depression which followed, described as of "unprecedented severity," became apparent. This meant difficult times for the young painter and his family. Fortunately, there were still a few people in Indianapolis and out in the state who could afford to have their portraits painted. And there were also others who were willing to exchange their services or their merchandise, or even board and room or farm produce, for portraits or other work from the artist's brush.

Steele exhibited his work whenever he had an opportunity at Lieber's store. But the Indiana Exposition held in connection with the State Fair in 1874 offered him his first opportunity to enter his work in a big show. It was an imposing exhibition. Copies and original works of some of the old masters as well as originals of contemporary artists were loaned by local patrons of art. On exhibit were works of a great number of painters from midwestern and eastern states and from as far away as Düsseldorf, Rome, Paris, and other art centers of Europe. It was an exciting occasion for Indianapolis, the most important exhibition held in the state up to that time, and it undoubtedly affected the tastes and broadened the cultural interests of the community.

Works by several Indiana artists were included. Jacob Cox had eighteen paintings, three of them portraits; Samuel Richards, then of Anderson, Indiana, had three including one portrait. Barton S. Hays had twelve including three portraits. Also represented were James M. Dennis, Theobald Lietz, Elizabeth Nicholson, Margaret Rudisill, and Lotta Guffin, all of Indianapolis. Steele showed fourteen portraits and two still lifes. Among the portraits were those of Jonathan M. Ridenour, president of the Indianapolis Journal Company; Charles E. Raymond, pastor of the Seventh Christian Church; Will Richards; and Liebermann I. and Solomon Mossler, proprietors of a clothing store at 37 East Washington Street. Steele received a gold medal for the two best original portraits in oil in the exhibition. It is not known which two were selected. The Indianapolis *Journal* of October 2, 1874, felt the award "undoubtedly just." It described Steele "as a young artist" who "has struggled with adverse circumstances from the outset, but through industry, patience, and application to his profession, has already risen to a proud eminence among Western artists, with fair prospects of going much higher before his career closes."

Steele did a great many portraits in 1875; among them one of his mother. Early in the year he was painting portraits of members of the Fletcher family of Indianapolis. Toward the end of January he had also commenced a portrait of a Miss Bratten and a few days later one of a Mr. Taylor whom he described in his journal as "a magnificent subject—grand in features like Angelo's Moses; hair and beard superb," the latter "angrily sandy and auburn." Early in February he painted a study of his son Brandt sleeping, finished the Taylor portrait and put it and one of Dr. William B. Fletcher on exhibit. Between the 9th of February and the end of March he was in Greencastle, and it was then that he painted portraits of Col. and Mrs. A. S. Farrow and Andrew and Elizabeth Lockridge. In March, after working on the portrait of "the elder Mrs. Lockridge," he jotted down in his journal a thought he wanted to keep in mind—one that reveals his pleasure in the experience of that day: "There are times when there seems to be to the artist a spiritual illumination when his spirit springs to the beautiful, and tasks he heretofore has been unable to accomplish become so easy that his work is the pleasant exercise of his power." And another day in a less serious mood he wrote: "Josh Billings says 'Every time a man laughs he takes a kink out of the chain of life and thus lengthens it.'"

Although the years in the mid-seventies were active and productive ones for Steele, they were accompanied by sorrow and illness. His third child—a boy—born then, lived but a short time. And it was probably in the summer of 1876, while the family was living in the quiet, tree-shaded suburb of

Irvington, that Libbie became seriously ill with typhoid fever. Their good friend Dr. Fletcher took her to his home, and there, under his care and that of his wife, she recovered. It was a long illness, however, and when she returned to her family the children hardly knew her, for the fever had caused her hair to turn from black to silver gray.

During the mid-seventies Steele frequently painted in other parts of the state. In 1874 he had returned to Rushville for a while and was often in Greencastle or back in Waveland and the neighboring countryside. During these years the Steeles lived in a number of places in Indianapolis. Late in 1874 they were at 47 Dougherty Street (now Woodlawn Avenue), and in the fall of the following year they were at 54 Spann Avenue. It is not known just how long Steele had his studio in McDonald and Butler's Block, but late in 1875 his address as a portrait painter was 82 East Washington Street, the store of H. Lieber & Company.

In 1876 the family moved to the Bradshaw Block at 73 West Washington Street. Their home was on the third floor, and it was there Steele also had his studio. On the first floor was the L. S. Ayres store, and on the second floor was the office and home of Dr. John E. Lockridge, the physician for the Deaf and Dumb Institute. The doctor and his wife, Lydia Margarita, had recently moved to Indianapolis from Augusta County, Virginia. They were older than the Steeles, but despite the difference in ages, they were drawn to each other through mutual interests and became close friends. The artist John Love also had his studio in the Bradshaw Block, next door to Steele's. He had just returned from Paris where he had studied for the past four years at the École des Beaux-Arts.

By this time Steele was enjoying something of a reputation as a portrait painter. He was described by a reporter on the local *Saturday Herald* as "a tall romantic-looking fellow," "an ideal artist in personal appearance, wearing his hair and whiskers long, after the manner of Bohemians generally," and "a general favorite with his fellow artists."

In January, 1877, he and John Love joined with a few others to form a short-lived Indianapolis Art Association—an organization which brought together some of the city's artists and patrons of the arts. It soon held an exhibition in which Steele's work was well represented. Though the Association did not last, interest in the arts and in art education was sustained. In October the Indiana School of Art, with James F. Gookins as director and John Love as assistant director, opened in Fletcher and Sharpe's Block at the southwest corner of Pennsylvania and Washington streets. Gookins, like Love, had studied painting in Europe—in the Royal Academy in Munich from 1870 to 1873—and had come to Indianapolis to join with Love in the founding of the school. In January, 1878, in an exhibition at the school, canvases by professionals, including Jacob Cox, Dewey Bates, Alois Sinks, and Steele, were shown. Work by the students was judged by Dr. William B. Fletcher, Herman Lieber, and Steele.

The following May a large loan exhibition of over two hundred canvases was sponsored by the school, with works by local artists and artists from the East. Ten portraits by Steele were exhibited which the Indianapolis *Journal* reported showed "a most extraordinary progress in his work during the last year." Portraits included were of Daisy (the artist's daughter), Dr. Samuel Davis, S. F. Lockridge, Alex Lockridge, Brandt (the artist's son), and James Whitcomb Riley.

But the most important happening in the Steele family during 1878 was the birth of another child, a son born July 15, who was named Shirley Lakin.

Before the end of the year Steele had moved his studio from the Bradshaw Block to Fletcher and Sharpe's Block. There the art activities and interests of the city seemed to center, and in this atmosphere Steele's deep longing for study abroad was sharpened. The enthusiasm of Gookins and Love for their experiences as students abroad undoubtedly influenced Steele and the other artists and students who went to Europe from Indiana in the eighties. They must have discussed together where they should study, how long they should plan to stay, and how they could manage it financially.

The years since Steele came to Indianapolis had not been easy. He had worked hard and continuously—painting portraits when he could, but also painting still lifes and making copies. There is a story, perhaps apocryphal, that during these hard times Steele joined the poet-to-be James Whitcomb Riley in painting signs; they worked together—Riley doing the lettering and Steele the ornamentation. It is known that Steele and Riley were friends and Steele's first portrait of the poet dates from this period. That Steele could earn enough money in those hard years of the seventies to provide for a period of foreign study seemed impossible. But no doubt he talked about it with Will Richards, Herman Lieber, and other friends, and clung to the dream that some day he could go.

It was probably in the late summer of 1879 that the family went to Stribbling Springs, a health resort in the Virginia mountains below Harper's Ferry.

Libbie had not been well and it was likely their Virginia friends, Dr. and Mrs. Lockridge, who recommended the place to them. It had a quiet, rather rustic atmosphere and sulphur springs, but to the Steeles it was the rugged mountain country through which they roamed and the pine-scented air that made the place forever memorable. They returned to Indianapolis in mid-October in high spirits and with Libbie's health much restored.

In the late fall of 1879 an opportunity for study abroad was presented to Steele by Herman Lieber. Just how the plan came about is not known, but it appears likely that Lieber developed it himself, or perhaps it was with the help of other of Steele's friends. At any rate, in November the plan had been agreed upon and on November 21, 1879, the following document was drawn up by Herman Lieber on a sheet of stationery of H. Lieber & Company:

Believing that Mr. Theodore C. Steele of this City possesses unusual talent as an artist, when the limited advantages he has enjoyed are considered, and that he only requires the benefit of study in European schools to develop into one of the first artists of this country and thus become an honor to Indianapolis and the State we hereby agree each to advance $100 to Mr. Steele, payable ¼ on or before July 1, 1880 and the Balance in 6, 12, and 18 months to enable him to spend one or two years in Europe in perfecting himself in his profession; in consideration of which Mr. Steele hereby agrees to repay the several amounts advanced in paintings from his own easel as soon as practicable after his return from abroad, guarantying satisfaction in each case.

Lieber and Dr. Fletcher were apparently the ones who obtained the pledges to the fund. Lieber was the first to sign, followed by Stoughton A. Fletcher, Albert E. Fletcher, Ingram Fletcher, Allen M. Fletcher, Laurel L. Fletcher (wife of Stoughton J.), John T. Brush, Francis M. Churchman, Stoughton J. Fletcher, Dr. William B. Fletcher, Emil Martin, Cyrus C. Hines, and — (?) M. Thompson.[2] Each pledged $100, making a total of $1,300.

With funds assured, Steele joined other European-bound Indiana artists

[2] Stoughton A., Albert E., Ingram, and William B. Fletcher were sons of the Indianapolis pioneer lawyer Calvin Fletcher. Stoughton A. and Francis M. Churchman were partners in the banking firm of S. A. Fletcher & Company. Albert E. and Ingram Fletcher were partners along with Thomas H. and Ebenezer Sharpe in the banking firm of Fletcher & Sharpe. William B. Fletcher was a physician in an office with W. H. Hubbard, and also a partner with Frank H. Carter in Carter & Fletcher, druggists. Allen M. Fletcher was a son of Calvin Fletcher's brother Stoughton A. At this time he was president of the Indianapolis Gas Light & Coke Company. John T. Brush was a member of the firm of Owen, Pixley & Company, a gentleman's clothing store. Stoughton J. Fletcher was a brother of Allen M., and in 1879 was serving as teller in S. A. Fletcher & Company. Emil Martin, a native of Germany, was a druggist. He later became president of the Indianapolis Chemical Company. Cyrus C. Hines was a lawyer and former circuit court judge, then a member of the firm of (Benjamin) Harrison, Hines & (William H. H.) Miller. Hines married Maria Fletcher, a daughter of Calvin Fletcher.

in making plans. It was decided that he and his wife and three children would go to Munich for two years where he would study at the Royal Academy and the two older children would attend school. During the seventies Munich as well as Paris had become a goal of American artists. Among those who had studied there and who may have had an influence on Steele were Indiana-born William Chase and Frank Duveneck of Cincinnati, as well as Gookins.

Libbie Steele entered into the arrangements with as much enthusiasm as her husband, and the prospect of keeping a family of five in a foreign land on a budget of $50.00 a month did not dim her eagerness for this new experience. Her letters and reminiscences have provided us with word pictures of their "Munich Idyll" comparable to the paintings of her husband.

In July, 1880, the Munich-bound group left Indianapolis and sailed from New York on the Red Star Line's *Belgenland* for Antwerp. On board were Theodore C. Steele, aged thirty-two years, his wife Libbie, then thirty, and their three children—Brandt, not yet ten years old, Margaret, who was eight, and the two-year-old Shirley; J. Ottis Adams; Samuel Richards and his wife Louise; August Metzner, an engraver associated with the William Burford Printing Company; and Miss Carrie Wolff.

2

WHERE THE RIVER SCHELDT widens to the sea, a great ship lay at anchor awaiting the tide which would take it into the harbor at Antwerp. The sun had set; the cloud banks broke up and floated out into the sky; several large vessels at anchor here and there came in beautiful relief against the west, and small sail-boats moved lazily over the water. In the tender twilight the scene was enchanting.

Then the night came down. Off in Holland, yellow lights gleamed like jewels in the velvety darkness. Something more of cheerfulness crept into the voices of the sailor lads as they sang at their tasks of making everything ready for the morrow's landing. Only a few hours and the voyage would be over.

When we awoke in the morning, light was breaking and Antwerp was in sight. Our sensations in those first hours were delightful, everything reminded us we were in the land of Art, the Mecca of our dreams, and we felt like a band of happy children. . . .[3]

The sea voyage afforded Steele a greatly needed rest. He had been overworked for the last six months, and until only two weeks before leaving Indianapolis he had been painting out of the city, most of the time in the western part of the state. The final arrangements that would permit him to be out of the country for two years had left him completely exhausted, but by the time the ship reached port he was rested and refreshed.

The Indianapolis party went to Cologne, then took a steamer up the Rhine, and nine days after landing at Antwerp the Steele family was settled in rooms in Munich near the Academy. Since classes did not start until October, Steele had an opportunity to explore the city and suburban villages and visit the galleries with his family and to do a little sketching.

When the Academy term opened Steele enrolled in the class of Gyula Benczur whom he described as one of the best draughtsmen in Munich. He studied life drawing for the entire year, working six to eight hours a day, from live models, laying a foundation for future painting. The remaining hours were spent in the Old Pinokothek copying the old masters. As the year passed he was conscious of the improvement in his work and rejoiced in his progress, but at the same time felt keenly the need for continued study and instruction.

In the spring Steele grew uneasy over his financial situation. Some of the people who had subscribed to his fund were slow in making their payments.

[3] Quoted from Mary E. Steele, *Impressions* . . . (Indianapolis, The Portfolio Club, 1893). For a description of this volume see below, p. 38.

17

The family simply could not live on less than the $50.00 a month he had budgeted and in March in desperation he turned to Herman Lieber and Dr. Fletcher. Again they responded generously, and in July, assured of being able to stay for another year, Steele wrote them, thanking them and their friends for their help "which is tenfold more valuable now than it would be later."

An exhibition of the students' work was held in July at the close of the school year. On the basis of his first year's work, Steele was promised a place in the painting class of Professor Ludwig von Loefftz the next year—just the place he wanted to be, for Loefftz's instruction was regarded as being far ahead of that of other masters in the Academy.

Throughout the winter the great city of Munich had provided endless diversion. In her *Impressions* Libbie wrote of it:

Munich is an eloquent city. Go in whatever direction you may, there is something to appeal to you. . . .

Naturally it was in the picture galleries where we spent most of our leisure time. The Old Pinokothek had a charm for us that no other place possessed. How many hours we spent feasting our eyes on the wonderful pictures by Rubens. No modern master can cover such great canvases with such tremendous forms.

And then the glorious color of Titian; the refinement and eloquence of Van Dyck; but it was Rembrandt who enchanted us. . . .

From color and form on canvas, to their corresponding qualities in the realm of sound, is but a step and there never was a day in Munich that one could not hear the best of music.

The opera, consecrated by the genius of Wagner, is world famous. The Odeon and numerous other concert halls testify to the high music culture, but outside of these it is a strong element in the life of the people.

Every day, between twelve and one o'clock, the band belonging to the royal guards, played in front of the *Rath Haus* in Marien Platz, while the guard was being changed. . . .

We went very often to the churches to hear the music. . . .

As summer neared they were anxious to get out of the city into the country. Since Steele would be free from July to October, they had planned to spend some weeks in the village of Schleissheim, six miles north of the city. But in June Daisy became seriously ill with scarlet fever, and it was not until late in the summer that she had become well enough for the family to leave town.

In the village of Schleissheim the well-known Boston landscape painter Frank Currier had lived and painted for twelve years, and it was Steele's intention to spend the weeks until October working under his direction. The

Steeles had fallen in love with the little village when they had made a day's excursion there shortly after coming to Munich. Some years later Libbie recalled this visit in her *Impressions:*

It was a dreamful August day when we first saw Schleissheim, and as we passed from the station down a carriage way lined with trees, through an archway into the great court of the old castle and over a stream of purling water so clear we could see the pebbles on the bottom and the fish swimming about, we felt deliciously happy, such a contrast was it all, to the narrow streets and high walls of the city.

The artists were in raptures over the color and picturesqueness of everything, and were continually finding *motifs* that drew from them exclamations of joy.

We went to the royal residence and spent some time looking through the gallery of pictures; sauntering through the lofty rooms; enjoying the fine tapestries; the rich mosaic of the floors; the grand entrance hall, with its famous marble stairway and stately columns of green porphyry.

Out in the park, where Nature and Art combine to make one of the most winsome spots on earth, we found Mr. Currier and Mr. Wenban, making charcoal studies of the mossy old Castanea trees, which line the walks.

Down through the long vistas of the *Allee* we could see the white walls of the hunting castle; the air was filled with melodious notes of myriads of birds; the cry of the cuckoo floated from the forest beyond, much to our entertainment, but to the disgust of Mr. Currier and his friend, who had long ago grown tired of the monotonous song. But in spite of the cuckoo it was idyllic painting ground, and we returned to Munich that night perfectly in love with Schleissheim.

Its nearness to Munich—six English miles—made Schleissheim a desirable suburban residence, and many artists spent their summers there, while a few lived there the year round. Mr. Currier had his school of landscape at Schleissheim— that is, Mr. Currier worked out there with some fifteen or twenty other Americans, he being the leading spirit.

During the day these artists would be scattered up and down the village streets; in the *Hof-Garten,* out on the moor, and even in the lesser villages of Unterschleissheim, Mittenheim and Lustheim. But at night, if you should have happened into the Hochenrieder inn, you would have found them sitting around a table sipping beer, and discussing the day's work.

The wealth of artistic material that Steele had found in Schleissheim and the nearby villages, the moors, and fields had called him back during the Easter holidays and again in June, when he made studies of the quaint houses and the hunting lodge. When the family finally settled there in the late summer the quiet charm, the parks, and open country around the village seemed to offer them so much more than the city, that they decided to stay on through the winter. When the Academy opened, Steele returned to Munich each day by train. In October Libbie was writing to her Indianapolis friend Mrs. Lockridge that "the cold weather has taken most of the Americans back to town. There are three left besides our family. In the morning [October 17] the academy opens for the year and Theo will have only a little time at home. He goes in town at seven o'clock in the morning and returns in the evening."

Until the spring of 1882 the Steeles lived in rooms formerly occupied by William Chase, Frank Duveneck, and Frank Currier. Previously, so the story went, they had been occupied by a Russian glass worker, and the house and garden were thereafter referred to as the "Russian Garten" or "Russian Villa." "The house and garden are just going to ruin," wrote Libbie to Mrs. Lockridge. "The fountains are still, the paths overgrown. There is a mournful feeling of neglect over all. It is much more interesting to an artist now for there is no interest in well kept things to them, and several American artists have lived here at different times. The pleasing part of it to us is that we have better health, and it is nearly one half cheaper; the children can play out of doors all day long and there is no better place for an artist's summer work."

The few weeks' painting Steele had under Currier's guidance had brought a noticeable improvement in his work, and he entered Professor Loefftz's class in October in better health and spirits and with greater confidence and enthusiasm than he had felt for years. This sense of well-being was heightened by a letter he received just before the academy opened from his cousin Will Richards. Will's openness and good will and his interest in Steele's career are evident in what he wrote:

Now Theo don't set any thing down against me for my long and mean neglect & don't delay writing in answer for a single day. I am daily asked about you.

Let me know just how your exchequer stands—such a statement as I can show to others—how long you can hold out on what you have—how long you ought to stay to make the principles and fundamentals of Art your own & laying aside your modesty state what your hopes are as to what you would be able to accomplish at the end of such a schooling.

It may appear as entire confidence of expression between us which will take away any element of egotism to others. I want such a letter from you between this and the approaching holidays to make up another batch of subscriptions.

This letter provided the opening Steele wanted. His two years would be up in ten months and he knew that he would not want to go home so soon. He replied to Richards at once, writing as frankly as he had been requested to do:

Now as to my affairs, I have been here a little over a year. The last payment that is due in Jan. will keep me until the 1st of April. This uses up all of my re-

20

sources. I will then have been here 18 months, and should stay at least 1 year longer from that time. This will require from $6 to 700 more, can it be raised?

I can hardly write to you how important it is that I should stay this full time. When I return to Indianapolis I want to be thoroughly & well grounded in my art, not for my own sake only but that I may be able to give to the people of Indianapolis in exchange for their money something of real artistic value.

That I can do this I am perfectly confident, but it will require time. Art is a long road. The study of Art is not comprized in the learning of rules or principles by heart, it is a growth, the development of a faculty and here is the utility of a school like this celebrated school of Munich.

The student works under the direction of thoroughly trained men in a direction that wisdom has shown to be the best calculated to develop the art faculty. I have worked just as hard at home with the same end in view but I must [MS illegible] the fact that most of my labor was useless because of my ignorance of the direction in which to work.

That I shall be able to accomplish in this time what is expected of me and what will be satisfactory to those that assist me I have no doubt. I was never more confident of success than at present. My improvement this summer has been so marked that it has decidedly increased my confidence and has been remarked on by the students with whom I have been associated.

Mr. Currier under whose direction I have prosecuted my vacation studies said to me today, "This summer you have made some decidedly big steps. You are now working in the right direction and next summer's work will tell." I value his opinion very highly for he is honest and frank, and a man of the first attainment in Art, and of the highest aims. He has studied here some 12 years for he considers himself still a student though I doubt if in landscape he has a superior in all Munich.

It has been my rare good fortune to be so closely associated with him in this summer's work, and it is probable I shall be still more closely associated with him in the future for we shall use the same studio.

I think my good friends in Indianapolis would feel gratified if they could see the improvement that I have made.

It was my intention to have sent some things home this fall, but the fact is I have been too busy to make pictures. I have felt the necessity of pushing my studies in certain directions. So the result is not pictures but studies. During this vacation I have made over 100 studies in oil from nature, averaging about 14 by 20 inches in size. So you see I have worked but by next spring, at any rate by fall, I shall send home some work.

If I can hold on for the length of time I propose, I am assured the result will be satisfactory all around.

I think we are upon the dawn of a grand day of art in our country. We have the subjects, the motives, and the material prosperity to support it, and there are hundreds of young men now being thoroughly educated in art, whose influence when they return will be a power.

I wish to take some part in this and though it will be humble I want it to be the right direction, to help and not retard.

On February 20, 1882, Will Richards drew up another agreement:

Whereas Mr. Theodore C. Steele of this city was believed to possess unusual talent as an artist and perceiving high honour to the city and state through him, provided he could enjoy the benefits of the best European schools of Art, and whereas certain public spirited citizens, promoters of Art, did by subscribing $100.00 each [to] send him there, said subscription is to be repaid in paintings on said Steele's return, and whereas now after near two years of study said Steele is desirous of completing the three years' course, having taken the lead of all American students in Munich, more than fulfilling the expectations of his friends and winning the highest encomiums from the Royal Academy, Therefore to enable him to complete a career so full of promise and of honor we the undersigned subscribe the amount set opposite our names payable in quarterly instalments said amount to be repaid in original painting by the said Steele to the satisfaction of each of said subscribers.

The first subscriber to sign was again Herman Lieber, and he preceded his signature with this statement: "I cheerfully head this subscription having advanced $200 before and consider that I am making a good investment beside helping the artist." Other signers included Richards; Jonathan W. Gordon, an Indianapolis attorney; John M. Butler, an attorney; Albert E. Fletcher; Charles E. Coffin, a real estate and insurance broker; William S. Hubbard, a wealthy real estate dealer and businessman; Henry C. Adams, deputy U. S. Marshal; Mrs. Stoughton J. Fletcher; and Francis Churchman.

A third year of study at the Academy was thus assured.

When spring came, the family was faced with finding new quarters, since the villa where they had lived during the winter was to be taken over by the government for a hospital. Rather than return to Munich, they decided to take rooms in the Old Cloister at the nearby village of Mittenheim. Again they were living in charming surroundings and among American friends, including William Forsyth who came over in 1882 to begin five years of study in the Royal Academy.

In a June letter Libbie described their new situation to Mrs. Lockridge:

... We have very pleasant rooms, everything convenient, our butter and milk we get from the man we rent of, and who with his wife lives in part of the monastery. A young German couple, and two of our American boys, (one Mr. Forsyth of Indianapolis) also live here. There are about twenty people including the servants occupying the building. The Landlord and his wife are very nice people, are from North Germany and well connected, being related *by marriage* to people of high degree, German nobility. I have never been in their rooms but I have been told they are very large and beautifully furnished.

The building itself inside and out is an object of beauty to the Artists. Its vaulted ceilings supported by arches and pillars, its old brick and stone floors, its unevenly shaped rooms, and antique windows are inviting studies for rainy

PLATE I

Pleasant Run, 1885, 19¼ by 32¼ ins.
© 1989 Indianapolis Museum of Art, Gift of Carl B. Shafer

days. Its outer walls stuccoed and rich in most harmonious and delicious colors. Its sunlit court with ancient well, and picturesque figures moving about, is equal so the artists say to any Eastern scene. The Cloister and garden are inclosed with a high strong wall. At night all gates are closed and locked, and guarded day and night by two big dogs. Uh! don't you think one ought to have sensations here living in a home three hundred years old, inhabited for two of those centuries by monks? I really and truly expected to be overpowered by romantic sensations, but alas! Well there *are* plenty of strange, weird things here such as bugs and spiders. If Mr. Riley were only here he would find plenty of poetic manna. There are, too, plenty of rats dwelling in the attic right above us. They are rather mysterious in their habits, and make strange noises in the wee small hours of the night, but we recognize them at once as rats, (if we only had a more vivid imagination,) and not the disembodied spirits of monks dead a century or so ago.

I think we are here surrounded by as beautiful country as can be found anywhere. It is so varied, too. Along our western horizon lie the Ampfer river hills. The village of Dachau crowns the highest one and on clear days its white buildings gleam in the sunshine and appear so near, that it seems we could really walk there in fifteen minutes; but it is six or eight miles distant. Then in other places the heavy pine forests outline dark against the horizon, or we can see the square patches of freshly plowed ground, or the light green of the fields of grain, and from the foot of the hills stretching toward us for miles, lie the moors or turf fields; dotted here and there with desolate looking black sheds for drying the turf; fringes of birch wood forests skirt the streams, and here and there a few white walled cottages. There are no villages west of us until we reach the hills. There seems to be a line of villages reaching from Munich to I do not know what point north of us, that seem to form the boundary line between these vast marshes and the farming land. Our village is on that line. North and northeast of us lie villages innumerable; and in that direction we can distinguish the course of the Military road which runs from Munich to Ingolstadt by its line of lombardy poplars the most military looking tree in existence. East of us we have no extensive view on account of the forests. Immediately south lies Schleissheim with its Castle, seeming to be the biggest thing this side of the Alps, but if we go out on the road west of the monastery we can easily see the two domes of the Frauen Kirche in Munich, and the villages which lie between here and there, then southwest the plain seems to go on and on uninterrupted by anything until it reaches the Alps. Everything becomes insignificant beside those wonderful works of creation. There is hardly a day that our eyes are not greeted by their majestic forms. They can look perfectly indestructible, and then again of such delicate loveliness that you could imagine that they are of such stuff as dreams, and a puff of wind would dispel them.

That summer the quaint Mittenheim Cloister and its quiet garden, the farmyards, the moors, and the grain fields became subjects for innumerable paintings and for sketches in charcoal and pencil before the Steeles moved back to Schleissheim in the late autumn. This summer's work was to provide the basis for many of Steele's best-known canvases. The family left Mittenheim reluctantly. Back in Schleissheim they took rooms with the Kuttendreir family, whose house faced the old canal that made its way through the village between tree-shaded banks and under arching bridges, and were settled when Steele's third year in the Academy began in October.

During his third year Steele concentrated on improving his technique and skill, and wrote down briefly, but frankly, in a little notebook Professor Loefftz's critical comments on his work. Often he added his own thoughts, as if to strengthen his determination to discipline himself and overcome his faults. For example, on December 16, he wrote:

Have had a number of criticisms upon my brushing. In the last particularly criticized. The Prof. found the tone and character good but my methods of painting bad and uninteresting. Explained at some length his ideas upon this, how the brush should follow the form. How that color should here be laid on sharp and "Schniederent" and here soft and passing gently into local tone or color. There is but local tone shadow and highlight with perhaps suggestions of connecting tone between local tone and shadow. In painting the color is so laid on that it loses the character of paint and becomes flesh. There are many methods in painting. Indeed every artist of originality develops a more or less original method. The great thing —does it represent the thing painted in true and interesting manner. I find unexpected difficulty in acquiring a method of brushing, but *will* have it eventually if persistent efforts will accomplish it. . . .

And then again he jotted down his own thoughts on matters other than painting.

As a general thing, a man is successful in proportion as he feels his responsibility. If it is a question of success or death, he will succeed. Herbert Spencer remarks upon this do or die expression in American faces.

There is an ennui that comes from want of intellectual exertion and a more terrible ennui that comes from the jaded faculties, from overexertion. And again from ill health, from the failure of some of the physical powers to fully do their duty.

Acquire if possible the enviable habit of getting rid of your work in the interest of it. Take an interest in anything else—gardening, amusements, etc.

Later, in reference to another study, he wrote:

The great fault he [Professor Loefftz] found in this study was the tendency to sweet unsound color and want of refinement in drawing and method of brushing. Upon the last point it will take unceasing watchfulness and study to correct. Always keep a watch for the hard and soft brushing. In a general way, the receding parts become soft, the advancing harder, or, better expressed more pronounced in the brushing. The highlights often quite distinct hard shapes. Nearly every touch should be harder here and softer there as it indicates the form. These points are those upon which I have often been criticized lately. I must correct them at once. A sharper eye, and quicker feeling would certainly correct them.

These excerpts show how absorbed Steele was in his work, and this is also reflected in a letter to Herman Lieber written on February 28, 1883. He wanted more time at the Academy and he wanted Lieber to help him manage it.

Well my third year will soon be up and I am not yet ready to return home. By the close of the year in July I want to see my way clear for about eight or ten months longer. From the figures that Major Richards has just sent me I find I will have enough money to keep me until about the 1st of Jan or possibly a month or so longer. I will then have to make the money to keep me the rest of the time some five or six months and to bring me home.

This will require about $600. Now the question is can I make this by the sale of some of my work. I am going to try it.

In just about a month I will send you about a dozen of the best things that I have done. Will you be so kind as to put them on sale and do what you can with them.

Now I will briefly state some of the reasons why I desire to further extend my time here. In the first place I have as yet made no copies and want a few good copies from the Masters, particularly heads by Vandyke and Rembrandt. Second I want to spend several months in securing sketches and studies of interesting places and motives for future pictures. Things that will not only be interesting and valuable to me when I return but that will be novel and interesting to the people at home, and that in the end will probably be worth to me many times their cost. . . .

But the principal reason is that I wish to push my studies further, that I know that I am not fully developed. I feel that I am making my way into a higher and more suggestive style of art, and wish to push it further while under the good influence of this art atmosphere.

The stronger I am when I return the better, for there will be but little chance for me to study for several years. It will then be to paint pictures.

I suppose that I have the good fortune to be under the best teacher of painting in Germany. The only thing his eye is so sensitive to tone and color and his ideal of technique so high that none of us can come up to it, but we are all the better for the effort. Mr. Metzner and Mr. Adams are now in the same class, while Mr. Forsyth and Mr. Richards will come in next fall. So all the Indiana boys will have their training from the same master.

You will see by the things I will send you that I am making my art culture broad. Interiors, figures, landscapes as well as heads.

When I return it is my intention to do as much landscape work as portraiture. I have a great feeling for it and find the outdoor work adds very much to my health and strength. . . .

I am anxious for you to see my work and want you to write me what you think of it, and what is generally thought of it. I will send it immediately after the Easter holidays about the 10th of April.

In the meantime I should be glad to hear from you. What do you think of the further extension of my time? I have no doubt you would like to see me at home as soon as possible and I certainly should like it myself, but the point of the whole thing is I want to be thoroughly prepared for what will devolve upon me when I return. This thing is not to be done over again. It is now or never.

Accordingly, Steele sent Lieber several canvases. Among them were "A Corner in the Old Kitchen of the Mittenheim Cloister," "A Winter Afternoon in Old Munich," "The Cloister Garden, Mittenheim," "Winter, Old Roman Road near Munich," "A June Morning, Village of Unterschleissheim," "Bavarian Farmyard," and a nude figure. Obviously they represented much of his previous summer's work. On May 24, Lieber wrote to him:

I suppose you are anxious to know that your pictures have safely arrived but also how they are received by the Indianapolis people. Now, the pictures have come. They arrived yesterday, being delayed in the New York customhouse. I put them on stretchers and placed a plain pine frame around them. So far they have been seen only by a few persons, as I thought it best to invite your subscribers and other friends to see them, before they are exhibited for the public.

Mr. Churchman of Fletcher's Bank is so far the only one of the subscribers who has seen them, and he expressed himself very much pleased. The same I can say of the clerks in my store, they are all full in their praise.

I am glad to say to you that I could state to Mr. Churchman "Mr. Steele has learned something." I can hardly say which one I like the best, have therefore said to Mr. Churchman I don't care which one he selects, would give all others the preference and take for myself the one which is left. This refers to every picture except the nude picture, which I admire as an artistic effort, but not enough to place it in my house.

I find it proper and right that you should stay another year amongst the artists. I consider this necessary, so that you may gain that freedom of action, which distinguishes the successful and progressive artist. I will do everything I can to assist you and think will be able to interest others for you.

The summer of 1883 thus started on a cheerful and optimistic note. To add to their pleasure, Otto Lieber, the eldest son of Herman, arrived for a brief visit at Schleissheim. "He is a genial and noble young man," wrote Libbie to Mrs. Lockridge, "and we felt sorry that his visit to us was of short duration. He says everybody is painting in Indianapolis, that they can hardly supply the demand for material. I do not know just exactly what that means, whether it is that people are trying to really cultivate themselves in that direction or whether they have become very economical and gone to *manufacturing* pictures for home use." In the same letter she asked, "Have you been to see his [Steele's] pictures at Mr. Lieber's? And what is your opinion of them? You better believe we await news of how they were received generally with no little interest."

When the public was given an opportunity to see the paintings sent to Indianapolis, all seemed to agree that the expectations of Steele's patrons were being realized. The local newspapers reacted enthusiastically, and Libbie was unable to restrain writing confidentially to her friend Mrs. Lockridge in June:

We have received from Mr. Lieber three papers containing notices of my husband's pictures and a noble letter from him. I am *so happy* over the good words I can scarcely contain myself. And my husband goes around in his calm way, with a joy beaming face. And he also had today quite a compliment from Professor Loefftz, and that is indeed a joy to receive a compliment from him. Oh Mrs. Lockridge you must not think this out-burst in bad taste. I know it is not considered the right thing to praise ones nearest kin. I would not let myself out to every one so, I have so much confidence in you, and I know you will understand me and rejoice with me. And I feel so thankful to every one who has helped my husband, who has had sympathy with him. May God bless you all!

Libbie's letter to her sister Laura Richards, written a couple of weeks later (on July 17), struck a serious vein and reflects her concern for her husband's future and that of the family:

So much depends upon Theo pushing his studies here just as far as he can. His future in Art, and the future comfort and happiness of his family are the two main things. You are a reading woman and have not failed to observe that Art in America much to the honor of America, is making progress. It is no longer represented alone by the ignorant and uneducated whose pictures are the laughing stock of the world, but by *artists* who have in many instances braved hardship in order to place themselves under the teaching of masters in the old world, and have made their art a long and conscientious study. The uneducated unprogressive artist cannot hold out against the latter. It is not right that he should.—While Theo has made good progress and has reached that period in his education where he begins to feel strong, that he is really doing something and to feel a satisfaction in what he is accomplishing, he does not feel that he has reached that period where it is safe for him to leave the influence he is under here. He wants to become *so* strong that all the counteracting influences he may meet with away from here will have no effect, and that there will be no danger of his settling back into his old way of working. . . .

I am anxious that his things shall command a good price when we return home. We must have a better and surer living in the future. We have suffered the inconveniences of too little money long enough. That is another thing that makes me willing to remain here although the life here has many hardships.—We want to have a home when we return to America. I do look forward to that so much—a home where we can find comfort and rest, where we can for our children's sakes have music and books and some of the refinements of life.

During the summer and fall of 1883 an International Exhibition was held in the Glaspalast in Munich, and the Steeles returned again and again to study the paintings. At the close of the summer they spent a few weeks at Schliersee in the Bavarian Alps. Here Steele added sketches to his collection for future work. Just before the holidays more canvases were dispatched to Indianapolis. Among them were three landscapes: "Haying on the Koenigs-feld," "Village of Schliersee," and "Brook in the Bavarian Alps," and two copies of old masters—one after Rembrandt and the other after Rubens. These along with some of his studies had been exhibited at the American Club in Munich and were well received. "Professor Loefftz was highly pleased with them," reported Libbie.

By March, 1884, this second lot of Steele's paintings had arrived in Indianapolis and were placed on exhibit at Lieber's. "They are specimens of his work which have won the artist high rank in the Royal Academy of Munich," and they "evince a genius . . . fully equal to that of [William] Chase at the time he left home," commented the local *News.*

Steele's last year in the Academy, which ended in the summer of 1884, was a successful one. At the exhibit of the students' work at the close of the term in mid-July he won a First Class Prize, a silver medal, for his painting "The Boatman" (Fig. 10). To be awarded one of the top honors was an eloquent climax to his four years of hard work. But a far higher honor came to him when authorization was given for the purchase of his prize picture for the walls of the Royal Academy. Naturally he and Libbie were overjoyed with this recognition of high achievement, but hard pressed as they were for money, Steele decided to send the picture home rather than sell it and have it remain in Munich. He felt that the best of his work belonged in Indianapolis.

Shortly after he won the prize Steele wrote Herman Lieber about it and soon sent him photographs of "The Boatman" and of one of his landscapes. He also wrote that he wanted to stay in Munich to paint more landscape studies under the guidance of Professor Loefftz and other masters.

Libbie had not been well that summer of 1884. Steele felt a holiday in the mountains would be good for all of them, particularly for her, so late in September back to Schliersee they went. Steele stayed with her and the children for a few days and then returned to Schleissheim. His letter to her, started that same evening, is the only surviving letter to his wife in this period. It shows the warm sympathetic relationship they enjoyed and also gives a good picture of the work he was then doing.

My dear Wife, I arrived home upon the 4:40 train. I say I arrived *home*, but it is not home though it looks like it. Everything as neat as a pin, and everything convenient, but there is no wife, nor children here, and it is so quiet and lonesome that it seems almost fearful.

The lamp is burning brightly and a pleasant glow is over the room, and I have arranged several studies upon the chairs around, but there is no Bessie to bore with my calling attention to this point or that and what does she think of the other. Yet everything in the room makes me think of her, the wings spread out over the whatnot and the graceful tea urn standing before them, its clear brightness its white gold somehow brings up the image of the wife that put it there. But it is no use to dream about it, my house without my wife and children is simply a lonesome place. I never saw Schleissheim so dreary. A perpetual drip of rain upon the muddy streets. No wonder the boys have all deserted and gone into town as I hear they have. After the things I saw at Schliersee even this morning in the rain and fog, this place seems very uninteresting—the plains barren, the foliage and trees commonplace, and things generally poor and with no juice in them (except water).

I enjoyed the ride from Schliersee very much. All the way to the plains the foliage was magnificent. The hills and distance lost in the gray mist, the foreground coming out mellow and clear and wet and shining. As I passed along many a beautiful picture was suggested. Would that they could remain in the memory but impressions so quickly received are not very permanent and I presume finally fade out. Possibly not entirely lost, but dimmed by time, others take their place, and they are gone. But they are not in vain even if finally lost as distinct pictures, their spirit remains and they have unconsciously to the beholder done a work in his culture, in the development of his taste and love of the beautiful, in his knowledge of form and color and the character of things. . . .

9½ o'clock next evening

This morning got up at 6 and found to my surprise a marvelously beautiful morning. I made a study of the water looking toward the bridge for my picture in the morning. Then spent the rest of the day in copying it into the picture. Have succeeded first rate with it. One more day and it will be finished. Got in the figure of a woman kneeling washing, will put in another standing upon the bank. Painted this evening upon the poplars. . . .

I do not know of anything new that has happened. I hope you have all enjoyed this beautiful day. I can imagine you have taken a fine walk and come home tired and hungry. I hope when I see you again your cheeks will be rosy and your calves will have grown (I mean of course the children) immensely. Hunt me some subjects. Wood interiors, &c. . . .

Well it is getting late and I must close. I want to urge you to drink beer a good deal. I think it will be good for you. You are now in a different climate and may take cold, & so a little beer prevents everything, and eat plenty of good food. You must do it. . . .

P. S. Thursday Afternoon. I got up too late to take my letter to the depot this morning. It proved to be just the day for my Lustheim Garden picture so I hurried down there. I was very fortunate in getting through with it. The left side now equals the other side, and in my room it appears superb. In the two days' work I have succeeded well. If things go so well for two or three days longer I shall be through, and then I shall pitch into my studies for the winter at Schliersee with enthusiasm.

Received a good letter from Mr. L[ieber] which I enclose. He seems to have been delighted with the Boatman. I will write him tonight. Take care of yourselves and have a good time. Love to all

THEODORE

Lieber's letter of September 9, 1884, that Steele enclosed for Libbie was cordial and encouraging as usual:

MY DEAR FRIEND, Since you wrote me that you would send a Photograph of the Prize Picture, I have been waiting patiently for it. At last it came and I must say I was surprised. . . . I really did not know what to expect, but I truly confess that I did not expect to receive such a satisfactory picture. You have struck out boldly and successfully. The Boatman is truly a study, a study of life, so true to nature that judging from the photograph the painting must be what Prof. Loefftz requires of a good picture, a reproduction on canvas as near to truth as possible. It seems to me also, that you have been quite lucky in selecting your subjects. The representation of the hard working man is pleasing and interesting. I also like the landscape as far as I can judge from the little photograph. Of course the photog. only gives an idea of the conception.

I am now anxious to see the originals and hope you have them started before this reaches you.

Those of the contributors I have seen make no objection of your remaining, so you have to fear no reproach from that quarter.

Now Mr. Steele, Good bye. Give my regards to your wife, who stands so nobly by you. Your friend,

H. LIEBER

In November Steele packed "The Boatman" and several other canvases and sent them off to Herman Lieber. He was counting on their sale as well as the sale of the ones he had sent earlier to carry him through until the following summer when the family would return to Indianapolis. Weeks passed and he heard nothing of them, and then in February came a card from Lieber

Fig. 1. Portrait of Thomas Lakin,
1873, 19½ by 15 ins.
© 1989 Indianapolis Museum of Art,
Gift of Mrs. Edward L. Pedlow

Fig. 2. Self-portrait,
c. 1874, 23 by 19 ins.
T. C. Steele State Historic Site,
Indiana State Museum Collection

Fig. 3. Brandt T. Steele,
c. 1875,
17¼ by 14¼ ins.
Theodore L. Steele

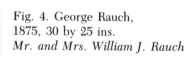

Fig. 4. George Rauch,
1875, 30 by 25 ins.
Mr. and Mrs. William J. Rauch

Fig. 5. Portrait of
Susan Jane Farrow Bryan,
1880, 27 by 22 ins.
Sheldon Swope Art Museum,
Terre Haute

Fig. 6. Road to Schleissheim, c. 1883, 25 by 36 ins.
T. C. Steele State Historic Site, Indiana State Museum Collection

Fig. 7. Study of a Negro,
1884, 27 by 22 ins.
Ball State University Art Gallery, Muncie,
Permanent loan from the
Frank C. Ball Collection,
Ball Brothers Foundation L29.078

Fig. 8. Schleissheim, 1884, 13 by 18 ins.
Theodore L. Steele

saying that they had not arrived. Alarmed, Steele went to Munich to see if he could find some trace of them. Poor Libbie wrote in agitation to Mrs. Lockridge: "They are the result of more than a whole summer's work beside his prize picture, and two or three heads. You can imagine how troubled we are over them . . . we had expected so much from them, and if they are lost do not know what we shall do."

To add to their distress they had learned that only one of the pictures that had been sent earlier had been sold. "I cannot tell you how disappointed we are," wrote Libbie with a touch of bitterness,

I assure you the prospect of success in Indianapolis does not look very bright. It is indeed discouraging, so much so that it makes me heartsick. I think there is but one other American who ever received from the Academy here so high an honor as he, (beside winning a silver medal), that of having one of his pictures bought by the Academy, but what success has his truly honourable standing here brought him in Indianapolis? I do not understand it. Well I am proud of the success he has had here. It has not been an easy victory, but all the more gratifying on that account. I am happy to know that those who have helped him to come here will also gain by it. He has been urged to send his work to London or some of the Eastern cities of America, but felt that he was under obligation to send the best he did home.

Eventually the pictures were located in the New York Customs House and finally reached Indianapolis. In April an exhibit of canvases sent by Steele and William Forsyth from Munich was held at English's Hall. "The Boatman" was included and the Indianapolis *News* of April 18 pronounced it "a striking picture, sufficient of itself to give its author a permanent reputation."

During the winter and spring Steele continued to submit his work to Professor Loefftz for criticism, and recorded what Loefftz said in his notebook. He often included a sketch of the particular study he was speaking of, either landscape or portrait. And as he had often done before, along with the criticisms he jotted down a few lines from his reading that had caught his attention. One day he wrote, "What Genius does is to inspire the soul with power to persevere in the work that is needed. Ninety per cent of what men call genius is a talent for hard work." Another time, " 'Contemplate your subject long,' says Buffon. 'It will gradually unfold itself 'till a sort of electric spark convulses the brain for a moment and sends a glow of inspiration to the heart. Then comes the luxury of genius.' "

The "Munich Idyll" was drawing to a close. Steele had earned enough by painting copies of the old masters to pay the expenses of the last months in Munich. He continued to paint until mid-April, 1885. Just before they left a number of his studies, mostly landscapes, were placed on exhibit in the American Club, and Professor Loefftz gave him his last criticism, which Steele carefully recorded in his notebook as he had always done—the last Munich entry.

In mid-May the family said farewell to Schleissheim and Munich and all their friends and went to Antwerp. Before they embarked they had an opportunity to see the fine collection of paintings at the International Exhibition which opened there in the middle of the month. On the 23d they sailed on the Red Star liner *Nordland* for New York.

One day out of port a case of smallpox developed on board, but the vigilance of the ship's officers prevented a spread of the disease and on reaching New York the family was permitted to pass through a rigid quarantine. The ship docked on the 6th of June and within a couple of days the Steeles were back in Indianapolis.

What their years in Munich meant to them all could never be reckoned—to the painter, to the sensitive and poetic-minded Libbie, and to the three children. T. C. Steele's pictures survive as tangible witnesses to what he saw and accomplished, and his wife some years later wrote of her memories of their sojourn in her *Impressions*. But now, back in Indianapolis, a new period in their lives began.

3

WILL RICHARDS was on hand to meet the Steeles upon their arrival in Indianapolis aboard the New York train. Libbie and Theo no doubt looked somewhat older than when they left, but, of course, the greatest changes were in the three children—Brandt, fourteen years old, Margaret, thirteen in another month, and the "baby" Shirley, almost seven. The children had been away long enough to feel shy and perhaps a little self-conscious in their "foreign" clothes.

The Steeles' joy at being home and seeing Will was soon cut short, however, by the crushing news that while they were on shipboard fire had destroyed the building where their possessions had been stored when they went to Munich, and that everything was lost. This distressing blow was softened, though, by Will. He had rented and furnished a house for them—the old Tinker home or Talbot Place, as it was known—on the north side of Seventh (now Sixteenth) Street at Pennsylvania, just across from his own home. It was a beautiful house in a parklike setting of lofty forest trees, flower beds, and shrubbery bordering on open lawn. There Theodore and Libbie courageously began a new life.

Theodore lost no time in setting to work. He had to make a living for his family and he had paintings to do for those who had contributed to the fund for his Munich study. He established a studio downtown in the Vance Block immediately. The Indianapolis *Journal* of June 14, 1885, reported that he would hold an informal reception there on the following Monday, Tuesday, and Wednesday, and that some of his work would be on display. For several months thereafter this studio was open on Saturday afternoons.

Early in July a reception in Steele's honor was given by the Art Association of Indianapolis which had been organized in 1883 while he was away. It was held in the home of the Association's president, Dr. Nathaniel A. Hyde, pastor of the Congregational Church. The Steeles were thus seeing old friends and making new ones. Unfortunately Herman Lieber was away; he had left in May for a visit with his family and friends in Düsseldorf and he would not return before September.

On June 27, Steele started a portrait of Governor Albert G. Porter which was exhibited at Lieber's on July 20, and by the end of August had been hung in the State Library. In September Steele and Miss Sue Ketcham, a re-

33

spected teacher of art, launched their art school in the old Plymouth Church. In mid-October he was at work on a group of portraits of members of the Fletcher family.

If Steele experienced any letdown on his return from the stimulating atmosphere of the Academy life and the Bavarian landscape, there is no indication of it. He had a remarkable capacity for finding painting subjects at hand. While much of his time was spent necessarily in his studio painting portraits and in teaching, he always had his eyes open to sights around him. One day shortly after his return he jotted down the following on a scrap of paper:

One of the most beautiful subjects that I have seen for many a day I saw this evening from the center of Circle Park: the young sycamores that run around the park with their finely drawn and characteristic lines, the play of light and shade and wonderful color upon the ground; the range of hack & express wagons with groups of figures that lined the outer rim of the Circle, and back of all this play of light and color, the background of dull neutral tones of the buildings in shadow upon the other side of the street. It seemed to me to have all the elements for a powerful and effective picture.

Indianapolis seems to me to be full of such subjects. There are dozens of such motives of equal interest. And then the beach forest about the city. There is no lack of subjects and picturesque subjects in every direction. I suppose of course I see things with a fresh eye, and perhaps with a keener appreciation of their picturesque qualities than formerly. At any rate I have been delighted with everything from New York bay to Indianapolis. Of course, there is a marked contrast to scenes in the old world, but it is equally fine.

In August Steele had found time to do some sketching around the city—the canal, the City Hospital, Pleasant Run (see Plate I)—and apparently out in the country, also, for under the date of August 18, he wrote in his journal:

In the few studies I have made I find a marked difference of effect from those I have been studying in Bavaria. I find more color, intense contrasts, and less atmosphere, or tone, and the effects of haze are thicker and when luminous rarely have that thin whiteness so common in the fine Bavarian afternoons.

Then, describing one of the sketches he had just completed which he thought "most promising," he wrote:

The afternoon effect, the warm sunshine, the cool shadows. The sunshine having the quality that haze gives to the beams that pass through it [in] late afternoon. The gray of the distance, the light shimmering over the cornfield of the middle distance and the stubblefield until it culminates in the luminous tones upon the white cattle in the foreground. The color too becoming very pronounced until it reaches the cattle and brighter and deeper still in the sunlit grass of the foreground.

In May, 1886, three Steele paintings were among the one hundred and twenty that made up the Eighth Annual Exhibition of the Society of American Artists at the Metropolitan Museum of Art in New York. The New York *Times* declared all three had "decided merit." "'A Birch Avenue near Schleissheim' and 'Afternoon in Early Spring,'" said the critic, "are closely related; the perspective in both is admirable, and so is the management of the lights and shadows, a cool brightness pervading the two scenes. 'The Boatman' . . . shows a grizzly oarsman, with plenty strength in his half-averted face and plenty muscle in his thin, weather-tanned arms, pulling at an oar, the figure standing out sharply on a gray sky."

During the same month, in the Third Annual Exhibition of the Art Association of Indianapolis, Steele had four canvases including a portrait of the granddaughter of Judge Cyrus C. Hines. In it, the Indianapolis *News* observed that the artist seemed to catch "the not-quite-steady attitude of a child that has paused a moment in its endless activity to be looked at or spoken to."

In 1886, probably during the summer, Steele built a studio in the yard at Talbot Place, northeast of the house, where there were no trees to interfere with the light, fulfilling a long-held wish of Libbie's that, when they returned to Indianapolis, the studio could be at home.

In late September Steele made what was the first of many painting trips to Vernon, Indiana, and the Muscatatuck Valley, and at least three of his paintings from there were in the Steele show sponsored by the Art Association in November: "On the Muscatatuck," "Beech Avenue," and "Afternoon on the Muscatatuck." This exhibit, held in Pfafflin's Hall at the corner of Mississippi Street and Indiana Avenue, included nearly one hundred and fifty of his sketches and paintings, many of them from the Munich period.

A long article in the Indianapolis *News* of February 19, 1887, titled "The Artist Steele," is revealing of the man and his work at this stage of his career. It describes him as "of striking appearance . . . above the average height, with prominent features, high and broad head, finely though modestly poised above broad sloping shoulders, full dark-gray, kindly eyes, large shapely hands, and the easy quiet manners of a man who has seen the world but lived more within himself." After giving a brief account of Steele's life and of his Munich period of study, the writer continues:

Since his return from Europe many of his pictures painted for home patrons have been portraits—a branch of art in which, though he excels in it, he has less delight than in landscape painting. . . . The Fletcher, Vonnegut and the Coffin group of portraits have been greatly admired, as much for their faithfulness as portraits as for the genius displayed in their artistic grouping and faultless coloring. The portrait of Mr. Lieber, just completed [Fig. 17] is not only a very striking likeness, but has a personality which none but a true painter can fix upon canvas. That of Gov. Porter allows the more rugged and positive characteristics of the man to pervade and give tone to his otherwise smooth and suave exterior.

Perhaps the greatest tribute to Mr. Steele's genius is the recent purchase by the Boston Art club of his "View on the Muscatatuck," a scene in Jennings County, Indiana. It was purchased on its arrival in Boston before it had been placed on exhibition. . . . The fact that this is the first work purchased from a western artist does not detract from the honor. A large picture sent to the New York exhibition last year, was sold at once, and his "Late Autumn on the Moor" and "Misty Day in Spring," sent this year, sold the first evening of the exhibition. He has two others in the Boston exhibition, "The Winter Thaw" and "A November Day," both of which have attracted much attention here. "The Oaks at Vernon" [Fig. 19], now on his easel, is a marvelously correct representation of an Indiana autumn scene. . . .

In general conversation on the subject of art, Mr. Steele remarked that one great difficulty in our city, as in most western towns where art is a new thing, is to get people to look at it seriously and reverently. . . . It is commonly thought that a picture is an ornament—a decoration for the walls. Now this is putting art upon its very lowest plane. A brass plaque or a Chinese fan will do this fully as well or better. Art, if it is art at all, has something to say to you. It expresses thought, feeling, sentiment often, that words will not express. It comes as an interpreter from the out-of-door world, of that continual miracle of beauty that also might have escaped your observation.

Landscape painting, he remarked, is a modern art. There are comparatively no old masters in landscape, certainly none that exert any influence on the great modern school. . . . The artist does not now sit in his studio and conjure up a weak suggestion of out-of-door life. He goes at once to nature herself, not as a mere copyist, for while he holds himself rigidly to truth or effect in atmosphere and light, his trained eye broadly generalizes, his imagination works with his hand, and the result, though it may be ideal, embodies the truth of reality. In fact it is the interpretation of Nature into the more impressive language of Art.

In 1887 the Indiana General Assembly created the Monument Commission which was to be responsible for the erection of a memorial honoring Indiana's war dead, a Soldiers' and Sailors' Monument, and appropriated $200,000 toward its erection. Steele rarely expressed himself publicly, but was moved to do so on this occasion. The Indianapolis *News* of March 22 carried a letter to the editor written by him which was captioned, "It Should Be a Work of Art." "Money does not necessarily buy good art," warned Steele, and stressed the importance of the appointment of honest and capable men to the commission. "In the last few years so notorious have become the 'misfits' in the selection of commissioners and committees, and the bad results following their dishonesty and incompetency that . . . [monument building] has almost fallen into contempt. Many of the best architects and sculptors have sworn never to compete for a public monument." Then he continued:

In the great mass of soldiers' monuments over the country the average excellence is not good. In some of them the name of neither architect nor sculptor figures, but such and such a marble or granite company who 'took the job' and made all they could out of it. If Indiana is to escape the disgrace that has fallen upon the well-meant efforts of so many communities, if she is able to build a monument whether the work of architect or sculptor, or both combined, that will fittingly embody the monumental spirit, that will never grow common, but command forever the reverent respect of the passerby, it means that rare men will be put upon the commission.

What Steele thought of the commissioners who were appointed, or of the finished Monument, is not known. He served as one of the art advisers along with William Forsyth and John H. Mahoney in approving certain of the sculptural decorations, and many years later Monument Circle was to provide subjects for some of his most pleasant canvases.

The Steeles spent the late summer and early fall months of 1887 in the Vermont hills, on the ancestral homestead of the Fletcher family, near Ludlow and Cavendish. Allen Fletcher and Judge Hines had commissioned Steele to paint landscapes of the countryside near the old home. He painted several while he was there, one of them "Vermont Hills, Village of Cavendish" (Plate II).

The year 1888 opened sadly. The Steele's last child, Mary, who was born early in January, lived only about six weeks.

In April Steele held an exhibition in his studio, and around the middle of June was at West Baden Springs. He had not been well and went there hoping the waters would benefit him. He found the surrounding hills and forests superb and wrote to Libbie that he could be satisfied there for the summer if she and the children were with him. He did some sketching up in the hills where he recorded some "glorious forest interiors—beeches and oaks." Later that summer the family camped in Montgomery County near the old mill at Yountsville, and below it, on Sugar Creek in the region called Pine Hills north of the Shades. Among the canvases in his studio exhibit in October were several done that summer: two inspired by a group of calves in a farmyard corner, some scenes on Sugar Creek, and "The Potato Harvest," which, said the Indianapolis *News*, was remindful of Millet.

In the fall Steele was occupied with writing, and in December he read his paper, "The Development of the Connoisseur in Art," before the Indianapolis Literary Club to which he had been elected in March of the preceding year. It was the first of four papers he was to present at that club. In February, 1892, he read "From the Painter's Point of View," and in May, 1896, "The Trend of Modern Art." This last may have been the paper he presented earlier that year in Chicago, at the Art Institute, on February 4, and in St. Louis on February 22. Although he remained a member all his life, his last paper for the club, which was entitled "The New Movement in Art," was read on January 6, 1902.

In January, 1889, he read "The Development of the Connoisseur in Art" at a meeting of the Art Association. He continued to read papers and speak to audiences in Indianapolis, out over the state, and occasionally in cities out of the state throughout his life. Steele's ability to write seems to have been almost the counterpart of his talent for painting. He wrote with great perception and skill, clearly and effectively, and always with restraint. Occasionally he expressed his thoughts in beautiful poetic imagery reminiscent of his writings in his journal in 1870. He was in the forefront of thought and discussion of art matters in his day, a champion of the impressionist movement, and concerned with the role of the artist in society.

In May, 1890, the Portfolio Club, whose object was to "bring the various art interests of the community together and promote a spirit of art interest and appreciation," held its first meeting in Circle Hall. Husbands and wives both could belong and Theodore and Libbie Steele were active in its organization. In May, 1893, the club published *Impressions*, the paper read by Libbie on March 16 of that year. It told of the years in Munich and was illustrated with pen-and-ink sketches by members of the club who had studied there, William Forsyth, Harry Williamson, J. O. Adams, and Steele, and carried a title page designed by Bruce Rogers, the eminent printer and book designer. Steele read papers before this club on twelve occasions, beginning with the second meeting when he read "The Connoisseur in Art," and ending in February, 1921, with "From the House of the Singing Winds."

Steele spent some time painting in and around Indianapolis in 1889; paintings entitled "On the Canal" and "Old Schofield's Mill," were done then. In August he returned to Montgomery County and painted in the area around Yountsville. In a letter to Libbie from "Mother Gunkle's" where he boarded he commented about his work:

PLATE II

Vermont Hills Village of Cavendish, 1887, 36¼ by 25 ins.
© 1989 Indianapolis Museum of Art, Long-term loan
from the Indianapolis Literary Club

I got home a little late for my study yesterday and in not a very good mood for work, so did not accomplish much, but today have had the best of luck. This morning was glorious and my subject in the woods fairly sang its silver song. If I can have but two more mornings such as this, I will get about through with it. The old strawstack I have painted in beautifully, and the dewy foreground promises well. This afternoon painted in the roadway, and with quite satisfactory result. A very unusual thing—the cows came stringing down the hill while I was painting and I secured some color notes. I am keeping it more luminous and fuller of color than the first study.

It was in 1889 that Steele opened an art school in Circle Hall at the northwest corner of the Circle and Market Street, which he called the Indiana School of Art, the third school to bear that name. He was soon joined in this endeavor by William Forsyth, but served as director until the Art Association assumed management of the school in 1891. Steele continued to teach, however, until February, 1895, when he resigned to be able to devote more time to painting.

In late August, 1890, he was in Delaware County, staying about a mile west of Muncie proper, where he found some subjects that delighted him. "I have seen nothing finer in Indiana," he wrote, "and think they will be saleable as well as artistic. I am anxious to see them under a sunny morning effect."

That year, 1890, Steele published *The Steele Portfolio*, a volume of photogravure prints of twenty-five of his canvases, seven painted in Munich and the others after his return from there. One portrait only was included, that of his niece Maude Lakin called "Just a Slip of a Girl." Among the paintings illustrated were "The Boatman," "Haying on the Koenigsfeld," two of Dachau Moor, and several of scenes around Indianapolis. The others had been done in Jennings County, Montgomery County, and elsewhere in the state.

Steele spent most, if not all, of 1891 in Indianapolis. "Talbot Place" (Fig. 24) dates from that year as does the portrait of his mother (Fig. 23), which was painted when she was in Indianapolis for a visit that year.

Steele returned to Old Vernon and the Muscatatuck for his painting seasons the next three years. Forsyth also painted there in 1892, and in mid-November he and Steele held an exhibit of their summer's work at Lieber's.

Steele sent two of the paintings shown in that exhibition, "On the Muscatatuck" (Fig. 26) and "September" (Plate III), to the World's Columbian Exposition in Chicago in 1893, where they were accepted and hung. It is said that he was the only western artist to have a work marked No. 1.

In 1893 Steele spent most of October in Vernon. His autumn exhibit at

Lieber's, held late in November, was again titled "Old Vernon, Hill and Stream," the same as the exhibit of the year before. This year, however, the invitation to it was designed and executed in pen and ink by Steele's friend Bruce Rogers. On the invitation was pictured Steele's painting, "Bloom of the Grape" (Plate IV).

In 1894 he was back again in Vernon from early August through September. That year he was not as content there as he had been in the past. Brandt had left in July to study in Europe, where he stayed until January, 1897, and Libbie was with her husband only part of the time. She had become ill soon after Brandt left, and Steele was greatly concerned about her. It was the beginning of an illness from which she was never to recover, rheumatoid arthritis, and by the following spring she was painfully crippled.

In November, 1894, the Art Association sponsored an exhibition of the work of Steele, Forsyth, Richard Gruelle, and Otto Stark at the Denison Hotel in Indianapolis. It attracted considerable attention and led to a similar exhibition in Chicago in January, 1895, under the sponsorship of the Central Art Association. The Chicago show also included paintings by J. Ottis Adams.

Early in May, 1895, Steele took Libbie to a sanitarium in Spencer, where she found some relief. While she was away he spent two days in Huntington, Indiana, where he read a paper entitled "The Tendency of Modern Art," a defense of Impressionism, before the Convention of the Indiana Union of Literary Clubs. It was an exhilarating experience for him. Hamlin Garland, the novelist, who had played a leading role in arranging the Chicago show held earlier in the year, was also one of the speakers. An exhibition of paintings by Steele, William Forsyth, Richard Gruelle, and Otto Stark was held in connection with the convention. Steele's account to Libbie of the events of the two days shows that his reputation outside Indiana was increasing, and that there was an awareness of a "Hoosier School" of painting, of which he was considered to be the leader.

Everything went off well, and unquestionably it has been a great thing for me. Had an hour and a half talk with Mr. Garland yesterday, and it was very encouraging. He says all the men in the East, or especially the most advanced men, Tarbell, Robinson, Benson and [MS blank] compliment my work in the East very highly, and he said very seriously, with no intention of flattering me so he said, that he expected me to be generally recognized as the leader in the landscape art of the west within the next year. There were some strong men coming on in Chicago, but that I had the start, and that it would be around my name the general reputation would settle. He thinks within a year I will be able to drop portrait painting entirely if I want to. . . .

Went to the lecture. Hamlin Garland took occasion in his introduction to speak of what Indiana was doing in Art and Literature, to speak of the Indiana School of Landscape painting &c. Later when speaking of the duty of the creative artist to take the things near at hand for his material, he spoke of what Mr. Steele who had come with the seeing eye had found in the state in the things near at hand, that others had not seen. Fortunately the people around me with a few exceptions did not know me and I kept still you may be sure. Dr. Hyde in the afternoon session had taken occasion to also say some pleasant things. Mr. Griffiths also in his lecture last night on "Read the Best Books" took occasion to say something in his introduction upon recent achievements in Indiana Art and Literature, and quoted what William Chase had said to him last spring that the best landscapes on the Academy walls were by Steele of Indianapolis. At this the people cheered, and later one of the delegates wanted to know if I had made my private arrangements with the speakers at this convention before hand.

I got through nicely I think and the people were much interested. An audience of over 600. . . .

In the spring of 1895 Steele was represented in the Cincinnati Art Museum's Annual Exhibition of American Art with three paintings, "On the Muscatatuck," "Lifting of the Fog," and "An August Afternoon." Thereafter he had paintings in these annual shows nearly every year until his death.

During the summer of 1895 the family and some of Steele's students were all in Spencer. Hoping Libbie might continue to benefit from the treatment at the sanitarium, Steele rented Ludlow Hall, the former estate of Calvin Fletcher on the north edge of the town. The eighteen-room mansion with its handsomely landscaped grounds made a delightful summer home, and it was a lively one, with Daisy, Shirley, and the students there.

In spite of the summer heat, from which Steele often suffered intensely, he worked hard, for hard work, he said, had "become a second nature to me, in fact I am unhappy if not working." But at this time he did not feel that he was having a successful painting season. "The subjects I find in Spencer," he wrote to Brandt, after returning to the city in early October, "have not proved the best for me and of course the constant anxiety in regard to Mama, who became much lower in health than we let you know, has had its influence. The work looks worried and shallow. The most of it is not even good realism let alone poetic interpretation. However I will have a month and hope to redeem myself. . . . Things are looking exceedingly beautiful, in fact just entering their full glory."

Shortly after their return from Spencer Libbie went to Kansas to visit her brother and sisters, and Steele joined J. O. Adams to paint along the Mississinewa River at Black's Mill. "We have a delightful place," he wrote Brandt, with "an old mill and its surroundings," and in a letter to Libbie, on October 18, he said:

Have got a very good start on two pictures, one quite japaneseish in color and composition. The other some large sycamores on the banks of the river with broken reflections in the water in full sunshine and very rich in color. Am very much interested in both of them. The weather is very fine now with a little too much wind for comfortable work, but good atmosphere and color. Of course every thing seems beautiful now. Gold and purple, blue sky and water. The sycamores seem to be the prevailing trees along the river and are now in their best. Some fine oaks not yet crimson but beginning to turn. I wonder if the crimson oaks will ever look so fine, burn with such inward fire, and toned with such an envelope of ashen gray as those we used to see at Vernon. Somehow the things at Vernon seem to be the standard by which things are judged. . . .

He and Adams painted along the Mississinewa until late in November, "up at dawn and at work until sunset every day," he wrote his son. At that time he was still not satisfied with the results, but, as he said, "kept plugging away." Adams, he reported, had "been doing some capital work and has become quite an impressionist."

Back in the city again, Steele held a Studio Exhibit from December 11 to 15, of thirty-seven paintings from Spencer and the Mississinewa Valley. By then he felt much better about the year's work. "The four days of exhibition have worn me out," he wrote Brandt. "There has been a constant stream of visitors this (Sunday) afternoon and sometimes the studio was so full that it was difficult for the newcomers to get in until the others left. There is no doubt I have made a step this year. I wish I could send the whole exhibit to Boston or New York, but it will be out of my power this year to do, possibly next year I may be able to do it."

And Libbie wrote Brandt that "certain it is that Papa never painted more poetical pictures, and I don't know but what it is the best work he has ever done." And to add to their happiness Steele heard from Harry Meakin, the Cincinnati artist and a fellow student of Steele's in Munich, that the painting that had received the No. 1 mark at the Chicago exposition had been awarded a medal at an exhibition in Atlanta, Georgia.

That winter seven of Steele's pupils rented Jacob Cox's old studio. There they worked in the mornings, and, when he could, Steele visited them in the afternoons to see their work and offer criticism. But he was very busy. During that winter and until the following fall he found it necessary to devote most, if not all of his time, to portraits. While he did not enjoy them in the way he did landscapes, he made himself "take an interest in them."

Libbie became markedly worse that winter; she was often unable even to be brought downstairs. Steele was being drawn more and more into the activities of a broader art world, and in February was in Chicago to speak at the Art Institute. Since Libbie could not be with him, as soon as he arrived there he wrote to her and described the scene from the window of the train as it passed through northern Indiana and neared the city:

It was a very beautiful ride. It seems to me that I have never seen more impressive landscapes than those in the neighborhood of the Kankakee as they came into the day's *stimmung*. Great plains, gray and brown, strong and vigorous in the foreground broken into pools of water or ice and fading off through wonderful modulation into vast distances, delicate violets and grays, and over all, low skies gray, broken, misty. Delightful and beautiful as I have seen these plains in summer, and I have always felt their beauty, the effects of today were a revelation.

I do not know just what it was, but somehow they were dramatic, and I felt the seriousness of an art that would attempt the portrayal of these great plains. Their immensity and the appeal of the low toned somber earth and weeping skies. After leaving the Kankakee region touches of snow began to appear and gradually increased until near the city it became six or eight inches deep. This changed the sentiment of the landscape, it gaining in picturesqueness and variety and losing in impressiveness.

As we neared the city it was nearly dark and misty, and the great foundries and factories dim in the smoke and mist added another series of effects. These too were beautiful but the somber tone predominated. Once we passed a street with great dark buildings on either side with great wheels here and there in the street. Foundries they were perhaps, and here again it touched the dramatic. It was a black and white, I thought of a charcoal impression, but it had mystery.

Steele spoke at four o'clock the following afternoon. F. Hopkinson Smith, the New York landscape painter, lecturing there the week before, had taken a negative stand on French Impressionism, and while Steele's subject was "The Trend of Modern Art," and not strictly Impressionism, he gave a good deal of attention to it and defended it. He had some reservations about how his talk had gone. "My voice failed me considerably," he wrote his wife, "and several people had to hollow louder. It was a miserable hall to lecture in. . . . I had some very warm comments after, or compliments and several told me it was the finest thing ever delivered there. I had the closest attention, but I am no speaker and will retire now." After his talk Steele was entertained by

Henry Fuller, the novelist, Lorado Taft, the sculptor, the Hope brothers, architects, and his old friend Hamlin Garland.

On February 21, Steele attended the opening of the month-long exhibition of his and J. Ottis Adams' work at the St. Louis Museum of Fine Arts as a personal guest of the Museum's director, Halsey T. Ives, and spoke the following day at the Museum on Impressionism. Their pictures were well received and he reported to Libbie that Ives had said that "he could select a half a dozen from either Mr. Adams' or my work that he would consider the equal of any Monet he ever saw and he would just as soon own them. This is saying a good deal. . . ."

On the 11th of March Steele was back in Chicago to help organize the Society of Western Artists. Indianapolis artists Steele, Adams, and Forsyth joined with three artists from each of five other midwestern cities—Chicago, Cincinnati, St. Louis, Cleveland, and Detroit—to form the society. Its purpose was to foster interest and understanding of art in the Middle West. That evening he dropped a card to Libbie saying "everything satisfactory at last, but there have been some trying situations during the day. . . . Frank Duveneck of Cincinnati has been elected president, Forsyth Vice-Pres. The nominating committee urged my name with two others . . . for Pres. but I refused to allow my name to be voted on. . . . I have met some very fine men, and it has been very pleasant. . . ." Steele was elected president of the Society two years later. Its annual shows were held in each of the six cities from 1896 through 1914, and Steele exhibited regularly in them.

Portraiture continued to occupy Steele during the spring of 1896, despite his yearning to devote his time to landscapes. In May he finished the portrait of Oscar C. McCulloch, late pastor of the Congregational Church, and shortly thereafter finished one of L. S. Ayres. Both were painted from photographs which he found particularly tiresome and trying. In contrast, the portraits of Will Richards and Henry Spaan done from life about the same time gave him considerable satisfaction.

Steele found a diversion that spring from his studio routine. Cycling was then the thing in Indianapolis, and he fell in with the craze. "He is having some fun . . . if you call some pretty heavy falls fun," wrote Libbie to Brandt. "He had some difficulty in learning, but gets along all right now. There are several thousand wheel riders now. At night Meridian Street is entirely given up to them and they make quite a display as they go flitting by with their lanterns of different colored lights. It is a great pastime."

In mid-July Steele took Libbie, Daisy, and Shirley to Bloomington with him where he was to paint portraits of several of the late professors of the University. They drove down in the new "studio wagon" which was big enough to accomodate the whole family. It was like a gypsy wagon, with seats along the side and big windows through which Steele could paint. Libbie was pleased with it because it had a "high-backed softly cushioned seat" where she could "ride in comfort and state." "I really think," she wrote Brandt, "that the studio on wheels is going to be a great success for it will enable papa to paint out of door effects in all kinds of weather, and he can easily have a little stove in it for winter and all sorts of accommodations and comforts." Steele had wanted such a wagon for years, and while he was planning it his friend Adams insisted "it should be able to jump fences as the finest subjects were always on the other side."

Steele was weary with the months of portrait work and finally in the middle of October, with Libbie and Daisy, he loaded up the studio wagon and went to Metamora, the little Franklin County village in the Whitewater Valley to paint landscapes. Adams and Henry R. MacGinnis painted there with him that fall. It was a successful trip. The hills reminded them of the foothills of the Alps at Schliersee, and Steele felt he would never tire of painting them. Since he could work from the studio wagon in good weather and bad, they remained until the day after Thanksgiving.

Steele and his wife and daughter were back in Metamora early in August, 1897. Being in the country was good for them, particularly for Libbie. She was out in the open air all the time, and often rode in the buggy around the countryside. "I am very busy trying to get my hand in again," wrote the painter to Brandt who was back in Indianapolis again. "It seems to me I have to commence over every summer."

Steele's studio in Metamora was in a house immediately opposite the one where they were boarding, but between them were the canal, the railroad, and the street. "Though it is not more than a hundred feet away," wrote Libbie to an Indianapolis friend, "we have to go fully three times that far to reach it. . . . But we call across. . . . I can go over every day and enjoy the progress of his work, and I am very happy to tell you he is coming on finely with it. I cannot tell you how grateful I am that it should be so. I have been afraid that my constant ill health and other worries would have a depressing influence on him and retard his work. But it is so gloriously beautiful here . . . his enthusiasm knows no bounds. . . ."

45

The Whitewater Valley—the bordering hills, the river, Metamora with its old canal, and the town of Brookville on the high tongue of land between the east and west forks of the Whitewater—appealed increasingly to Steele and Adams. It seemed to them to be an area to which they could return for years to paint, even live, and before the end of 1897 they decided to buy the old home of William W. Butler at Brookville. It still stands on the bank of the East Fork of the Whitewater, with the town on the hill behind it. It had been built by the owner of the old mill that then still stood across the road. Early in February, 1898, the purchase was consummated. Because it was isolated and the artists could work there without interruption, Libbie called it the "Hermitage," the name by which it has ever since been known.

Many years later—perhaps at a meeting of the Portfolio Club—Steele told this story about why he and Adams bought the Hermitage, and there was possibly considerable truth in it:

The chief reason was that we might grow our own foregrounds. Foregrounds are composed principally of weeds, and are not always easy to come by in the well cultivated farms of the Whitewater. The first year there was a little garden as a side issue, at least we called it a garden, but from a little distance off, we saw only weeds. Luxuriantly green in summer and tawny and golden in the autumn. Magnificent horse weeds five or six feet high and Spanish needles and wonderful specimens of the noble family of burrs. If upon closer inspection one discovered a hill of corn or a wandering melon vine, or a lonesome tomato, it was only proof that our plans had miscarried a little, and the gardener was to blame for that. But in truth it may be said these aberrations did not count in the general effect.

In mid-July Libbie and Theodore went to Brookville to oversee the remodeling of the house, and they stayed through the summer, boarding at the Edringtons'. By late August or early September the work was completed, even to installing the stained-glass doors which Brandt designed to separate his father's studio from the rest of the house. Each artist had a studio and living quarters, the Steele's occupying the "downstream" half of the building. While the work was going on Libbie was able to walk to the Hermitage and stroll through the garden she had planned where mignonette and verbena were in bloom. "You can expect to be very much pleased with it," she wrote Daisy. "It is not wonderfully beautiful nor wonderful in any way, but I think if we all keep well we can have many happy days there. It is a very restful place. . . ."

Although probably never completely free from pain now, Libbie was still deeply sensitive to the sights and sounds around her and her powers of poetic

Fig. 9. Munich Girl,
1884, 20¼ by 16¼ ins.
© *Indianapolis Museum of Art,*
Gift of Mr. and Mrs. Alpheus Snow
in memory of Mr. and Mrs. John M. Butler

Fig. 10. The Boatman, 1884, 38 by 46 ins.
Private Collection

Fig. 11. Evening Poplars,
1884, 31¼ by 24¼ ins.
© *Indianapolis Museum of Art,*
Long-term loan from the
Indianapolis Literary Club

Fig. 12. Interior of a Cloister, 1885, 16 by 20 ins.
T. C. Steele State Historic Site, Indiana State Museum Collection

Fig. 13. Path between Birch Trees, 1884, 19½ by 29½ ins.
Heirs of Brandt T. Steele

Fig. 14. Munich Model,
1884, 26¾ by 22¼ ins.
© 1989 Indianapolis Museum of Art,
James E. Roberts Fund

Fig. 15. Late Afternoon, Dachau Moor, 1885, 25½ by 38⅛ ins.
© *Indianapolis Museum of Art, Gift of Mr. Frank Churchman*

Fig. 16. Fall Creek at Meridian Street, 1887, 30 by 45 ins.
The Burke Family

description had not been dimmed. "The last few days have been wonderfully beautiful," she wrote to her daughter,

The haze makes this country seem like some enchanted land, and as we ride about I feel more as if I were listening to some beautiful story and that my fancy was picturing it—that it was not real at all. The little town of Brookville stands upon its hill like some quaint old world town, and when the mellow bells of the Catholic Church and court house are ringing the delusion is complete. But—it isn't always so. It takes the mellow haze, and the mellow hills, and a mellow mood to make it so enchanting. There are clear days when things come sharp, and you even notice how rasping and unmusical the people's voices are, and how your own buggy wheels rattle, and the little church with the high pitched nasal voiced bells always holds service on such a day.

During the following winter and spring Libbie's health failed seriously, and in the early summer of 1899 it was found that she had contracted tuberculosis. Thinking that cool, clear mountain air might help her, Steele took her and Daisy to the village of Roan Mountain in the Tennessee Appalachians. The three-day journey by train was exhausting, their situation was not very satisfactory, and Libbie's condition worsened. Three weeks later they moved up the mountain to Lost Cove where they were much more comfortable. Steele managed to do some sketching and painting, but Libbie did not improve. She grew homesick to see her sons, and in mid-September, when the heat of the summer had passed, they returned to Indianapolis.

In the fall of 1899 Steele was honored by being named to the commission which was to select the American paintings to be hung at the Paris Universal Exposition the following year. It was to meet in New York the second week in November, but by then Libbie was critically ill and Theodore gave up all thought of attending. However, she insisted earnestly that he go, and on the advise of her physician who felt that knowing her husband was there would give her strength and hope, he finally acquiesced. He returned home as soon as possible, however, to be with her. Two days later, in the evening of November 14, she died.

Libbie was only forty-nine. The beauty and sincerity of her nature had been an inspiration not only to her husband and children, but to many others. Though she had remained outwardly hopeful and courageous during her painful illness, she apparently was aware that her life was drawing to an end, for the following words written in her hand—probably in the summer of 1898 —were found some years later in the desk at the Hermitage: "In the dusk of life, as the spirit nears the night which is to enthrall it for a time, and the dissolution from its past comes ever and inevitably nearer, the mind takes up that past as a precious volume of pictures, and one by one and slowly the pages are turned and dwelt upon with unutterable tenderness."

4

AFTER LIBBIE'S DEATH T. C. Steele and his children continued to live in Talbot Place, which she had helped to make into the delightful home none of them would ever forget. Many years later Daisy recalled their life there in a long letter to an old family friend, revealing the beauty and the warmth of the family feeling that prevailed:

    . . . It is not the surroundings of the Tinker Place, so much as the interior and the life that took place there that I wish you to see. Father and Mother soon made the home *our* home. Picture to yourself a large living room, its broad windows reaching nearly to the ceiling. The walls were a soft gray that made a splendid background for pictures, and the wide mantle was black. A cheerful note was furnished by a warm toned rug. Even with the many doors and windows there was plenty of wall space for pictures. . . . Father and Mother often changed the arrangement of our pictures and for a while only black and whites were seen in the living room. There were prints of Van Dyke and Rembrandt and etchings of Frank Currier and Wenban. To the right of the mantle was a broad window seat, that followed the west and part of the north wall. In the corner of this window seat, with the light falling upon the head and shoulders stood a cast of the Venus de Milo and upon the piano in the opposite side of the room was an ivory colored copy of the beautiful head of Michel Angelo's Slave. A music cabinet, well filled with Beethoven, Schuman, Schubert and Brahms, a whatnot and a bookcase overflowing with books also found comfortable space in this room. Upon the piano rested several flutes and a cello stood nearby. . . . Father and Mother were both exceedingly fond of music. . . . One of my sweetest memories is hearing Mother play Handel's Largo in the evening hours before the lamps were lit. Mother loved the twilight and when it became too dark for Father to work in the studio it was his habit to come to the living room to listen to her or sit with her before the open fire, talking quietly or meditating. . . .

    After the evening meal, Father always read to us. . . . I do not know whether Father chose books that were particularly musical in their diction or whether it was his own rich intonation that made his reading so melodious. But I do know that I looked forward to the music of his voice as much as to hearing the contents of the book. . . . Mother's comments were listened to eagerly. She was so quick to recognize beautiful parts and her own remarks were often as fine as the author's. She was a poet at heart, a poet with great reverence for all things beautiful and true. Father enjoyed reading aloud. One winter, while I was recovering from a serious illness, he came to the sickroom regularly to read to me Riley's "Flying Islands of the Night."

    After the reading it was Father's custom to bring to the living room the pictures upon which he had worked that day. These he studied by lamplight, sometimes humming or whistling as he tried them in different lights. Studying the day's work before he went to bed was a habit I think Father kept up as long as he lived.

It was a happy day when Father's first studio was finished. The dream of years had at last become a reality. . . . Father and Mother soon made it a charming place —a studio to which friends as well as patrons eagerly came. Many of Father's best portraits were painted here. . . . After lunch Mother always accompanied Father to the studio, where her criticism was often of great benefit to him. He said many times to friends: "My wife is my most helpful critic, she brings to me a clearer eye, a more poetic vision." Mother's nature was one of infinite charm and those who came under her quickening influence were always inspired by her. She was generous and lovable, gave freely of herself and joyed in the giving.

In the summer of 1900 Steele returned to the Hermitage where he remained through the late fall. Daisy was with him and she recalled "carrying pots of coffee into the studio wagon where Father was ensconced with canvas and easel, a little stove nearby to warm numb fingers. As twilight came on we would wend our way back to the Hermitage fire. . . . Tired as he often was he always lingered . . . to see the effect of the evening sky against which Brookville's roofs and towers were silhouetted."

In 1900 Steele's "Bloom of the Grape" (Plate IV) won honorable mention at the Paris Exposition, and in June that year Wabash College granted him an honorary degree of Master of Arts. In December in the exhibition of the year's work at Lieber's landscapes of the Whitewater region predominated, but portraits of Benjamin Harrison (Fig. 33), Volney T. Malott, and Hugh H. Hanna were also included.

In October, 1900, Steele's younger son Shirley married Mira (Almira) Daggett of Indianapolis, and the next fall, after the Tinker house was sold to the Art Association, Steele, with Brandt and Daisy, moved to East St. Clair Street. In June, 1902, Brandt married Helen McKay, a teacher in the art school, and in July Steele and his daughter left for the West Coast to visit his mother and brothers in Oregon and Shirley and his wife who were living in Redlands, California. It was his first trip to the West, and while he was awed by the Cascade Mountains, where he spent two weeks, he found little there to interest him as a painter. On the other hand, he was fascinated by the Oregon Coast and spent a busy month at Newport and Nye Creek Beach. "Imagine," he wrote,

a mile or two square of broken country, a hill and slope and deep ravines, covered with a growth of dwarfed cedars of the coast, now deep thickets of odorous green and then again becoming a forest of good-sized trees including some firs and pines, and over this broken ground and through this variegated forest, paths and roads, winding and turning in every direction, seemingly without plan and going nowhere in particular, and all along these roads hundreds of cottages and hundreds of tents, and this is Nye Creek Beach. The place seemed to have grown just of itself and had that charm of irregular construction that falls into harmony with nature's plan. It was beautiful always, in the morning and evening and the full light of midday, but perhaps most of all in the starlight, or when the moonlight silvered the cedars and gave mystery to the winding roads and the white tents. . . . As you walked its dusty paths, there was no sound of footfall and the night air, dewladen, was rich with the odors of the forest, and now and then pungent with the smoke of the campfires. There were great depths of shadowy thickets, and here and there the tents gleamed white in the moonlight, or they were illumined by candle light, or were ruddy in the glow of campfires. There were happy voices of men and women and children, and now and then the music of some instrument or the voice of a singer and in your ears always, sometimes loud like distant thunder, again soft as the murmur of summer wind in the trees, but incessant as your heart beats, always, the voice of the sea. . . . I had gone to the coast unwillingly, but fell under the spell of its charm at once, and every day felt more and more the eternal challenge the ocean, like the mountains, makes to the painter and poet for a voice and interpretation.

From Oregon they went to Redlands where they remained until mid-November. Steele found the color in southern California to be "marvelous and unlike that of any other land he had ever seen," and due, he felt, largely to the atmosphere. "The air seems to vibrate with flashes of colored light," he wrote, "rose and violet, red and blue and orange, and this with a vividness and intensiveness I have never seen before. . . . It has in it something of unreality." He found painting in this land a stimulating experience. "I am marvelously well satisfied with my position here and shall try hard to give a good account of myself when I return," he wrote Carl Lieber, a son of Herman Lieber. "People, at any rate, will know I have been away from Indiana. . . . I think I can promise you the best exhibition I have ever had."

Steele returned to the West Coast the following summer to paint. He also served on the jury of selection and awards for paintings for the Lousiana Purchase Exposition which was held in St. Louis in 1904. Four of his own canvases were hung there.

During the summer of 1904 he was painting in Brookville, and in December he had his show of the year's work at Lieber's. In January, 1905, he exhibited with the Society of Western Artists at the National Academy of Design in New York; and in February he had a one-man show of twenty-nine landscapes at Pratt Institute in Brooklyn, New York. Also in February he had three canvases in a loan exhibit at Marion, Indiana, and in June, 1906, he won the Foulke Prize in the Richmond, Indiana, Art Association Annual.

Meanwhile, Steele had been concerned with the planning of the museum to be built by the Art Association of Indianapolis on the site of the Tinker house. In March, 1905, he and William Henry Fox, director of the museum, were instructed by the Board of the Association to visit a number of museums in the East and Middle West in order to study their facilities. In September, the Tinker house was torn down and on November 25, at a meeting celebrating the cornerstone laying of the new building, Steele spoke on "The Future of the John Herron Art Institute." In the following October the Institute was officially opened and Steele was represented in the Inaugural Exhibition by a painting entitled "October Afternoon, Whitewater Valley." In December, he had ten landscapes in an exhibition at the St. Louis Museum at which artists living in St. Louis, Chicago, Cincinnati, and Indianapolis were represented. William Forsyth and Otto Stark also had paintings there.

In June, 1905, Margaret Steele married Gustave Neubacher of Indianapolis, and that summer T. C. Steele spent some time painting near Zionsville and also at Brookville. The following summer he was back at the Hermitage for what was to be his last painting season there.

With his children married and absorbed in their own affairs and families, it was natural for Steele to marry again. He had known Selma Neubacher, Gustave's sister, for several years. She was a handsome woman of striking appearance, with a fair complexion and light auburn hair—a woman of rather aristocratic bearing and temperament, and of high ideals. She was born on October 21, 1870, the daughter of Ludwig J. Neubacher, an Austrian by birth, and Margaret Berg Neubacher, a native of Cincinnati. She was a graduate of Pratt Institute, had been a member of the local Sketching Club, and was in the circle of young people of the city interested in art, along with Margaret and Brandt Steele and Helen McKay. She had conducted Saturday classes at the Art Institute for public school teachers and in 1906 was assistant supervisor of art for the Indianapolis schools. She was to be a devoted, sympathetic, and energetic helpmate for the painter.

In 1905 or 1906 Steele apparently had taken time to make some brief excursions into the little-known region of Brown County, Indiana, in search of new painting ground, and had found the hill country with its hidden valley farms and meadows to have great possibilities. Early in April, 1907, he bought land there and built a studio-home. On August 9, he and Selma Neubacher were married, and as she relates in her recollections of "The House of the Singing Winds," they went immediately to their new hilltop home.

Steele's life hereafter is covered so completely in her recollections that it need not be detailed here. The Brown County period was a happy one for both of them and productive of a great number of canvases, mostly landscapes, some still lifes, and now and then a portrait. Highlights of these years included his one-man show at St. Louis in 1907, the Retrospective Exhibition at the Herron Art Institute in 1910, and a one-man show there in 1920. Honors continued to come to him, including his election in 1913 as an associate of the National Academy of Design, the award of an honorary degree in 1916 by Indiana University, which may have meant more to him than any other recognition he received, and finally the appointment as honorary professor of painting at the University in 1922.

The expansion of the Brown County home and the building of the big studio were experiences which gave both Steele and his wife great satisfaction and enjoyment. The landscaping of the surrounding hillsides was largely conceived and overseen by Selma. Although he lived in the semi-isolation of the Brown County hills, involved in his work, he always maintained a warm interest in his children, his seven grandchildren,[4] and his circle of intimate friends. And as the years passed he was delighted to receive the increasing number of people from Indianapolis, from the near-by University, and from elsewhere who came to see him, his studio, and his work.

T. C. Steele had always enjoyed exceptionally good health. He seemed to recover completely from an attack of rheumatic fever in 1918, and his comeback from a heart attack in December, 1925, was rapid. By the middle of January he was painting snow scenes from their cottage window in Bloomington and by April had started two or three paintings out-of-doors. Meanwhile, he was very busy getting pictures ready for the spring exhibitions and sending them off. He attended the opening of the second Hoosier Salon in Chicago in March and the exhibition of his pictures at Lieber's in May, and when he left Bloomington for the House of the Singing Winds for a few days it was not, he wrote, "for a rest, but to get some of the spring beauty. . . ."

In June, however, having come back to Brown County for the summer, he became seriously ill. After a few weeks at a Terre Haute hospital he returned home again "anxious to get to the out of doors and to the shade of trees."

Soon afterward he wrote to his daughter as he sat on the porch in the open

---

[4] Margaret Daggett Steele, daughter of Shirley; Horace McKay Steele, Theodore Lakin Steele, and Brandt Ferguson Steele, all sons of Brandt; and Lewis Lakin Neubacher, Robert Beatty Neubacher, and Theodore Steele Neubacher, all sons of Margaret.

air, "I think I am getting on as well as could be expected. . . . So long as I am on the upgrade, I am satisfied and do not get impatient." Workmen had been there that day and he could hear them in the distance. "It is good," he wrote, "to hear hammer and saw. It means somebody is well and at work." Those words seem to speak the longing deep in his heart to be up and painting again, but that was not to be. They were, perhaps, the last words he ever wrote, for ten days later, on July 24, 1926, at the age of seventy-eight, he died.

His years of joyful work were over.

THE HOUSE OF THE SINGING WINDS

THE HOUSE OF THE SINGING WINDS

BY SELMA N. STEELE

YOU WOULD HAVE ME tell you just how it happened—that this isolated spot of a wilderness—"God-forsaken" as someone put it—inaccessible, at times, by existing roads, should have been chosen by us for a place upon which to build a future.

Are there not moments of revelation that come to all of us? Do we not accept and trust these to an almost unlimited degree? Anyway, it was so with us. We felt and believed that here in this hill country were evidences of a character in the outdoors that would command of us our best and finest in spirit. This determined our belief in the wisdom of our choice. This belief carried us on, through each succeeding year, in spite of difficulties and discouragements.

And it came about that this bit of wilderness emerged from out its obscurity, and became a place of recognition over great distances of country.

SELMA N. STEELE

January, 1940

1

A FEW YEARS AGO, after the painter, T. C. Steele, had died, I agreed to the demands of my friends to set aside a few hours each day and put into writing some of the incidents of interest that led to the finding of the location and the final building of the home.

However, the constant necessity for devising ways and means to meet the expenditures involved in the further maturing of our landscape development, which always had been in the making and which I believed should continue to unfold and reflect the characteristic inspirational quality of beauty of the locality, did not allow time to do this. For, inasmuch as the isolated locality, through its varying moods and inexhaustible subject material, had remained an ever-unfailing source of inspiration to the painter, with his almost unlimited capacity for creative work, I believed it justifiable to continue the studio home as a Sanctuary of the Future. I came to believe that others, given the privilege of living intimately within this Sanctuary, could achieve, likewise, a distinctive expression to their own creative powers.

But at present no exacting duties loom ahead. Why not, then, reveal in reminiscences—forgetting the present-day world with its war conditions—and slip back in memory some thirty-four years, into that wilderness out of which the Sanctuary was slowly evolved? Then try to discover just how it all happened, to have accepted so many hard, untried experiences, and yet be willing to have them placed in the light of just a new adventure.

Then came the question—could I possibly recreate the mood of that day—so long ago, a day in early April of 1907? Would I be able to recapture the hour, when I stood in all humbleness, listening to the voice of the painter, as he said: "My dear, if you think you can manage to live in this wilderness, we will build our home here—on this hill"?

Not to be able to recall the glory of that moment? Not to remember the depth of that conviction that made me say in answer: "I am quite sure living could be made very simple, living so far away from everything—just among the trees and clouds"? Not to remember standing there, and visualizing the home that was to be—so high!—so far away! Not to remember the stretch of forests and my battling against the strong winds as they carried the cloud shadows from hilltop to hilltop! A home in the wilderness! What an adventure it would be!

A precious hour, in which one accepted all without reserve or question. Strange, too, how quickly decisions can be reached, even when you realize that they are to affect and change the whole course of your life.

So it was there and then, on that April day, standing on the hilltop which could not even boast a footpath, but was covered with a thicket of underbrush through which we had torn our way, that I met the challenge to assist in creating a new home.

At the time I sensed no difficulties. Pioneering had always held a charm for me, as I read of it in books. Neither was I aware how inherited family traditions very frequently were to complicate my original plan for simple living. I believe, most thoroughly, that I could live contentedly any old way, as long as I had a daily panorama of forests and great skies spread before me.

Up to that day my knowledge of Brown County had been limited to hearing my brother Walter talk enthusiastically about its primitiveness and picturesqueness which he had discovered on hikes through the country. My curiosity becoming aroused, I would ask to be allowed to go with him on these expeditions, for we did much hiking together. To this, however, he would never consent, begging off by saying that accommodations were too primitive for me to be comfortable.

So matters stood, up to the fall of 1906, when, one day, Mr. Steele informed me that he felt the need of a new painting ground. Judging from Walter's Kodak pictures and his descriptions of the quality of the beauty in the Brown County hills, the painter believed there might be suitable material there for landscape work. He concluded by saying he would investigate, and should it prove to be so, he would look about for some purchasable land where a studio-home could be built. We were to be married the following August.

In the spring of 1907 he went to Nashville, county seat of Brown County, and stopped at the Ferguson House. While here, he was driven about by the real estate dealer, William (Bill) Ferguson, to see various tracts of land which were for sale. At that time Marcus Dickey[1] had already acquired consider-

---

[1] Platform manager, private secretary, and biographer of James Whitcomb Riley. Born in Fayette County, Indiana, in 1856, Dickey attended Fairmount Academy in Grant County, State Normal School at Terre Haute, and Harvard. He published the first volume of his two-volume biography of the Hoosier poet in 1919 and the second in 1922. He had acquired his Bear Wallow site in 1905 and the following year built his "house of thirty windows" on the hilltop. In 1942 Dickey and J. K. Lilly, Sr., presented their adjoining holdings on Bear Wallow, totaling 555 acres of heavily wooded land, to Indiana University to be used for botanical studies. Mr. Dickey died in 1950.

able acreage for a future home on Bear Wallow, three and a half miles to the north of Nashville. Before Mr. Steele left the county he had decided to consider one of two tracts of land.

Needless to say, as an artist in heart and feeling, he had come away convinced that there was inexhaustible material in the county for his work. In discussing with me the two tracts of land which he believed might be made adaptable to our needs, he spoke of the one tract as possibly preferable, for more than one reason. This tract lay about a mile and a half off of the main highway that led to Bloomington, the university town.[2] Bloomington, with its variety of stores, offered facilities for shopping for ones everyday needs, and our shipped goods could be handled through the express and freight offices of that city. Furthermore, there would be great convenience in being very near the post office station of Belmont, which was in the immediate valley on the Bloomington highway.[3]

There and then we decided that this particular tract of land would be of first consideration.

Within a couple of weeks, on a Saturday afternoon, April 10, I was taken in tow by two men, the painter and my brother Walter, to be given a meaningful picture of Brown County. We took the train to Helmsburg,[4] and from there we drove by hack to the county seat of Nashville.[5] Twilight was gathering as we started on this drive, over a road of mud deeply rutted and with shelves of rocks. I was long in forgetting the horror I felt on this first drive into the county. The road wound in and out of the valleys. The hills seemed dangerously high. The horses were constantly whipped to keep up to a certain pace. At times they stumbled going over the rocky road; then again, because of the deep mud, they seemed to experience great difficulty in mak-

[2] Bloomington, seat of Indiana University and county seat of Monroe County, had a population of 8,838 in 1910. The University was growing rapidly. For the academic year of 1906-1907 it had a total enrollment of 1,821. In 1910 the enrollment reached 2,113, an increase of 30 per cent over the preceding year.

[3] The post office at Belmont was established in 1884 and discontinued in 1916. Thereafter Nashville served as the post office for the Belmont area.

[4] Helmsburg was the only passenger railroad station in Brown County, the county's lone railroad being the section of the Illinois Central running from Indianapolis to Bloomington, which cut across Jackson Township. The first train passed over this track on August 31, 1905. A post office, Helms, was established here in 1904, the name being changed to Helmsburg the following year.

[5] When Brown County was organized in 1836, out of territory taken from the surrounding counties of Bartholomew, Jackson, and Monroe, the village of Jacksonburg, platted in 1836, became the county seat. The name was changed to Nashville the following year. It was incorporated as a town in 1872 with a population of 286. In 1910 it had a population of 354, having declined from 393 in 1900 and 395 in 1890.

61

ing the climb over the hills. Various rest periods became necessary. After reaching the top, they galloped down the other side. The vehicle kept rocking back and forth. I wondered how the horses were managed so that they kept on their feet, and how the travelers were kept from being thrown out. Cautiously I asked Walter whether he knew if such things ever happened? The answer came from a native sitting in front of me, who said, "Oh, yes, ma'am—this same hack turned over last Saturday night," "Anyone hurt?" "No, ma'am," came back in reply.

By now the night was dark. So I held on, all the tighter. Eventually our destination was sighted with flickering windows appearing, now and then, out of the darkness. I wondered why I had not been prepared for the very rough, high hills and the almost impassable road. Maybe I had been told but did not wish to be convinced and purposely suppressed all memory of it.

We stopped for the night at the Ferguson House, kept by the wife of the real estate dealer. Mrs. Ferguson was one of the interesting characters of that day: vivid, quick of tongue, and born with a native curiosity and frankness. It was she who told an artist friend of ours that if she were ever to go to Europe, "she would go in the summertime, when the waters were low." We had a bountiful country-style meal, sat awhile around a wood-burning stove, and then asked to be allowed to retire, for we were planning for an early start in the morning.

Weary from bewilderment rather than from enthusiasm, I climbed the stairs to the room which had been reserved for me. It proved to be an un-heated one, one, I am sure, that had not been used all winter long. As I opened the door, the accumulated cold air rushed out, as of a solid chunk. Was it cold! I opened the bed. Oh, horror! icy sheets, too! Reasoning that it would be wiser not to grow peevish for fear of bigger and more disturbing things to contend with on the morrow, I crawled into bed under a huge featherbed and was not long in finding sleep.

The next morning the whole world, and I, too, had undergone a trans-formation. As I walked outdoors I found myself transported back into a period of long ago, quite remote from the one I had left barely twelve hours before. How out of the ordinary the little hamlet was! Such charm! Such quaintness!

At breakfast we were seated at a long table, piled high with a variety of foods. There was trivial conversation, but, on the other hand, plenty of in-formation for me. We did not linger long at the breakfast table for we had

Fig. 17. Herman Lieber, 1887, 36 by 20 ins.
Curtis and Mary Liechty

Fig. 18. A June Idyll, 1887, 18 by 29 ins.
© 1989 Indianapolis Museum of Art, Gift of Mrs. William B. Wheelock

Fig. 19. Oaks at Vernon, 1887, 30 by 45 ins.
© Indianapolis Museum of Art, John Herron Fund

Fig. 20. Governor Alvin P. Hovey, 1889, 50 by 34 ins.
Indiana Historical Bureau, State of Indiana,
Photograph by Robert Wallace

Fig. 21. The Creek (Sugar Creek near the Shades),
1888, 22 by 40 ins.
Private Collection

Fig. 22. Twilight, Cattle Crossing a Ford,
1889, 19½ by 31 ins.
Private Collection

need to be up and going. The tract of land which we had come into Brown County to see and consider as a purchase possibility was, we were told, about nine miles from Nashville. Before the day was over, I "reckoned" the mileage was nearer fifty than nine.

Our traveling experiences were practically the same as those of the day before coming from Helmsburg, with this difference, however: we were seeing the country in a morning light and not through a hazy atmosphere of a late afternoon. We went by "hack," two-seated and drawn by a pair of horses. They were whipped to get into the ruts, and whipped to get out of them. We were told it had rained more or less continuously during the last few days and this had put the roads into an almost impassable condition. So we got out frequently, the painter, Walter, and I, and walked to lighten the load for the horses, letting the driver use all his energy for urging the horses on.

The winds were high, which sometimes made walking difficult, nevertheless, exhilarating. The forests were not in leaf, but silhouetted against great expanses of sky. I was overwhelmed by the beauty of the countryside. I had no idea the Indiana landscape could be so fine.

As we left the valley and reached Kelley Hill, at the top of the ridge, I was stunned by the dramatic spectacle spread out before me. There was a sweep of great distances. There were cloud shadows of deep purple hue passing rapidly over one range of hills to the other. It was all so wonderfully appealing in its bigness, so full of meanings, and so alive, with the stir of a coming spring. As I stood before it and thought of the prospect of a future residence among such loveliness I grew very humble, indeed. I could well grasp the painter's desire to live and paint in this region where there would be untold possibilities, and an isolation conducive to intensive work.

The road down from Kelley Hill into Schooner Valley seemed long, steep, and difficult for the horses. However, we rode, instead of walking, for the mud was deep and time was passing. We talked enthusiastically about the valley views, and the painter thought they would be fine subjects for his work.[6]

At last we reached the small post office hamlet of Belmont, consisting of a general store, blacksmith shop, and a few houses. At Belmont we turned south to go up the worst road imaginable. It was so deeply rutted through

[6] The road which the party took from Nashville to Belmont followed the route of the present State Road 46.

the valley section that it became quite a question whether the horses could pull our load through. For we could not walk. Finally, through slow stages, it was accomplished. Just before we reached the bridge there came as a joyous interlude the sound of waters rushing over a dam which had furnished in its day power to the wheel of an old gristmill, ruins of which were still standing.

Then over the bridge, through another stretch of muddy lane, through a creek bed that had to be forded, and we began to ascend another hill. This, too, was accomplished with great difficulty. After a short drive we came to what was then known as Bracken Hill. At that time Bracken Hill was so steep and so full of gullies made by the winter rains that even the horses could not be whipped into carrying our load over the shelves of rock in the roadbed. From there on we three walked the remaining distance through mud up to our ankles. We stopped at the cottage of Wash. Parks. A tract of land of forty acres, with cottage and a few log buildings, owned by Parks, joined the acreage to the north which we had come to see as a possible purchase.

Upon our arrival we were asked to stop for a rest and also to join the Parks family at the midday meal. This we did. We had been told that they were a very hospitable people. Mrs. Parks was of Pennsylvania Dutch parentage.

After a friendly visit we started out for our walk of inspection over the adjoining land. I cannot say that any one of us had much enthusiasm for the difficulty with which we had to fight for a way through thickets of brambles and underbrush that covered practically every inch of ground. Already I had begun to question whether I was equal to making a home in an isolated wilderness such as this. However, whatever doubts I had were fast dispelled when I reached the brow of the hill and faced the panorama of hills and skies spread before me.

While I looked at this unobstructed view of a nearly complete horizon, in an atmosphere of fantastic blue with pulsing clouds, there came the conviction, to which there could be neither question nor argument, that a way must be found whereby the painter could use this particular spot for the continuance of his work. There was everything here to meet his requirements. There was an incomparable quality of beauty to the hills. There was a great variety of subject matter. Above all, everything seen and felt conjoined to sing its way into our hearts, divining that here there would always be inspiration for the tasks that lay before us.

How prophetic of our future this was!

On the way back to Indianapolis we were already considering the type of house best suited for this high windswept hill.

Now, at this particular time the painter still had ownership in a studio-home. Some years previous to this he and J. Ottis Adams,[7] the landscape painter and a member of the Hoosier Group,[8] had bought the old mill property on the banks of the Whitewater at Brookville. They remodeled the old mill house into a double, with each side containing a studio and living quarters. It became known as the Hermitage, and, as such, is still owned and used by Mr. Adams' widow.[9]

During the fall of 1906, Mr. Steele was painting and living in the Hermitage at Brookville. Writing to me in September of that year he said, in view of our plans for a future home,

But artists, above all people, ought to have and do have, if fortune allows, homes of the greatest individuality and beauty. . . .We will try to have ours such a home. . . . I think it is all right to love people and the life of the city, so much richer in many things than country life. I take it, one should not be bound to either, but alternate, as the mood and the need come. When I go back to the city, I feel the electric thrill of its crowded streets and the stimulus of meeting its splendid men and women, and the outdoor life becomes all the more beautiful for the change. But my life work, the thing that interests me most, and that I am persuaded I am most successful in is under the blue dome of heaven when the bugle notes of color are sounding and the world seems big and mysterious—a vision, half from the realism before my eyes, half from the dream of my heart.

In the spring of 1907 the Adamses were in need of more room for their growing family and expressed the wish to purchase Mr. Steele's share in the Hermitage. The sale was consummated April 14. At the end of that week when he started for Brookville the painter wrote to me: "I want to pack things out of the way. It is going to be a tiresome, vexatious job, from the fact I do not know what things I need at our new home in the wilderness. How much I wish that you were here with me, with your clear, practical initiative."

[7] Born in Amity, Indiana, in 1851, Adams studied in London from 1872 to 1874 and, like Steele, at the Royal Academy in Munich, from 1880 to 1887. He had a studio in Muncie for a few years and taught in Union City, Fort Wayne, and the John Herron Art Institute in Indianapolis. He painted on the Mississinewa River, at Metamora, and around Brookville, and, as related above (p. 46), joined with Steele in buying the Hermitage at Brookville for a studio. Adams later painted at Leland, Michigan, and in Florida. He died in 1927.

[8] A school of Indiana painters that included J. Ottis Adams, William Forsyth, Richard B. Gruelle, Otto Stark, and Steele.

[9] A native of Muncie, Indiana, Winifred Brady Adams studied at Drexel Institute, Philadelphia, and the Art Students' League in New York. She was a student of William Chase. Mrs. Adams was known as a painter of still life. She died in 1955.

A few days later, April 17, he writes from the Hermitage:

I thought perhaps you would like to know how things appear to me now, at my last visit to the Hermitage, for it is my home no longer, and I am just a visitor. Well, in the first place, I feel I have made no mistake, at least as an artist. Brookville—the hills about it—the river—the view and the Hermitage, as I have seen them today, do not appeal to me so much as the wilderness of Brown County. At any rate, I am satisfied. But the dear rooms—so large and so fine—it is hard to give them up. . . . I spent the evening sorting books. . . . I have had a big fire in the fireplace, and its beauty appeals to me greatly. I am satisfied I have done for the best, and I believe I will find it so. . . . I hope to get through by Friday morning. . . . I find everything in perfect order, but I am surprised at the number of canvases I have here.

A few days later he writes: "It is not at all certain that I will be home for tomorrow night. I had no idea there was so much here. . . . Have a room uptown, and will store everything but the phaeton, which I will send over immediately."

During the time that the painter was at Brookville I was at work at home on a preliminary plan for the new house so as to have it ready at his return. It had been decided that the house must be of a low type that would withstand the high winds prevailing on the hilltop. It would be small, just enough for our needs. Of first consideration in the plan would be a well-lighted room, large enough to be used for a studio.

So the floor plan was laid out to contain one large room across the north end, facing the great view, with provision for ample north light. Back of this large room three smaller rooms were to provide for a kitchen, a dressing room, which later could be converted into a bathroom, and an indoor bedroom. There was to be an open terrace porch on the north side, which would not obstruct the north light from the studio room, with screened porches extending around the whole length of the other three sides of the house. These porches could be used for outdoor dining and sleeping purposes.

There were two features which I asked to have incorporated into the original plan; various others could be left for consideration. One was a cellar under the house, for I could not accept the type of cellar in use in the hills. This latter type was an outdoor pit, dug into the side of a hill, and very frequently a distance from the house. As I now remember, our type of "under-the-house cellar" was the first of its kind in this section of the country and stirred up a great deal of interest among the natives, who came from distances to see it. I had to admit that although I still clung to the idea that I would enjoy pioneering to its fullest, when I saw some of its aspects, I did not hesitate to insist that I wanted to avoid them if at all possible.

The second feature of my choosing was of an entirely different nature. I had always thought of a house in the wilds as incomplete without a fireplace. In my school days the old Gaelic tales of Fiona Macleod touched me deeply not only because of their sheer beauty but because they made me aware that life could be sensed only in its fullest through a keen understanding and enjoyment of the great open spaces. The previous year, on his birthday, I had given this collection of tales to the painter with certain marked passages. I believed one of these passages was particularly suited for an inscription over our new fireplace—"Every morning I take off my hat to the Beauty of the World."

In the house plan the fireplace was to face the great north view, and the inscription "Every morning I take off my hat to the Beauty of the World" could become a philosopher's stone and make each new day a golden one.

Eventually both features became a part of the house: the cellar under the house to store the food for ourselves and our friends, and the fireplace around which we were to have so many intimate hours. In time the inscription, too, was put into place by Gustave Baumann, the artist, for a few years a resident of Nashville but now of the art colony of Santa Fe, New Mexico.[10]

In the meantime, Mr. Steele had purchased the tract of land.[11] The house plan took definite shape and he went to Nashville to find and hire workmen who could build the house. He arranged for the building to be done under the supervision of William Quick of Nashville. Mr. Quick and his two assistants proved to be very versatile in their work, for they did practically everything necessary to complete the house, with one exception, the plastering was done by workmen brought out from Bloomington.

During the building period of the house Mr. Steele was painting the por-

[10] Born in the Prussian town of Magdeburg, in 1881, Baumann came to the United States in 1891. He studied at the Art Institute of Chicago and in Munich. In Brown County he not only found the quiet and seclusion that he sought, he also found the inspiration which turned him from commercial art to wood-block printing and he became the acknowledged leader in this field in America. Through his efforts the first exhibition of American block prints and wood engravings was assembled at the Chicago Art Institute in February, 1916. He maintained studios in Nashville and Chicago, and in 1918 moved to Santa Fe, New Mexico. On March 8, 1966, he wrote to the Indiana Historical Society from Santa Fe: "Am beginning to feel like a Prehistoric at eighty-five. You know the only stone carving I ever did was over Steele's fireplace, one of the Thanksgivings I spent there—marvelous days they were in 1910–1916."

[11] Steele's Brown County holdings by 1920 included 240 acres in the northwest corner of section 18, T 8 N, R 2 E, Johnson Township, and 40 adjoining acres in section 7.

trait of William Lowe Bryan of Indiana University.[12] He divided his time between painting in Bloomington and supervising the building operations in Brown County.

I did not see the house at any time during the construction period, largely because we were keeping our approaching marriage a secret. We knew too well of the grapevine method of spreading news.

It is not easy at this day to envisage the difficulties that were involved in erecting the first simple structure. To begin with, there was not even a path leading up the hill where the house was to stand. The first semblance of a road was made by the first team that brought the first load of building material from the mill in the valley to the building site on the hill. The building site, too, had to be cleared out of the forest's undergrowth. The roads through the valleys below and up Bracken Hill were all dirt roads, made up largely of deep ruts and shelves of rocks. It was not unusual for the teamsters to be compelled to stop to fill up the ruts before they could go on with their loads. Very frequently two teams had to be used to one load of material.

But here I am going to stop and let the story of the building period be told through letters written to me by Mr. Steele during that time. On the 4th of May, 1907, he took the train at Indianapolis for Helmsburg. From the Ferguson House at Nashville he writes on that evening:

This has been a very beautiful day and the ride down this morning was delightful. I have wanted you with me all day, in all I have done and in all I have seen. First, I will tell you all I have done. Arrived about 10, leaving my trunk, in which I had brought bed clothing etc. at Helmsburg. I find my carpenters cannot go out until Tuesday. This suits me all right, as I can get my trunk over tomorrow, and all can go over to Belmont together. Talked over matters with the carpenters this morning, and made partial arrangements for the purchase of a horse. The horse I have in view is not the one I saw last week, but will be, I believe, a more satisfactory one, though perhaps not so good looking. His history is however splendid, and I can get him for $125. He is a horse that Mr. Dickey drove a great deal last year, and Mrs. Dickey, too, and is perfectly safe.

I have arranged for three men to start grubbing out the underbrush Tuesday morning. So there will be six men at work, and things ought to move very lively, and I shall see that they do.

[12] Known affectionately as the "Grand Old Man of Indiana University," Bryan served as its president from 1902 until his retirement in 1937. He was born in a farmhouse two miles east of Bloomington in 1860 and graduated from the University in 1884. He continued his studies at the University of Berlin and in Würzburg and Paris, and received the Ph. D. degree from Clark University in 1892. Returning to Indiana University, he taught Greek and philosophy, served as vice-president, and then as president. In 1899 he married Charlotte Lowe of Indianapolis, and added her name to his to become William Lowe Bryan. He died in 1952. See Fig. 43.

This afternoon, took a walk of three or four miles over the hills south of town with Ferguson and Quick. Saw some very beautiful subjects and two or three with rather grand qualities. Got back to town in a shower. A young woman from Indianapolis was here looking for a place to buy, and will probably buy a place about a mile from ours—a tract of 280 acres. A man and his wife came on the train this morning, and rode out part of the distance with us in the hack. They, too, were looking for a place. The interurban prospects,[13] also, seem a little brighter, though I don't count on that a bit. This is all the Brown County news, I think, except that my address will be Belmont, Brown County, until I find more definitely as to the rural delivery.

Enclosed are some flowers picked from a bank by the roadside. Perhaps they will bring up to you the hills with their mingled light and shade—and of fuller leaf, and the gray trunks and the abandon and suggestion of the tangled underwood and thickets. They were beautiful today and I have brought my things and expect to sketch some.

I am eager to begin. What a fine subject would be that of the men working in the underbrush grubbing it out, and burning it, with the blue smoke rising up between the gray trunks of trees, with the flush of the spring color coming. Maybe something will come out of it.[14]

I hope you have had a pleasant day and ever happy. . . . believe me, dear heart, that I am here working for our home, the place and conditions I trust will make us happy.

On the next day, Monday, he writes that he has just bought the horse for $125, "that he is not pretty, but he is good and safe. So I am satisfied. Phaeton not yet here. Everything moves slow. I find I have to get behind everything and push to make it go."

On the next day, May 6, he writes again from Nashville:

This is a soft gray afternoon, dove tinted is the atmosphere, and how exquisite the surrounding hills are. The beauty of the day is the one thing that cheers me, and inspires me in the midst of the many perplexing problems that come up to be decided in getting things started.

However, everything I can do here is now done, and as far as I can see, well done, and I can only wait until morning when we go to the Hopper Farm. That is what the place has been called for forty years, I understand. We will change the name for that would never do for a place where an artist's dreams are to be planted, and pictures grown instead of corn and wheat.

I grow impatient when I think of all that is to be done before our life is to commence there. But all good things cost, and perhaps it will be better that it has cost sacrifices and care and anxiety, even.

I will be glad to get away from Nashville. It is a rather tiresome place, and I find it difficult to get much in sympathy with it. Better the real country. . . . But while it is only three hours distant from home, this place feels as far away as

---

[13] No interurban line was ever built into Brown County.
[14] See Plate VII for Steele's treatment of this subject in 1910.

California. . . . Many natives I suspect have never been out of the county. The people seem kindly, but not progressive, except in a small way. It is a little corner that the great strenuous world has swept around and missed. Whether they are contented with their lot, I do not know.

The young woman who was looking for a place telephoned to Ferguson she would take the place, and he has started to Indianapolis to close up the deal. It is her intention to make it a sheep and fruit farm.

Ferguson has 160 acres just a half mile west of us, that he would sell for $350. I wish some of our friends would take it. It comes out closer to the valley than ours. So the views would be probably finer. If I felt I had the money to spare, I would take it myself. However, a man that is building a house must not think of anything else until he is through.

Mr. Dickey is over at Bear Wallow for two or three days, and learning I was here, sent over his "Hello! and good luck." I only wish he were nearer to us. We do not want many people though. We are running away from towns and people, for the hills and woods and the sky, and we can get people when we want them.

The woods were full of red birds and blue birds yesterday, and I heard several times the jolly vigorous call of the bobwhite. I hope we will have plenty of birds in our thickets—think, acres and acres of thickets with all kinds of shrubs and trees. I shall get our carpenter to tag a lot of them, that we may learn their names.

On the next day, Tuesday, he writes:

A gray misty morning with a little sprinkle of rain. It is not cold, and we are going to start in all right, without it rains hard. As a start to housekeeping in the old log house, I have bought a cot, a broom, a hatchet, padlock, wheel barrow, water barrel, etc. Have my own bed clothes brought in the trunk, and lots of determination to make things go. I have made the plunge and the timidity is gone. Now it is the fight for success.

It so happened that at this time there was a squatter's cabin on the place—a one-room cabin. This stood at the left of the great oaks that you pass coming this way from our present gateway. This cabin the painter had renovated to the extent that it could be used by him for sleeping when he was out here supervising the work and could also be used in that capacity by the workmen.

So on Wednesday, May 8, there is a letter from him written from "Hill Farm."

I am writing this in the old log cabin, sitting on my cot with my trunk for a table. A gentle rain is falling, spoiling things. So far the five men and one team keep on working, but if the rain increases, they will have to stop. We have got things well started, but the difficulties have been, and will be, great.

I am grateful that somewhere back among my ancestors were people that wouldn't give up, and that some of it has come down to me.

We have the home beautifully located, and now as the underbrush is being

PLATE III

September, 1892, 30 by 45 ins.
Theodore L. Steele

taken out, one can see how beautiful is the lay of the land and the trees. Three men have been grubbing since Monday morning. Though it tears up the ground like plowing almost, it is the only way, and I will immediately sow it into grass.

The team is hauling stone for the foundation and cellar. We have finally gotten a road that is fairly easy to the top of our hill. The main road from Belmont, however, is as bad as ever, and I may have to have that worked before I can get my lumber up.

The main carpenter was sick Sunday, and has not as yet come, but probably will be here today, but the other two have done very well. The whole body of men are splendid workers, and put in ten hours a day.

I was surprised to see a team driven into the grounds about four o'clock yester-day, and a couple of young men got out and came up the hill. One of them had tried to get me all day. He telephoned to Indianapolis, then Helmsburg and Nashville, and finally had located me. So you see a fellow can't get lost, even in Brown County. He was a member of a committee from the senior class of the State University and wanted me to paint a portrait of Dr. Bryan by Commence-ment. This I have agreed to do. So I will have to be in Bloomington some of the time, while the house is building. Think I can arrange my time so as to be here every few days. It will help out with the cost of the house.

I find it is only about twelve miles to Bloomington, and from our house we can see the smoke of the town and hear the engine whistle on the road. So it does not seem so far out of the world.

The log house is cleaned out, and quite comfortable—a cot in each corner, a trunk, a tool chest or two. Last night was quite cold, but a tray of my trunk fitted into one window, and an extra quilt covered up another. The doors are all right, and yet we have plenty of ventilation. You may be sure the hardest problem seems to be in getting teams for the hauling, and it will take four horses to get an ordinary load up that miserable hill, which is worse than when we saw it. How-ever, the people here are used to the hills, and are very skillful in getting over difficulties.

Things will come out all right, I am sure. . . .

The boys are getting out some splendid rock for the foundation and chimney. Have to haul it about a half mile. The woods are full of dogwood and there are many fine wild haw in blossom. These will be kept, of course. I am keeping more of the trees than should be, I have no doubt. In fact, not cutting many trees or saplings. We can tell later what is to come out. It is the sassafras thickets and sumach which I am having grubbed out, blackberries and wild haw where they have scattered and become thickets.

The next day he writes of going down to the store at Belmont to see if he can prevail upon the road supervisor to have something done about "that infernal hill road, which threatens to stop everything. I have offered to do-nate $15 to help gravel it." Otherwise, he says, "he is inchin along and keep-ing up courage."

On May 10, he has gone to Nashville to get the phaeton and plans to drive

71

to Bloomington early the next morning to see Dr. Bryan about painting the portrait.

On the 16th of May, after having been in Indianapolis and Bloomington, he writes again "From the Home in the Wilderness":

Just a few words as to how I found things. All satisfactory at Bloomington, where I returned for a few days' work on the portrait.

The roads were bad—a hard rain or two since. I felt a little blue until I climbed the hill and saw the noble prospect open out under the afternoon sun, and looked around and saw how much had been done at home. I was very much surprised. The cellar is finished and the foundations all in, and part of the floor framing (joists).

Three carpenters, three grubbers, and two teams have been at work all week and things are moving rapidly. The payroll is $17.50 a day, but things are going fast, and I am satisfied.

There is a splendid foundation, made of those fine stones that I thought were to go for the fireplace. However, we will get more for that, and the house cannot fall down with such a foundation.

The view this afternoon was wonderful and the forests all about are glorious. If they would stop just where they are I certainly would be pleased, but, perhaps, new beauties will develop as time goes on.

May 17

Good morning. A bright sun and a hazy atmosphere makes things very beautiful. Slept fairly well last night, but find I will have to get a mattress at the first opportunity.

The teams will begin hauling the lumber on Monday. The horse is not well. Won't eat this morning. We are going to try him on grass, which I think he needs.

I shall try sketching this morning. I wish I could see these things with you. . . .

And in the evening of the same day:

I am alone in the cabin tonight. The boys go home Saturday and it is getting back to primitive things more than I like. All about is the sound of the whip-poor-wills and a cheering bird note, and from a distant farmhouse comes the barking of a dog; which is a reassuring sound, for it means a home and family life and cheer of one kind. Parks invited me to his house, but I would rather stay here.

This morning there were great storm clouds, deep and bluish, and as I took a walk up the hill road deeply enjoying the forest, now so wonderfully beautiful, there flashed into my mind the line from one of the New England poets: "The harvest of a quiet eye." I thought of our hopes of seeing things together, these impressions from the wonders of nature, and hoped the harvest would be all we wished, here in this solitude.

I have been sketching the last two days with rather indifferent success. Not time to get my hand in. I shall go to Bloomington tomorrow afternoon, so as to be in good condition for the portrait, which I hope to commence Monday.

The house is getting along all right. The sills for the whole house are now in, with the exception of the back porch. The cellar is finished with the exception of the steps. It has taken six barrels of cement, though I believe some of this was used in the foundation of the chimney. . . . Sent to Bloomington to get me a mattress for my cot, as I was not finding it comfortable. You see I am telling you all the details of my little housekeeping.

My horse is still not right, though better. He will not eat as he should. I shall drive him into Bloomington and have a veterinary see him. I think I have been cheated in the horse, and that it is a bad bargain. At any rate, I cannot help it now. . . .

Sunday morning, May 18

A bright beautiful morning, after a night of storm. Terrific thunder and did not sleep much, and found your lamp such a comfort.

Walked down in the east ravine this morning. It was very beautiful. The little rill was rushing full, and numerous falls. There are many beautiful wood interiors there, I think,

Found the cellar with several inches of water from the rain. It is now, of course, uncovered. I think by next Saturday the house will be under roof, or partially so, at least.

I am now getting things together for my drive over to Bloomington, and putting my bedding in the trunk, etc. Horse is eating this morning.

Sunday evening, May 18

Arrived in Bloomington about 4:30, and am enjoying the comforts of civilization. The uncouth surroundings of Brown County affect me unfavorably. Of course, it will be different when we get a home, and things more as we want them. That will come.

I am not discouraged, and, after all, it is only a part of our life—to be put off when we want it, or need the change. And again, two hearts that love and work together make a world of their own, with their own quality. That is our consolation and joyous anticipation for the future. It will come, do not fear.

It is true I sometimes regret selling the Hermitage and coming here. But still I think it will work out for the best, though it is causing so much worry and anxiety. In the end it will come out all right. I will close now, as I am trying to arrange an early interview with Dr. and Mrs. Bryan.

I will be here until the latter part of the week.

On May 20 he wrote from the Hotel Bowles, Bloomington: "Mr. Brooks [15]

[15] At this time Alfred Mansfield Brooks was serving as head of the Department of Fine Arts at Indiana University. Born in Saginaw, Michigan, in 1870, he received his A. B. and A. M. degrees from Harvard and studied in the School of Architecture of Massachusetts Institute of Technology. He came to Indiana University in 1896, and in 1911, in addition to his University post, he became curator of prints at John Herron Art Institute. In 1922 he went to Swarthmore College as head of the Department of the History and Philosophy of Art, retiring in 1937. He died in Gloucester, Massachusetts, in 1963. Among his several published works were *Architecture and Allied Arts* (1914), *Dante How to Know Him* (1916), and *Our Architectural Debt to Greece and Rome* (1923).

came into the hotel this morning and handed me your letter. How much good it did me. I wanted to sit down immediately and answer it. Dr. Bryan came for me and took me over to the University and assisted in getting the things I wanted for the temporary studio." And later that same day:

In thinking about your letter—it was so cheery and loving and hopeful of the home on the hill, I think I do understand how you feel about it, and appreciate it. And it is the one great thing that sustains and inspires to go ahead, and make it a success. I know we shall be happy there. It is only a question now of ways and means to bring it about.

Financially, I cannot tell how it is going to come out. I cannot calculate the cost of the labor and the hauling, which is a bigger item than I thought. But I hope not to go much over $1,000 for the house. Perhaps $1,200, when entirely finished. People here are very much interested in it. Dr. Bryan, Will Howe,[16] Mr. Brooks and others of the professors went home with Dr. Bryan for luncheon.

Worked from him for about two hours this afternoon, and have two sittings tomorrow, and also Wednesday. Then Monday and Tuesday of next week. Then off until the following week when I must finish. He is quite a good subject, and a very kindly considerate man.

Will Howe is the enthusiastic, bright-minded interesting man he was at Butler, only a greater field and responsibilities have further developed him. He is at the head of the department of English literature with several assistants. He told me today he has some aspirations toward a home in Brown County.

Dr. Bryan wanted a place on the ridge between Helmsburg and Bear Wallow, but the man wanted $100 an acre and he gave it up. He, indeed everyone, says the time will soon come when all these hills will be valuable, and I should not wonder if some of these people do not invest this summer. My buying has started them all to thinking about it.

Yes, we will have the fireplace. Ogle, one of the carpenters, is going to build it. He is also a stonemason and a blacksmith—one of those men who can do anything. His father is a chimney builder, and he will get him to come down for a day when he is building the throat of the chimney. I have no doubt it will prove successful.

They think they found stone for it on our place in one of the ravines. This would please me very much. There is some sentiment in using the products and materials found on your own place to build a home.

The cellar came out beautifully. Is yet to be plastered with a thin coat of cement and sand. By the way, no sand is found in that part of the county. It will have to be hauled from Bean Blossom or Helmsburg. This will make it cost $3.50 a yard. The great amount of hauling to be done is where so much of the expense comes in. Well, when it is once done it will be done and the expense will stop.

[16] Born in Charlestown, Indiana, in 1873, Will David Howe graduated from Butler College in 1893 and received the A. B. and A. M., and Ph. D. degrees from Harvard. He served as professor of English literature at Butler from 1899 to 1906 and at Indiana University from 1906 to 1919. Going to New York, he helped establish the publishing firm of Harcourt, Brace and Howe, and from 1921 to 1942 served as editor and director of Charles Scribner's Sons. In 1942 he was a visiting professor at Emory University and the University of Georgia. He died in 1946.

The House of the Singing Winds

The letter from "The Hill Cabin, May 26," begins with a pencil sketch and then continues:

Is it a bungalow? It looks a little like it from the rear, of which this is an imperfect sketch. The back porch is going to be charming, and so will the east porch, but the north side will look bare, though the five windows may relieve it.

This is Saturday at 4 P. M. and the boys have just quit work and started home. Things are working out all right. They commenced shingling this morning and did about a quarter of the roof. Enough to protect the lumber which we have moved in, though the doors and window frames are here in the cabin for better protection. About all the lumber is now on the ground and paid for, or nearly so, and takes a lot, for after all, it is a big house.

The studio room will be a magnificent room, and in fact, I believe you will be pleased with all. Now, how does the country look, the surroundings and views? Of course, around the house it is all disorder as it must be, but aside from that, it is magnificent.

Today has been one of showers, and some of the effects of sky and distances have been very impressive, and the middle distances and foregrounds are fine. Green, perhaps too much green in evidence, but glorious, after all. There is plenty of material. It is new, and perhaps some experimenting will be necessary before I can use it effectively. But I look forward to the work here—this our new Eden.

A great many birds are singing here. Some new ones to me. Have seen a number of bobwhites, and now I hear the strong notes of his call over in the ravine. I understand this has been a favorite place for hunters, and I should like to stop it if I could.

It is said there are lots of squirrels in the woods, and I believe people in the county do not pay much attention to the game and fish laws.

I had a pleasant ride out yesterday afternoon. Horse seems to be all right. I will go back to Bloomington in the morning and expect to work some tomorrow afternoon, preparatory to the sitting Monday, and expect to return here Wednesday or Thursday. I expect to be needed here. There will be a number of things to be determined upon about that time. The week following the Bryan picture must be finished.

And from "Hotel Bowles, May 26, 1907, Sunday evening":

All day I have been wishing you had been with me in the ride over this morning. If you had been along, how delightful it would have been. It was beautiful, though the roads were in a terribly muddy state from yesterday's rain, and now it is raining again. A severe storm over to the south.

Sunday is a great day at this hotel. Have an extra dinner and a crowded house. A small orchestra plays the usual music for such occasions, which is very nice.

I met Marshall S. Mahurin of Fort Wayne while here Friday. He is the architect of the new courthouse building.

Worked this afternoon on the portrait so as to have it in good condition for tomorrow's sitting. I will have two a day for the next two days, and ought to get along rapidly.

Why! it is hailing! I do hope this is the end of the rain, for it will interfere much with the men's work.

I think I never saw a more beautiful afternoon than this has been. The view from the studio window was magnificent. A beautiful green meadow, a great plain of sunlit green, dotted here and there with children playing. Houses beyond it and a great sky of silver clouds. A beautiful stream runs through it, too. I have told you how beautiful the campus is here, with its cluster of stone buildings among the trees. A great many people were out walking in the grounds, and some kind of services were being held in the auditorium, which is in the building where I am located.

I keep away from these places, for I do not want to meet people, and run a risk of being invited out. Have evaded several invitations—and yet I like the air of culture and intelligence of a college town. What a tremendous contrast to the neighboring county seat to the east. They are a century apart, as well as twenty miles.

To slip to our Eden again. Last night I slept in the cabin again, and although I felt its loneliness, I enjoyed it. It was a beautiful moonlight night and I slept with the cabin door open wide to get the fine night air and see the moonlight. There are wonderful songs among the trees.

HOTEL BOWLES, May 27, Monday evening

. . . I cannot write but a line tonight. It is now ten and I have promised Will Howe to talk to his class on Impressionism tomorrow at 8 a. m. I did not wish to do it, but I like it so much and he wants it. It will only be a twenty-five minute talk, but I must make at least some preparation.

When I returned to the hotel at noon, I found Dr. Woodburn waiting for me, and he asked me to his home for dinner this evening, and to see his little girl, that he is talking of having me paint.[17] So I did not feel free to decline, though I was very tired, having had two sittings today, besides an hour or two of work before the sittings began. Have two sittings tomorrow, then I go to the farm, and probably return here Saturday, and, if so, will come to Indianapolis Sunday.

HOTEL BOWLES, BLOOMINGTON, May 28, 1907, Tuesday night

. . . Had my last sitting for this week, and will start for the hills early tomorrow morning.

Dr. and Mrs. Woodburn asked me last night if we had found a name for our place, and they hoped I would find one better than Bear Wallow. They are a very charming and cultivated people. Have traveled a great deal, and the Dr. has

---

[17] James Albert Woodburn was professor of history at Indiana University. Born in Bloomington in 1856, he received the A. B. and A. M. degrees from Indiana and in 1890 the Ph. D. degree from Johns Hopkins. He was a member of the faculty at Indiana from 1890 to 1924. Among his published works is a comprehensive history of the University. He served as president of the Indiana Historical Society from 1923 to 1931. Although Steele was unable to paint a portrait of Woodburn's daughter, Janet McMillan Woodburn, at this time, he did paint a portrait of Woodburn in 1916 which was shown in a portrait exhibit at the John Herron Art Institute in 1917. It is now in the University's collection of paintings.

quite a reputation as a historian, and is, I think, one of the strongest men in the University.

Got through my talk this morning very easily. About one hundred people in the class, and they seemed interested. It seems Brooks has the reputation of having the best-prepared lectures of any member on the faculty. I heard a part of one the other day, and it was very good. His rooms lined with engravings and reproductions are very interesting.

I find Dr. Bryan a delightful sitter, a delightful man and charming. Next week I can have him every day, if I need him.

THE CABIN, May 30, 1907

. . . As we are early risers here, we had breakfast before six, and the boys were at work by half past six. They are laying the ceiling above the rafters in the big room this morning, and enlarging the half windows in the large room to be certain to have enough light. The two teams have gone to town for sand for the fireplace and flue. Think of paying $9.00 for two loads of sand. They have gotten out some beautiful stone for the fireplace and have it on the grounds, and that will be built next week. Things are going all right, and now is the interesting part of the work, and I am sorry to have to be away so much.

We expect to harrow the ground, and sow some grass seed this morning, although it is late and probably will not do much good. There are millions of young sassafras shoots starting where the grubbing has been, showing a lot of work cut out in eradicating them.

This is a glorious day, and things were wonderfully beautiful. The road up through the place is not the least interesting thing here, with its numerous compositions.

HOTEL BOWLES, June 4, 1907

. . . When I left town [Indianapolis] this morning, it was a gloomy-looking city, with a depressing downpour of rain, but it has been a good day after all.

I spent the morning in fixing up the supplies of materials. The teams were in and took out two loads. Come again tomorrow for brick and lime for chimney. Have just had a talk with a plasterer who wants $130 to go out and plaster the four rooms. It is about twice what I expected, but it is the best I can do. However, everything costs twice what I estimated, and the sooner through the better, for then I will quit worrying about it.

Have had a good afternoon with the portrait.

Dr. Woodburn was up, and asked me to paint his little girl, but I told him I could not do it now. Friday night is the president's reception, and I will have an invitation, I suppose.

Ben Greet [18] is here Saturday afternoon and evening, brought by the senior

---

[18] English actor-manager Sir Philip Ben Greet (1856–1936) was a convinced believer in the educational value of good plays and produced and acted at many schools and local communities in the United Kingdom and North America. He concentrated on the presentation of Shakespeare.

class who expect to raise the money from these performances to pay for the portrait. Suppose I shall buy a ticket, although I expect to be at our place.

Students had a lawn fete on the campus this afternoon and it looked very beautiful through the trees, and the music came to me as I worked, with its melancholy appeal, for it seemed so to me, though doubtless the gay young people got quite another sentiment out of it.

I see the weather bureau promises settled weather and seasonable in a few days. I shall feel grateful.

HOTEL BOWLES, June 5, 1907

. . . I wanted to have things all done, and ready for you, but things have been larger and more difficult than I expected, and some things must be left undone, and we will finish them together. But one thing must be done. The house must be so that we can live in it, for I could not take you to Mrs. Parks's.

But it won't be long now. The bricks went out today for the flue, and the laths tomorrow and the plasterers Monday. Paper hanging we may have to defer and inside finish, that is baseboards, windows and door casings, etc.

I can't tell you how I long for the rest and recreation that will come from our wilderness home. But to get that, we must have things so as not to disturb us too much.

I shall try to go to Brookville this coming week and have things shipped over. I think I shall have to go, cannot well send for them.

I hate to give up the Woodburn portrait, but I see no way to do it.

HOTEL BOWLES, June 6, 1907

. . . I am glad you are planning a garden. The house on the hill has a big flower garden in the way of a blackberry patch now full of bloom, and numerous weeds whose names I do not know.

I have only one or two days more on the portrait. Brooks saw it today and liked it—and Mrs. Bryan. Just exactly what she thinks I do not know, but she seemed to like it. Two more days at the furthest ought to finish it.

Will go to the place Saturday, and return Sunday. Week after next shall see the house finished, and I believe this will be the case. The stains have come, I understand, and will go out tomorrow, with some lime and the rest of the doors, and it will not take long to finish up.

HOTEL BOWLES, June 7, 1907

. . . Hope it will clear by morning, for I shall be obliged to go to Belmont tomorrow. Hope to start early in the morning.

Have had two sittings today and the portrait is virtually finished, though I shall retouch it a little Monday morning. It gives very good satisfaction, and Dr. Bryan is well pleased with it, and all his friends who have seen it.

The day has passed pretty well and I have taken things leisurely, and without stress. I hope the ride to the country and back will do me good, and I believe it will if I do not get caught with another freshet and high water.

Fig. 23. The Artist's Mother (Harriet Newell Evans Steele), 1891, 27 by 22 ins.
T. C. Steele State Historic Site, Indiana State Museum Collection

Fig. 24. Talbot Place, Indianapolis, 1891, 27 by 40 ins.
Columbia Club, Indianapolis

Fig. 25. View of the Ohio River from the Hanover Campus, 1892, 26 by 38 ins.
Private Collection

Fig. 26. On the Muscatatuck, 1892, 30 by 45 ins.
Columbia Club, Indianapolis

Fig. 27. Woman Washing Kettles, 1892, 22 by 27 ins.
Private Collection

Fig. 28. Mary Elizabeth Lakin
(Mrs. Theodore C.) Steele,
1894, 27 by 22 ins.
Theodore L. Steele

Fig. 29. Portrait of Rev. Nathaniel A. Hyde,
1893, 45 by 34½ ins.
© 1989 Indianapolis Museum of Art,
John Herron Fund

The plasterers sent out a load of laths yesterday, and I heard from the boys who came in for the paints that they got stalled on the hill and had to get help. The teamsters have taken out twelve loads of material in the last two weeks. It is surprising where it all goes. The plasterer claims it will require sixty bushels of sand to plaster the five rooms, and about an eighth that amount of lime. One has no idea the amount of material that goes into a house. Sorry the stains could not have been put on before this rain, but guess it will be all right.

The Ben Greet people are disappointed in the weather, and will have to go indoors.

I shall be glad to see you in your new simple dresses, which you think are just the thing for Brown County. A sunbonnet is the thing with a dress to match.

One has to be very careful in Brown County not to put on style. Envy is the sin of all such communities, and to act, talk, or dress better than the people there, is one of the things they do not like, for it is like an expression of superiority to them, and they are apt to resent it. However, I think we will get along with our neighbors, though it must be admitted they are a curious people. Dr. Bryan says they have a few students from there, and their schools are on a low plane. A lack of ambition.

Met the music dealer here, and he introduced me to his wife, and they informed me they thought of investing in Brown County, with the raising of fruit in view. And a man at the supper table tonight said he was looking for a place to raise sheep, and he was going over to Nashville to see what he could do.

I gave him Ferguson's name. Some day that country will be made over, but it will be when a new class of people get in there.

The contrasts between these two counties is very great. Here land is from $75.00 to $100 an acre, and good houses and roads. It is surprising the influence does not extend to the neighboring county.

BLOOMINGTON, June 14, 1907

. . . Have spent the morning fixing up things, and getting my easel and paint materials to the livery, where I keep my horse and buggy.

Saw Dr. Bryan, and he told me again that all his friends liked the portrait very much, and that it gave great satisfaction. He inquired if I had gotten his letter, in which he had written me to join a luncheon party of almost twenty-four in the college building. He was giving it to Mr. Watterson of Louisville and Mr. Riley—just before Mr. Watterson's address and a conferring of a degree upon Mr. Riley.[19] This for next Wednesday. I thanked him and declined, although it would be enjoyable. It was exceedingly kind and thoughtful in Dr. Bryan.

Met Mr. Parks in the street here, who said I would find the chimney completed, and the house painted, and the plasterers at work. They just went out this morning,

[19] Henry Watterson (1840–1921), editor of the Louisville *Courier-Journal*. He has been called the last of the great personal journalists. Watterson was the chief speaker at the Indiana University commencement on June 18, 1907, his subject being "Abraham Lincoln." James Whitcomb Riley (1849–1916), the Hoosier poet, was awarded an LL. D. by the University at the commencement exercises.

and should have been there yesterday. Whether they will get through by Sunday, I think it is doubtful.

Have been feeling very well today and look forward to the country air and the week's work there with the deepest interest.

Things *have got to go* and *got to* come out all right.

This letter contained a clipping of an editorial from the Indianapolis *Morning Star*. Of it he said that it means something to us both, and asked that the clipping be saved. I quote from it: "For the normal man his work, with whatever eagerness and fidelity he may follow it, is not as near to him, not as essential to him, not as satisfying to him, as the life he leads at home and with his friends, among his books, among his memories, among his dreams."

AT THE COTTAGE ON THE HILL, June 15, 1907

. . . The home will be finished possibly this week, certainly by the middle of next week. Then I will get our goods over from Brookville, and we will be married immediately, and come here to live. No more beautiful place can we have for our honeymoon, and no more delightful work getting things into shape.

THE CABIN, June 20, 1907

. . . I was up at four this morning, and it is not yet five. A gray, cloudy half misty day. I must go to Bloomington and back today, and there are many things needed. As the house nears completion, numerous things come up that seem necessary, but I certainly am near the end. It is going to be a great place for quiet nerves. What is better than good air, sunshine, and the woods. Good water we need, and will have to be brought this year in jugs and stored in the coolness of the cellar.

I thought it possible I would have gotten the carpenters away this week, but it will take a part of next week. The casing and fitting of ten doors and ten windows and screens for nearly all of them takes a lot of time. It is hot and sultry, and I see the men are getting tired. I believe they will be glad to quit by the middle of next week, when I expect things to be finished.

I expect to move my trunk and bed up to the house this afternoon, and will sleep there from now on.

LATER—BLOOMINGTON

I had a fine ride in this morning. Country marvellously beautiful. I am trying to select wallpaper for the studio, and I wish you were here to share in the search. Think I have it in a gray green, in a 25-cent paper. The room will require about twenty-five rolls. It will be necessary to do it now—to get the benefit of one of the carpenters who is a good paperhanger. It means a saving of five or six dollars.

Things are going on satisfactorily. I have had some days painting.

The House of the Singing Winds

. . . Business commenced on the hill at 6:30 promptly. I was up at four, and saw a most wonderful sunrise. There is a great morning subject looking from the spring to the northeast, along a winding path that leads to the cabin. Great oak trees and picturesque arrangement of foliage and path giving a human interest to it—and the cabin lends itself admirably to the sentiment. Then, beyond the morning sky, and the great Lord Sun in his Splendor.

The road to Bloomington is for four miles through the valley, and I think is far finer than anything around Brookville. Between us and Belmont are some wonderful things as you go down into the valley.

Mr. Shulz was particularly taken with these subjects. I think I have not told you about him. He is an artist from Delavan, Wisconsin, taking a walking trip with an Indianapolis teacher through Brown County. At Belmont he heard of my building here. He immediately came up and spent a couple of hours. He was immensely pleased with Brown County, and this region especially, and said if he could find a place to board, he might bring his family and spend the summer.[20]

Some day artists will come to this county. So possibly you and I will be pioneers to blaze the way for future artists. I have written about this, because I know you will put the interest that I do in the artistic material we will find here. I know there will be no disappointment in this respect, for the longer I am here the more I see, and with horse and buggy we can easily reach localities of a different character.

The house is getting along beautifully. The big room will be a great room, and the paper I selected (a sage green) promises well, with the stain on the floor and ceiling. The boys are making things very convenient. I wish much you were here in the finishing up. I am doing the best I can, but doubtless you will see many things to change, and this can be done. But it looks to me as if living here might be simple, and with the minimum of work.

A soft breeze is coming and going through the trees now, and it is all delicious music.

The House on the Hill, Sunday night, June 24, 1907

. . . I tried to get a letter off to you yesterday morning, but owing to the many things to do I failed and this cannot reach you now before Tuesday.

I have been sitting for an hour or two in the twilight and moonlight. And wishing you were here. I have been very busy trying to get things into shape, for you know I will not be here again until I bring you with me. I want to have things passably so, and so you can take hold and arrange and change and experiment until you make a home.

You know I came to Bloomington Thursday morning. I got some draymen there to bring out the things; by dark I had everything here but the pianola, which the draymen forgot. The three drays, a darky driving the canopy wagon with two bales

---

[20] Adolph R. Shulz (1869–1963) studied at the Art Institute of Chicago, Art Students' League in New York, and at the Julien Academy in Paris. He came to Brown County shortly after the turn of the century and returned for visits until 1908 when he settled permanently near Nashville.

81

of hay, and myself with the phaeton with a big sack of corn made up the procession. We arrived in the midst of a furious rainstorm and had difficulty in getting up the hill.

Friday morning Mrs. Parks and Mr. Parks and the boys started to clean house and unpack and have gotten along very well.

Friday afternoon, about three o'clock, I was surprised by Clarence Forsyth,[21] Allan Hendricks,[22] and Mr. Ferguson coming in. After a little while I went with them to see the 160 acres Hendricks was talking of buying. We found it about two miles from here, and not very satisfactory. There was no good building site, and back from everything. It seemed out of the world.

The boys went back Friday night and came back at noon, Saturday, bringing Mrs. Forsyth with them. They stayed until this morning. They were delighted with my place. Unfortunately there were no other places as good about here; but Allan Hendricks has virtually bought a very picturesque place of twenty acres about half way between here and Belmont, joining Mr. Parks on the north. This will give us a good neighbor. It has a good orchard and shade and some fine timber.[23] He pays $300. The Forsyths have not been able to find a place near here— so far, at least. I spent this morning and yesterday afternoon going around with them. The Forsyths are old friends, and I should be glad if they could find a place near us.

Monday morning

I slept on the porch last night, and it was cool and refreshing.

Parks will be up again this morning, to finish up. They have been very kind. Pianola has come. I believe it is all right, but out of tune. We will have to have someone over from Bloomington to tune it.

How wonderful the winds sing in the trees here, and the great views do not grow old. The friends were wild with delight over them. After all, I expect I got the finest prospect in this part of the county, and, sweetheart, how I long to have you here to enjoy it, and put your heart in it. Just a little patience now, and it will come.

THE HOUSE ON THE HILL, Monday, June 25, 1907

. . . I was so tired yesterday. We had a fearful storm in the afternoon—thunder and lightning, wind and sheets of rain. I was not afraid, but it was lonely enough. Even Parkses were gone.

The storm has kept the men from coming this morning. The other two and myself have been busy putting up the stove, which is a beauty, though it got wet, and is a bit rusty.

As you know, I am sleeping at the house, and like it. The night views are wonderful and the night air delightful. The names for our home?—Some of them you

[21] A native of Johnson County, Indiana, Clarence Forsyth (1859–1912) attended Butler College and the Cincinnati Conservatory of Music. In 1889 he founded the Indianapolis School of Music. From 1902 until his death he was associated with Butler College as professor of music. He was a well-known composer, particularly of children's music.

[22] Born in Madison, Indiana, Allan Hendricks (1864–1949) studied law with his father and became the first secretary of the Indiana Law School.

[23] The tract purchased by Hendricks was in Section 8, T8N, R2E, in Johnson Township.

suggest are good, but not of Steele's make. I think when you see the place, it will suggest to you more than to me, because it will come to you fresh and with an interest that I cannot feel now. Three months of hard work, with so much care and anxiety about it, have had their effect, and it will take a little time after we are settled to get back the interest and delight that I feel must come. I am not an executive, and this work has told on me. The reason I painted the other day was to get away from it, and back, for a few hours, into the only life I know.

Three days more will end it up. The outbuildings are now being put up, and the general cleaning up outdoors will have to be done later.

It is still oppressive and more rain is to come.

To sum it all up, I believe you will be happy here, besides we are not tied here as at a permanent home, but can come and go as desire or need makes best. The prospect for the interurban seems brighter.

THE HOUSE ON THE HILL, June 26, 1907, Tuesday

. . . It is hard to realize that seven weeks today this house was started in what was truly a wilderness, and had I known what I had to go through with, I would never have had the courage to go through with it. But thank heaven, it is almost through. I will probably be home by Saturday.

I am glad you visited the Art Institute. I am homesick to see things again. It seems a month since I was at home.

The boys are rushing things now, but still much to be done. The room is being papered and is successful. I see mistakes about the house now that cannot be remedied, but it will do, and in the main is successful.

I have to start to Belmont immediately. We ran out of nails, etc. It isn't like running downtown to get things here, and lots of forethought is necessary, or lots of trouble takes place.

The storm seems to have passed and this morning is cooler and there is promise of clear weather. The morning is superb in its sun and air, and I feel its hopeful influences.

The carpenters have sent for a wagon to take their tools by tomorrow noon. They are very busy, finishing the stable, dredging and boxing up the spring, and dozens of the ends of things that I want to get into as good a shape as possible. It is almost impossible to get a carpenter or any other help I think in this neighborhood.

I shall have things pretty complete, I think. Yesterday I insured the house and contents for $1,700, so I will feel safe in leaving it, if my application goes through.

If I can get off by twelve, I can make the train for Indianapolis. If not, it will be the next afternoon.

The painter returned to Indianapolis that same week—but more tired and weary than he had realized. Believing it for the best, he consulted his doctor friend—Dr. Alembert Brayton,[24] who, after an examination, ordered a period of complete relaxation from work.

[24] Born in Avon, New York, in 1848, Alembert Brayton graduated from the Chicago Normal School in 1869, attended Cornell University, received the B. S. and M. S. degrees from Butler

The memory of the incompleteness still surrounding the house in the country, with the thought of the amount of work waiting to be done, made him decide to delay going back for a few weeks. Anyway, he had been absent from his Indianapolis studio for some time, and as a result there was an accumulation of various sorts that needed immediate attention. Also, there was a delayed portrait commission. This, too, he decided, he would rather not postpone and have it come as an interruption to his fall landscape work.

On July 29, 1907, comes his first letter from Crawfordsville, where he had gone to paint the portrait of Colonel Elston.[25] In part he wrote:

Just a line this beautiful summer morning to tell you how things are going. Had two good sittings yesterday, and the portrait is progressing finely. The Colonel is well pleased with it, and his sister, Mrs. Lane [26] is also pleased. . . . Crawfordsville is one of the prettiest towns in the state, and with the distinction that comes from an old college life, its traditions and spirit of scholarship. Have met some fine people here. Dr. Mackintosh [27] and a number of college trustees are personal friends. Wabash College a few years ago had the kindness of conferring upon me an honorary degree of M. A., which I think I have never spoken about. I do not value such things much, except as evidences of good will, etc.

On August 3, 1907, he writes from Crawfordsville:

Now my work is about finished here—only one more sitting and I have a chance to think and plan for next week and after. I have purposely kept from doing this, because I wanted to be through with this first. . . .

It will please you, I know, that the picture is a great success. The few friends that have seen it are delighted with it, and the Colonel himself is satisfied.

I have refused to take any orders now, though several have been virtually offered to me. They can wait, for I have another and more important engagement.

College, the M. D. degree from Indiana Medical College, the M. S. degree from Indiana University, and the Ph. D. from Purdue. He practiced medicine in Indianapolis and from 1882 to 1912 also served as professor in the Indiana Medical College (later Indiana University School of Medicine). An enthusiastic naturalist, he taught botany in Shortridge High School and Butler College while attending medical school. He died in 1926, the year of Steele's death. Steele painted a portrait of Dr. Brayton in 1898 which was among the works hung in the Steele Memorial Exhibition in 1926.

[25] Isaac C. Elston, Sr. (1836–1925), Civil War veteran, banker, and successful businessman, was president of the Elston National Bank of Crawfordsville. Colonel Elston was born in Crawfordsville and attended Wabash College and the University of Michigan.

[26] Joanna Elston (1826–1914), who married Henry S. Lane, Indiana governor and United States senator.

[27] George Lewes Mackintosh (1860–1932) served as president of Wabash College from 1907 to 1926. Born in Nova Scotia, he graduated from Wabash College, attended Lane Theological Seminary, and was ordained a Presbyterian minister. He served as pastor of the Fourth Presbyterian Church in Indianapolis for sixteen years. He joined the faculty of Wabash College in 1905 and was elevated to the presidency two years later.

I have promised Mr. Gregg [28] to go with him to the college and advise him as to the hanging of the college pictures.

And later that same day:

It is evening. Spent an hour with the men at the college building, and finally brought them to see what was the final solution. There is one room that with little expense can be made a Memorial Room, and their portraits, about a dozen, can hang there. It can be made very interesting. Helped them select paper for a background, etc.—I think they will carry it out. . . .

Well, you will soon see your dream house and hills. Don't expect too much in the beginning. It is a home in the making not completed. Perhaps better on that account, in some respects. I know you look forward to the building of a home out of this shell—for a home is more than a house, however fine and richly furnished it may be. Houses may be bought, but homes grow and out of the heart's depths. Memories cluster about them, so that when we give them up, there is a pain that will not down. Rest and contentment and recreation live in the home, and out of it we get the inspiration and strength for the work in the world that tells. I look forward to this home for both of us, as a source of inspiration.

I still have the small pencil sketch of the house which the painter had sent me in a letter. How idyllic the setting was, with the large forest trees about it. Although I had never seen the house, I had already begun to assemble various things I believed appropriate to the type of home we were planning. As the craft work of the interior was to be under my supervision, I had made ready for use portfolios containing stencils, drawings, and the like.

In the early part of August—on August 9—we were married at a simple morning ceremony. I liked my wedding dress, which was also my going-away dress. It was of French importation, a soft gray jacket suit of silk crepe with a colorful hat.

We took the noon train out of Indianapolis and stopped at Gosport to wait for the Monon connection which would take us to Bloomington. It was here that I faced and was made to realize that the supreme interest in the painter's life would always be his work—and that it would dominate every fibre of it. As we left the Indianapolis train at Gosport, the painter suggested that until the Bloomington train arrived he would like to show me a part of Gosport which he had visited as a boy with his father. As I was interested, we started out. We had not gone far when he stopped short and out came a sketchbook. As far as he was concerned, I no longer existed—completely forgotten. After

[28] Orpheus M. Gregg, a Crawfordsville manufacturer and civic leader, and an alumnus of Wabash College and a member of its Board of Trustees. His wife was Julia Mills, daughter of Caleb Mills. Gregg died in 1927 at the age of seventy-eight.

a while, tired of the silence, I spoke—casually—so as to remind him I was there. No answer—then I walked away—looked back—walked farther. Nothing happened. Supposing I were to take the northbound train back to Indianapolis? Would I be missed? So ran my thoughts. I was still dawdling and walking when I heard steps behind. "I've finished," he said. "Look— I'll come back some day to paint it." It was lovely. But it made me think. The train was soon due. So there was no further mention of the purpose for which he had set out.

Reaching Bloomington, the painter suggested that we had better take along some supplies. "I am not so certain that the Belmont store will have all you need," he remarked. "We will see," I said, and bought sparingly. How should I know, when my experiences had been restricted to buying from well-stocked groceries in the city?

Then followed some hours of driving, for we stopped frequently, not to lose a single effect of the ever-changing afternoon scene. When, at last, we came to the last climb up the big hill—Bracken Hill, or Belmont Hill, as we now speak of it—we felt a benediction resting over our homecoming.

Mrs. Parks awaited us, asked us into her cabin kitchen while the young sons took our luggage to our home and stabled the horse.

In deep twilight the painter and I started on our final climb to the house, still a quarter of a mile away. It was over the rough road the teamsters had made: I in my wedding clothes and wedding shoes.

2

IN A LETTER WRITTEN to me by the painter during our second year of residence on the hill while he was away carrying out a portrait commission, he asked, "Will we ever forget our first year there, all we saw, and heard, and felt?"

In coming to the hills the change for me had been very great. I had gone from one extreme to another; from the close-up life of a city to a wilderness that seemed boundless in scope; from an exacting daily routine of teaching to a place so complete in its isolation that our time of day was reckoned by the sunrises and the sunsets, and our lives so flexible that we could arrange our hours, for work or relaxation, as it seemed best.

I came here inexperienced in the ways of an isolated region. I found myself transported from a familiar world into a scene of life that seemed very unreal. Always, I felt a quickened pulse, as I viewed the great distances, with their ever-changing light and color effects, encircling the hilltop home.

I stood in awe of the nearness of the great untamed forest about us. There was much wildlife, and it was unafraid. So much that little Anna from a hill cabin brought her mother to see "the tame birds Mrs. Steele kept in the trees about the house." No hour of the day was free from the song of the wood thrushes and other forest birds. The whip-poor-wills came with the twilight in such numbers that they broke into our conversation and had to be chased from our doorsteps. The early mornings brought evidences of an extensive and active night life throughout the forest.

How could one help becoming aware of the existence of great and silent forces at work in the outdoors about us? How could one resist the desire for a better and deeper understanding of the world into which we had come? Thus the whole beautiful region took on a halo, and I fancied myself within a fairy world, whereof each day would be one of anticipation on which I would go forth in an inspired mood of discovery.

Autumn was on the way. The forests were mellowing. Mornings and evenings were delightfully cool. The weather continued open and dry. Walking became delightful and exhilarating. Thus followed many planless hours, in which the painter and I tramped through the forests and over the hills. As we centered our interests largely in the outdoors, I seemed to have had no scruples about relegating my indoor duties to as short periods as possible.

87

From this life of the outdoors we garnered moments of such poignant beauty that not even the passing years could wipe them from our long line of memories. There were the first hours of our homecoming. There was my first view of the house in the solemn stillness of a late twilight. There was the coming of the dawn on the next morning. How marvelous it was!

Forest trees grew to the very edge of our sleeping porch. I was aroused at break of day by the stirring in the trees—always incited by the coming of the first rays of a morning sun. At first but an occasional burst of song—then a general twittering—and then, as the light grew in intensity, a great tumultuous chorus of bird song was upborne—heralding the new day. The forest had come alive—sending from its depths, sweet, inspiring melodies, proclaiming with every note the joy of life itself. Along with the birds' songs came the soft winds of the August morning singing their way—from low in the ravines to the trees standing about us. It came as a ritual. I thought of God sending us a heaven on earth. The occasion left its imprint—something akin to a prayer that I be given strength to hold and retain a sensitiveness for the beauty that must come renewed with each successive day.

At the time a memory remained with me of two other mornings of long ago, and of which I had to tell the painter. One, as a child, on which I went boating with my father to meet the sunrise on a river. Another, later in life, when I rowed from the shores of a great lake in the darkness before dawn to watch for the first rays of light to appear to see their effect upon the waters, as the night let go and the day came on. Both sunrises I remembered with a feeling of awe. This one I would always remember as an expression of great joyousness.

It was then we went into the open to see the sun come up from behind the hills. I longed to see the house in a setting of morning light. I had to be convinced that it could be finer than when I had seen it in the mystery of a deepening twilight. There it stood, on the brow of the hill, illumined in a morning light, with a great view stretching to the north and forests crowding close on three sides. A marvelous, natural setting for any house and this house left an impression of having grown up with the forests about it.

Then I turned and looked into the open country beyond— the scene stretched far over many ranges of hills, and from low on the horizon bands of golden light of transcendent beauty were ascending and flooding earth and sky.

It was a morning hour of exquisite loveliness—an idyll. The sheer beauty of it brought tears and made me sad. We stood in silence. A sanctuary indeed—a place of peace. A refuge to come to. Would it prove helpful to the painter in bringing his art to a culmination—something apart from that that had gone before?

As the sun rose higher and higher we felt the need of breakfast. So we stepped indoors to start making preparations for it. Seeing the rooms in the bright light of the day we were rather disconcerted by the confusion about us. The large studio room was well filled with a conglomeration of furniture and painting material which had come from the Brookville studio. Added to this were the trunks and unopened boxes sent down from Indianapolis. Laughingly we both admitted we abhorred the sight of a cluttered room.

While I unpacked the few utensils and tableware necessary for this our first breakfast in the wilderness, the painter laid the wood for fire in the new cookstove which he had, in one of his earlier letters, so eloquently described "as a beauty." Not long—and there was the fragrance of burning wood to mingle with the aroma of the coffee. Domestic life in all its charm. With this—to my dismay—a stifling heat began pouring out of the kitchen.

As the painter did not seem affected by it, nor speak of it, I, too, passed it by, in silence. Nevertheless, I began to ponder. It seemed unbelievable that there could be flaws in this hitherto perfect environment. Going into the kitchen I saw the reason for the extreme heat. Suspecting the great difficulty the painter must have had in trying to solve this particular kitchen problem, I again passed it by in silence. He had had one central flue built in the house. This flue was not only to serve the fireplace in the living room, but also the pipe coming from the kitchen stove. The kitchen was one room removed from the room containing the rear opening of the central flue. In order to connect the kitchen stove with the central flue it became necessary to use five elbows and quite a number of feet of stovepipe (about seventeen) along a tortuous way through the kitchen wall to the center of the next room and into the flue opening. Therefore the excessive heat. This, however, was not the time to be critical.

The breakfast was laid in our outdoor dining room—a screened porch adjoining the little kitchen. Here it was cool and sweet, with a morning fragrance.

As the early morning grew into the day, we divided our time between the outdoors and the unpacking of boxes and trunks within. Finally we realized that one meal, consisting of coffee and breakfast food and toast, had better be supplemented by more substantial foods. So it was decided to go to the country store to make purchases. I began to make a list of supplies while the painter went off to harness the horse. "Better bring the light wagon, instead of the phaeton," I called after him, "for I want to buy enough supplies to last a number of days."

We drove leisurely, for there were so many interesting, paintable subjects all along the way. As we approached the country store at Belmont, I became very conscious, as a "foreigner," of the groups lounging about, and I found it difficult to meet their stares with friendliness. We found a hitching rack for the horse, and went into the country store. I was introduced to the store-keeper—an awkward occasion for both of us.

To make immediate conversation I informed him that we had brought the wagon instead of the phaeton because there were so many things I needed to buy. I took out my list and began:

"I'll take a pound of fresh butter." The answer came: "I do not sell butter, for everybody makes his own." "Could I buy some from one of the farms of the neighborhood?" I asked. "Yes," he said, "Mrs. K— is a good buttermaker." After being told where she lived, I scratched that item off my list.

No. 2 on the list. "Let me have a loaf of bread." "I don't sell bread, every-body makes his own." No. 2 checked off.

No. 3 on the list. "Do you sell eggs?" "Sorry—the huckster was here this morning." No. 3 checked off.

No. 4 on the list. "Well, then—meat. Surely you keep meat?" To my sur-prise he said, "Yes." "May I see it?" I was taken into a rear room where it was kept. What I was shown was fat side meat (pork) pickled in a barrel of brine. "Oh no," I said in disgust, "I cannot eat such fat meat." In reply, hesitatingly, he said, "Everybody out *here* likes it. It would be purty good eatin for you both, bein as thin as you are." Questioning the advisability of trying this country method of putting weight on my husband, if not upon myself, I nevertheless bought some—deciding to stop on the way at the Parkses' and ask Mrs. Parks how to prepare it so as to make it "good eatin."

"Any fresh vegetables?" I queried. "No," came the reply, "everybody has his own garden." "Could they be bought?" I asked. "Hard to say," was the answer.

The day of canned and packaged goods had not yet arrived except for a very few kinds. The storekeeper called my attention to the various staple foods which he had on hand, but as these were all exposed in open barrels and boxes I could not bring myself to buy any of them. It finally ended by my buying a few crocks, soaps, jugs for carrying water, etc., and these we put into the empty wagon. I was sorry to have widened the breach between native and "foreigner." Fortunately, this did not remain so for long.

As we drove up the hill and out of hearing, we had a hearty laugh about my store experiences. As the wagon rocked over the stony road the loose parcels were tossed about in the wagon bed. We stopped at Mrs. Parks's to tell of our food shortage. Immediately she offered to sell us eggs, milk, and some butter, although, as a rule, little could be spared from what she needed for her own household she explained. She also told me how to prepare my "fat meat." I was "to soak it in cold water, drain, roll in flour, and fry in a hot skillet."

We were hungry at noon and ate the "fat meat" with relish. I was also told by Mrs. Parks that the farms about here produced little above what was needed for the individual households because, as a rule, the families were large. After that we were not so positive but that the local purchase of foods might not assume all the proportions of a problem. Still I hoped a personal visit to each farm might offset this.

By evening, however, we had decided an immediate trip into Bloomington would be necessary in order to lay in a good supply of staples. So up, on the second day of homecoming, with the call of the birds—away, through the dews of a morning, riding on an open seat of a light spring wagon. Our horse was not a rapid traveler and in spite of the early start it took us a long time to reach Bloomington—a distance of twelve miles. Throughout the day we went shopping, buying enough food supplies, as I believed, to last for a period of time. Besides the foods we bought a motley of other things.

Of the first concern were the requisites for bread baking: a baking board, rolling pin, flour, and yeast. I had been informed by the Belmont storekeeper that there were a number of gristmills in operation in the county, some very close by, where the farmer had his wheat ground into flour and corn into meal as it was needed in his household. As I had neither, the flour I used had to be purchased in Bloomington. Hot breads (soda biscuits) for each meal were used by the hill people in preference to yeast bread (light bread as they termed it). The only available yeast in the country store was a dry packaged variety which was to prove for me at times very unreliable.

I mention all this because our way of life, even the foods we served on our table, no matter how simple the meal, became a matter of general discussion throughout our hills. We became the subject of much "argufying," as we learned, and were pronounced as being very "queer."

I had previously decided, before we came to the country, that various things of my own (furniture, rugs, dishes, etc.) should not be sent down until I had seen the house and had determined what could be fittingly used. At the time we had little idea of making it into a permanent home. Some of the furniture that had come from the Brookville studio had been badly damaged and was in need of repair.

So, on this buying trip into Bloomington, we purchased a few hickory chairs, a plain wooden table, some dishes, and a few other necessary articles for the household.

At last the wagon was filled. We could take no more. It took on the appearance of a moving van, with chair legs and table legs standing up at various angles. We knew that we were making quite a spectacle, seated upon our wagon seat, but we hoped we would not meet anyone who would recognize the recent portrait painter at Indiana University. As for me, it made little difference, for I was unknown. At last, when we thought we had made a fortunate escape and were back on the country road we came face to face with H. L. S.[29]—driving back into Bloomington.

"Quick!" I said. "Can't you pretend? Look the other way." It was too late. There was a nod of recognition and "a questioning look." Just our luck, I remarked, why could he not have seen us two afternoons ago when we were in our city finery, riding in a cushion-top phaeton?

The next day, weary from the shopping trip of the day before, I clung tenaciously to the idea that life for us out here could and should be lived just about as we chose to have it. I refused to think of the days that were bound to come when I must bring order out of the chaos of things that were standing and lying about—of the day when the last loaf of bread would have been eaten, and the making of bread became a forced necessity. But this day must remain a day of days, and other days, too, I argued. Let's have them all carefree days.

So again we hiked and looked and found innumerable subjects which

[29] Perhaps Henry Lester Smith (1876–1963). Born in Bloomington, Smith received the A. B. and A.M. degrees from Indiana University and the Ph. D. degree from Columbia University. He served as high school principal and superintendent of schools in Brookville where Steele probably knew him. In 1909 he joined the Indiana University faculty and became dean of the College of Education in 1916, retiring in 1946. He then served as head of the department of school buildings and grounds of the Indiana State Department of Public Instruction.

the painter pronounced very paintable. So far, so good. I hardly expected the day of reckoning to come so soon—to the painter, when his temperament no longer could remain reconciled to his paints and brushes being idle. The final day arrived, when he announced that as these sunny hours were so full of marvelous atmospheric effects, and transient at that, he thought it a pity he was not painting them. He believed he would be up by the morning's sunrise and at least start one canvas.

I could accompany him, taking with me some of my own work. But I reasoned the sooner I faced some of my own problems the better. So we made a compromise. The morning was to be used for individual work; the afternoon, or at least, some of it, for tramps—seeing more of the country. Before many days even this plan was broken—for the painter was overwhelmed by the number of paintable subjects to be done. Soon there were enough canvases started to cover the hours of almost the entire day.

The day came when after an early breakfast the painter gathered together his materials and set out for his work. I stayed behind to poke more wood into the stove, heat the water, and wash the breakfast dishes. For the first time I had been left alone. Just as well, I thought. Face the situation realistically. You know very well housekeeping, under present conditions, cannot be accepted as the simple matter you believed it was going to be. In fact, what will prevent you from adopting the pattern in use in the hill-cabin home? The water problem for one did not differ one iota from that of any of the cabins. The painter, after his completion of the building of the house in June and before he had left the county, had given orders that a cistern be built and completed before his return. This had not been done. There were two small springs on the place that furnished water not only for our own horse but were used for other stock in the neighborhood. For our entire home supply we had to depend upon water hauled one and a half miles from a well at Belmont.

So, on this particular morning, after the painter had left, I concluded I would spend my morning in the kitchen and decide how it could be put into better shape. The water supply received first attention. Looking into a water pail standing on the kitchen table, I found it was empty. I remembered that I had not investigated the water jugs in the cellar. There I did not find enough of a supply for the day. Later, when I told the painter about it, he remarked that he could hardly understand how it was possible to use so much water in so short a time. I tried to convince him that I used it very sparingly. "All the more," I continued, "there is a positive need for a cistern." To this he agreed. After that, at regular intervals, word was sent to the "cistern man" at Nashville whom the carpenter had recommended as the best in the county. Each time brought back a promise of coming very soon.

Cisterns were not in use in our immediate locality. There were dug wells at the lower levels of the farms, also occasional springs. Both wells and springs were surface-fed, and dry during the dry periods of the year. Practically every hill farm had its puddled ponds, generally two of them: one for the stock and one for the household washing of clothes. Also there was the proverbial rain barrel which stood at the corner of the cabin. So cistern builders were not available outside of Nashville.

Finally, the late fall arrived and time for leaving for the city, and we were still without the needed cistern. Before leaving we had a very definite promise that the cistern would be ready for us upon our return in the spring. This did not prove to be the case, and I went through the many months of the second year handicapped by water shortage. We continued with the hill country method of hauling water from Belmont, and using the rain barrel, tubs, and other utensils to catch the water from the eaves whenever the heavens would let us have it.

At last, when the water situation became simply unbearable and no immediate change seemed probable, I had to resort to the threat that I would not return the next year unless the water problem had been definitely solved yet *this* year. This brought things to a climax. Within the next weeks a cistern was built by two men brought from Bloomington. They were supposed to be expert workers in their field. This proved true inasmuch as no criticism could be made regarding the interior of the cistern. Somewhere there had been a miscalculation and the crown of the cistern came out exposed and stood as a mushroom on top of the ground. In appearance it was disturbingly ugly. Besides, uncovered, it would have been damaged by a single winter's freeze. This was the first of the landscaping problem that had to be solved. But of this I'll speak later.

Remember, the water problem was not solved until the end of our second year on the hill.

Now to my other kitchen problems. The kitchen faced the southeast, with porches surrounding it on the south and east. The east-side porch was screened and used as the dining room during the open seasons. Located as it was in a corner of the house structure it caught the winds, and we had them

Fig. 30. Col. Eli Lilly, 1894, 45 by 34 ins.
Eli Lilly and Company, Indianapolis

Fig. 31. Brandt T. Steele,
1897, 40 by 30 ins.
Brandt F. Steele

Fig. 32. Tennessee Mountains, 1899, 22 by 29 ins.
Ball State University Art Gallery, Muncie, Gift of Mrs. Edmund Burke Ball, 000.346

Fig. 33. Benjamin Harrison, 1900, 40 by 50 ins.
The President Benjamin Harrison Home (one of four versions)

Fig. 34. Whitewater Valley, 1901, 22 by 27 ins.
Mrs. Harry Mallinson and Family

Fig. 35. Oregon Coast, 1902, 20 by 24 ins.
Theodore L. Steele

Fig. 36. Hunting Rock Oysters, 1903, 22 by 32 ins.
T. C. Steele State Historic Site, Indiana State Museum Collection

playing constantly upon the screen wires of the dining porch. It was this that finally suggested the name for the house: "The House of the Singing Winds." The kitchen was small (ten by ten feet). In it were two full windows, one opening on the screened porch to the east, and the other on the porch to the south. There were also four doors: two of them opened on the porches, the other two led to the inside rooms. The doors and windows, as arranged, used practically all of the wall space. No provision had been made for cupboards of any kind.

The most baffling of all the arrangements in the kitchen was the set-up of the cook stove. It was an elongated, antiquated iron type with a large reservoir at the rear; and, as such, used up much of the floor space. With a separate flue for the stove the large quantities of stove pipe would have been wholly unnecessary. The arrangement with the one central chimney was not only responsible for the excessive heat but was unattractive enough to suggest a factory workshop instead of a kitchen. With all this I began to understand why the painter had had so many discouraging moments during the time he was building the house. Here, alone in the kitchen, he had had to cope with an unfamiliar problem. I had not been asked for any help concerning details in the construction of the house, and it was only later that I learned that this had been his first experience in conceiving a complete house. I was sorry, too, for I could have been of help, because I had had previous experience when I assisted a brother through the building of a home.

Among the things we had bought for the kitchen on our recent purchasing trip to Bloomington was a kitchen table of average size. After it had been placed in the room it had become the repository for all kitchen utensils, dishes, etc., leaving little room for a working space. Making a further survey of the kitchen's limitations, I had to admit that with the chairs piled high with parcels and other things tucked on the floor under the table, with two water pails on the floor, and the stove wood piled high behind the cook stove, it was a masterpiece of unattractiveness.

The thing was I had to do something to change matters, and it was important that it should be done. But how? I sat down and looked into the forest for inspiration.

So far I had accepted the house just as a place to be lived in just by the hour. Now there must be definite plans and those must eliminate drudgery as much as possible. Some things would just have to stay. Much was to be gained from conserving foods very carefully, for shopping could not be done "around the corner." The cellar had a floor of solid stone, and kept foods remarkably fresh. Other than this I had no kind of refrigeration. So all perishable foods had to be carried downstairs and placed in containers on the stone floor of the cellar. The entrance to the cellar was on an exposed porch to the rear. It became apparent that many steps would become necessary to carry the food each day for the various meals to and from the cellar.

To the native women my cellar was a marvel. With one accord they longed for a similar one of their own. I agreed with them it was an indispensable adjunct to the kitchen.

That morning a tentative plan took shape that would establish, at least for the present, a semblance of order. At the same time I concluded that there must be no radical changes. Nothing must distract the painter. He had had enough during the early part of the year.

So, at noon, during the dinner hour, I stressed the way I felt about the untidiness of the kitchen. I told him I needed to provide some way of caring for the kitchen utensils. He looked the kitchen over and agreed. Then cautiously I asked how much, if any, of his assistance I could depend upon to work out a simple plan. His plea that he needed all the time for his own work was plausible. But, he concluded, if I had definite plans in mind we could ask Mr. Quick, the carpenter from Nashville, to come over and do the work.

A happy thought! I sent word that same day for him to come as soon as possible. In the meantime, the painter brought in some packing boxes which we placed on end and used these to hold the things that had been on the floor.

After a couple of weeks or so Mr. Quick arrived. A considerable amount of dressed pieces of lumber had been left over from the original building operations. So I found myself having much more work done than I had planned. I found Mr. Quick a skilled craftsman. He told me how fond he was of interior work. I was glad of that, for already I had become convinced that other changes would have to be made in the house sooner or later. For the present, however, all work was restricted to the kitchen. There were open shelves placed on the walls, wherever that was possible. Strips of wood, with hooks, were placed at convenient places for the hanging utensils. A wood box was made to hold the kitchen wood. Lastly, came the big moment when I told the carpenter and the painter that a place would have to be provided for my dishes and kitchen linens, that I believed the clothes closet in the adjoining room could be utilized for that purpose. When I told them, however, that the closet door would have to be reset so as to open into the kitchen, which meant that the plastered wall would have to be cut into, no words could describe their lament over spoiling a good and expensive plastered wall. In the end they were convinced it was a sound idea. The closet proved its worth, for it is still in use as a kitchen cupboard.

When the cupboard was being planned and constructed I had no idea it would become such a novelty to the natives. They had never seen a built-in cupboard. Theirs was a "safe" and stood in the kitchen. They came from far and wide to see it. A knock at the door or a call from the driveway and they would ask to see the cupboard.

The kitchen had been made over into a rather attractive room. One drawback remained—the stove with its excessive heat. To eliminate the heat, at least for part of the time, we bought a small two-burner oil stove. Somehow, due to my inability to operate it successfully, it did not prove very satisfactory.

The two small rooms adjoining the kitchen, the little bedroom with its dressing room attached, proved well suited to meet the needs for which they had been designed. The outdoor sleeping porch was ideal.

The original house had been conceived on very simple lines, for, at the time of planning there was no thought of using it as the permanent home. We believed the one large room could function in more than one way. It could serve as a studio for the painter, besides being utilized as a living room and for dining too, when the screened porch was no longer comfortable for the purpose. It was a beautiful room of fine proportions (twenty by thirty feet) with a beamed ceiling fourteen feet high. The fireplace had been built in the middle of the long south wall, with a tier of five windows opposite, flooding the room with a clear, north light. The other walls were unbroken by windows.

Into this room had been crowded all the furniture, canvases, and painting material brought by the painter from his Brookville studio. The room was so filled with a motley of things that no satisfactory artistic arrangement was possible. For the present I decided to bide my time and accept the limitations as they were. I knew only too well that long before the painting season was over the painter would come to realize that because the room had to serve other purposes it could not remain satisfactory as a studio.

Our original scheme concerning the room failed because we believed, in our isolation, the painter would be subject to but few interruptions. Although he was an outdoors painter, and by that I mean although his canvases were painted out-of-doors, there were times when they were brought indoors for study and future consideration.

Our ways of living differed decidedly from those of the hill people of the neighborhood. Naturally there was much curiosity concerning them. For instance, one of the things brought from the Brookville studio was a large oriental rug. This lay on the floor of the large studio room. In this the natives became very much interested. At this time there were a number of looms in the neighborhood on which rag carpets were woven. The women did the weaving and they were excellent weavers, too. The word went around that we had a carpet that was very "queer" in the way it was woven. So they came to see it. Both men and women. They "never saw the likes." They were pleased with it and would get down on their hands and knees to examine it, being very much impressed by the thickness. I remember one tall, angular man, a six-footer, who crawled like a child over the rug.

Also, in the room was a piano and an attached piano player. These were among the things brought from Brookville. The player, too, excited a great deal of interest among the natives. Some of them were really musical. This was especially true of two near-by families. Old ballads were still being sung. We would often hear music or "tunes," played on fiddle and guitar, carried to us on the winds of a summer evening as we sat out on the terrace below the starry sky.

The painter was very fond of music and found much relaxation in it. In fact he had played the flute in his youth, and there were stories told in his native town of how he would sit on a summer evening, out in the open, and play for the entertainment of school friends.

For his piano player he had acquired a fine group of music rolls, among them the great symphonies of Beethoven. He always began and ended the day with music. At intervals during the day classical music could be heard coming from the hilltop home.

It came about that people would stop and assemble in the road below the house to listen as long as he played. Word of the piano player went far and wide and distant families would drive up in their farm wagons. They would ask to see the piano player, then ask for some music. Some who came were not so much interested in the music as in the mechanics of the player. When questioned whether they liked the music being played (always classical), they replied by saying it was not a "common tune"—meaning, as we thought, that they could not understand it. Music, at that time, was not a part of the school curriculum. Those that sang and played did so by ear.

During these first weeks in which we were probing, weighing, and accepting conditions as they existed about us, the painter willingly complied to the visitors' request to stop his work "to make music for them." I, myself, found it difficult to manipulate the player. Somehow, the weather affected the pedals, and they were not easily "pumped." I was sorry for this; for as the visitors increased in numbers, the painter was compelled to put an end to the interruptions. So as not to give too much disappointment, I always took them in, showed them the player, explained how it worked, and assured them that the painter would play it on any Sunday that they returned. Thus was started "Our Sunday at Home," from which we were never able to break away.

During that first year many, many a wagon filled with county folk and many a one on horseback came to look us over and take back to their neighborhood an appraisal of what they had seen. "Hi!" would come a call from them as they stopped on the driveway, and "we came to see your house." Upon entering, they would ask to see the built-in cupboard, the rug, and the piano player. There was always a group of questions to be answered, something like the following: "Why did we sleep on the porch?" "Why did we not place a bed in the large room? It was large enough to have two beds." "Why did we paint the house red?" "Why had we no roof over the north porch?" "Were we thinking of having a grocery store?" (Only grocery stores used a porch without a roof.) "Were we thinking of farming?" "Why did we come to live here?" They generally pronounced the pictures "perty," but it was hard to explain to them why they were being painted.

As an ending to the visit, they asked to be shown the outbuilding, of which they had heard so much. It proved as great a novelty as the things they had seen indoors. Since we had no running water, arrangements for a toilet had to be taken care of out-of-doors. The little separate building had been constructed of unseasoned lumber. This, during its seasoning, had left the building with wide-open cracks. In my effort to make it flyproof I had laid a piece of old linoleum over the cracks in the floor, and had window and ventilator screened. Screens at that time were not generally used in cabin homes. Nor were toilets of any kind. So this curiosity of a building evoked much discussion, and contributed its part towards establishing a reputation among our neighbors of my being "queer" and "too particular."

It was not difficult, nor even impossible, to find out their reactions after they had visited our place. They would go out of their way to let me know what "Jack" or "Kate" or "Mary" said. I gathered that the general opinion of me was that, being a "foreigner" I was different, and could not be one of them. They liked the painter but were rather bewildered because of the "easy work" he was doing.

One day, however, Mrs. W— from a near-by farm, informed me that she was telling "them all" that I was "common," and continuing, she said, "I told them, I know you can understand the likes of us." At first I resented the status of being "common," but when in further explanation she said she knew I was "a lady" by the way "I walked," I accepted it all in good faith.

I learned to understand their vocabulary faster than they did mine. Old English was still being used to some extent. Some of the visitors had difficulty in understanding me. I found myself getting into the habit of talking slowly, and explaining just what I meant. In turn, I would ask for an explanation of the meaning of some of their words. As a result, I found myself much "visited" and became quite interested in the cabin life of the hill people.

One thing was puzzling me. I could not understand why they should be so contented with their lot. They enjoyed few comforts of any kind and apparently there was no initiative on their part to have it otherwise. The standard of living seemed low. They were unmoral. There was barely a family without the illegitimate child. This was accepted, as one mother told me, "as somethin natural." There was no stigma attached, and the child apparently was treated well by the family group. Later, in other years, when on more intimate terms with cabin life, I had to guard against becoming too much disturbed by the tragic side of their lives.

At the time conditions seemed incredible. Were we not but a few miles removed from a university center? And yet there were obvious reasons why this countryside should have been left untouched by the progress of the world outside. Its people were shut in by bad roads a large part of the year. Travel was slow and very difficult. Thus, but few had contact outside their hills. Many had not been to their county seat, Nashville, nor to Bloomington. There was no [enforcement of] compulsory school attendance. Very many were illiterate. Newspapers came to very few families. Intermarriage had been going on a long time. Child marriages were frequent. All the families that I knew were related. The one standard of living had become fixed. They had been given practically no chance to make comparisons until we came, as "foreigners," to live among them. For the first time inroads were being made upon their one-way path of thinking.

Thus a reason for the resentment on the part of some of the women was that their children and young people would frequently stop for a chat on their way back and forth to the country store. One day a mother came to tell me that she "allowed I would not larn her little girl wrong."

My first day's experience at the country store rather forecast that getting food supplies, especially farm products, would become a major problem. You will remember that I was told on that day at the country store of an excellent buttermaker who lived on our adjoining hill. As the supply of butter bought at Bloomington was coming to its end, I telephoned the buttermaker on the hill to see whether I could arrange to buy some. It was agreed that I could have two pounds on the following day. I was directed to take an old bridle path, follow it through the ravines, and I would come to the cabin as I climbed the last hill.

This tramp, which was the first to take me to a hill farm, was to remain an unforgettable one. Coming into the deep ravine I could not refrain from loitering and sitting on a log at the side of a forest pool. Blue skies were overhead, and these, with the waving branches of the tall, forest trees were reflected deep in the waters below. There were the autumn winds, singing "a song of songs" in the very high treetops. I was alone, and yet not alone, with all the beauty and the wonder which only a great, untamed forest can reveal. Favorite poets and familiar poems came to mind. And I recalled the lines of one who said: "Men are always for hurrying things on, but God lets them ripen."

With this mood still on, I finally but reluctantly continued on to complete my errand. As I left the forest path and reached the open hillside, I came to great views, extending far toward the east, enveloped in a morning light and mist. I turned when I saw the roof of a cabin. Still absorbed and haunted by the forests below, I went on—expecting much from a family privileged to spend its days in the midst of such extraordinary natural beauty. I believed, in general, all humanity was susceptible to beauty. Anything else I imagined impossible. I had yet to learn that a man-made world becomes stagnant if it continues to remain ignorant of the great living forces at work round about.

The unexpected happened. I was appalled and stunned at what I saw. I came upon a large table standing in the open before the cabin door. In the cabin yard were a number of dogs, cats, chickens, and a cow. The table had been used for breakfast, and the dirty dishes and leftover foods still remained as prey for the flies. I had never seen so many flies—there were thousands of them. The table looked as if it was set in a black cloud.

I stepped to the cabin door which was unscreened. I looked in and saw the light of the sky filtering through the cabin roof. I called, for there was no one in sight, although I knew the family had seen me. The dogs had barked loudly and announced my coming. Mrs. K— came to the door and informed me that I could have but one pound of butter, since her family had eaten the other pound without her knowing it. She was a very fluent talker. Over and over again she expressed her regret that this had happened. She went to the "safe" to get the one pound of butter. This, she said, she would wrap, to keep it fresh. After various steps about the room she found a clean cloth. Later on I identified it as a handkerchief. She came out with butter and cloth and went to the rain barrel at a corner of the house. At the barrel was the cow, having her morning drink. With much ado the cow was chased away and the cloth dipped into the barrel until it was well soaked. The cloth was then wrapped about the butter and placed in my basket with the statement that it would keep fresh nicely until I had gotten home.

Earlier I had been asked to "sit a while." I need hardly explain that was precisely the thing that I did not wish to do. Neither need I explain the reason of my immediate efforts toward locating a reliable farm from which dairy products could be bought. I succeeded in doing this, but I had to resort to various subterfuges to prevent the neighborhood gossip doing damage to the local reputation of the buttermaker.

My tramps continued to the neighboring farms in search of "things to cook." Finally I grew convinced of how futile my efforts in that direction were. The farm gardens had nothing to offer at this time of the year. Then, too, no more was raised than was needed in the individual household. I found there was but one planting of vegetables in the spring of the year—with the exception of cabbage and potatoes, of which there was an early and late crop. Some of the vegetables, common with us, such as carrots, asparagus, cauliflower, celery, spinach, etc., were unknown to them. As the sun grew hotter and the season advanced, the spring crop of lettuce would disappear for the year. In later years when a vegetable garden of our own became imperative, and I resorted to successive plantings, my efforts as a "book farmer" were widely discussed and laughed at. One day the country storekeeper

PLATE IV

Bloom of the Grape, 1893, 30⅛ by 40⅛ ins.
© 1989 Indianapolis Museum of Art, Bequest of Delavan Smith

came up "to see with his own eyes." Before he left he admitted "that I was larnin them about gardening, instead of them larnin me."

There was one orchard in the neighborhood. Fortunately apples were plentiful that first year. They came to appear on the table under many disguises. I had to make an effort to keep the menus from becoming unbearably monotonous which brought the painter to refer to the concoctions as "Steele's Mixtures."

Grocery staples could be bought in quantity at Bloomington, although it required practically a whole day to do the shopping. Fresh vegetables could be bought at Bloomington, but they could not be kept without refrigeration. They were not often at my disposal to be included in the menus.

It was not difficult to get eggs, but they were seldom very fresh. Milk could be gotten at the stock farms—but it was not very palatable. The stock preferred was of the beef type, and largely kept for the raising of calves.

In the cabin home the menu was a very limited one. Generally the meals consisted of fried foods, and hot soda biscuits, and pies. Finally I reached the conclusion that if all cabin households could be dispossessed of frying pans, it might assist towards making the very desirable radical changes in the people themselves.

Don't think that I had not realized that my system of carrying on the household routine was not above criticism. The cuisine remained far from commendable in its functioning. The kitchen was always uncomfortably hot. It took some time before I learned to use the wood stove intelligently, having been accustomed to the use of gas in the city. I had great difficulty in regulating the oven temperature. Either it was too hot, or it went to the other extreme. One day I stumbled on the fact it could be controlled by the kind of wood I used. Some woods produced more heat than others.

I shall never forget my first day of bread baking. It brought the first occasion for tears—also, my first decided resentment of the primitive conditions with which I had to cope. I had gone about each step in the process of breadmaking very carefully. At last the loaves, light and fine, were ready for the oven. I made an especial effort not to start with too much wood in the fire pot. The oven, by guess, seemed right in temperature, and the loaves were put in. A peep into the oven a little later showed that the baking was progressing finely. I was filled with pride. I left the room and turned to other work.

After a time I returned to the kitchen, when I believed the stove needed replenishing. To my dismay I found the fire very low, and the oven heat too low for the baking. My perfect loaves of bread had risen too high. They had toppled over and the dough had spread out in all directions over the oven floor and its door, too. It was not easy to accept this defeat. While the fire was starting anew, I took a walk on my "consolation path." Later I salvaged the best part. Chunks of toasted bread became a part of our menu—until there was another tomorrow, on which love went back into the labor of making another attempt at breadmaking.

When the stove was first used (during this first breadmaking period), it was "obsessed" with becoming too quickly overheated. That was my reason for a small fire. In time it did just the opposite. With use the stove refused to draw. The stovepipes, as arranged with the many elbows, became clogged, and we had to resort, every now and then, to taking the sections apart and cleaning the soot and ashes from them, out-of-doors. Then all was well, but only for a while. Without any attempt on my part to argue the matter, the painter, after a siege with the sooty pipes, declared one day "that something must be done about the stove." Silently I agreed.

As the weeks went on a plan matured in my mind for a complete recon-struction of the kitchen—to provide a separate flue for the stove and also to eliminate other defects. I even went further. I would ask, when the time came, for a new room to serve as kitchen and use the present room as a dining room.

Thus far I have rather emphasized the rugged side of homemaking—speak-ing of the obstacles that stood in the way of making the routine a simple matter. Although sometimes bewildered, on the whole I accepted them as but an interlude, and knew, someway or somehow, I would find a solution. And in that prospect of expressing myself, I found much joy.

For instance, there was the ever-present scarcity of water. Not enough at any time to have the laundry done at home. This meant that it would have to accumulate and then be taken to either Nashville or Bloomington to be done. When I found this took practically two days—one to take it and one to bring it back—I began immediately to devise ways of conserving the use of household linens. The large tablecloth was the first item to be discarded. For it I substituted scarves made out of hand toweling. These I could launder at home. So began my first adaptation to my rural conditions. Ever after I clung to a statement made to my friends that all new changes, whether within the home or without, were brought about by necessity; and if they stamped the home with an individuality—as was said—it was because limitations were so great that I had to use much ingenuity to get around the difficulties. The painter said that I was continually "keeping him guessing." Maybe so.

Naturally I craved an expression as much as the painter did. I wanted to realize my conception of the beauty I discovered about me, even if it was to be imaged into other forms than his. We both desired a home. I was happy in being privileged to create one. More than that, I was very anxious to create conditions that would reflect in his work.

There was a reason why all the windows remained so long uncurtained. I remembered, as a child, asking my mother why she made her own curtains instead of buying the lace drapes so much in vogue. In reply she said she liked to make them herself. I still remember how much they appealed to me because they were so colorful. I had decided to do likewise. In the city I had bought a whole bolt of coarse Irish crash for that purpose. The curtains were to be handsewn, hand-dyed in some cases, and design applied in some form or other. This was work which could not be hurried. The making of the curtains was bound to cover a long period of time.

However, although there was definitely planned work for me in the house and for the painter out-of-doors, we never allowed it to stereotype our way of life. Always we would find some time in which to wander aimlessly about and become inspired anew by our surroundings. At that time I wrote, "Up in the hills the roads are long and winding. To the hurried and the unseeing they are too uncertain and go too far. To those who care to follow they lead to sun-flooded heights and shadow-covered places—to where the wild things are, and have their day."

Our enthusiasms were kept keyed high. More was being contributed in these parts by external forces than we could ever begin to understand. So we turned to our more learned friends—the authors—and taught ourselves to identify more of the living things about us and indulged ourselves in discussions of the why and wherefore of all life and our relationships to it. Always the hour ended with the thought that fundamentally there existed an environment here which afforded sublime opportunities for a realization of the painter's ideal regarding his work.

I found a particular friend in the person of Mrs. Parks. The Parkses were our nearest neighbors adjoining us to the north. We grew very fond of them. The two sons, Homer and Jimmy, hauled our daily water supply from Belmont and took care of our horse. I saw much of Mrs. Parks and depended upon her for advice concerning some of the perplexing problems with which

I had to deal. Through her I learned much about the history of the neighborhood. I learned of the tragic side of life as it existed in the hills. I drove with her to distant neighbor friends, and learned much about the ways of living among the better households. I took many walks with her through the woods in search of herbs and plants with which she compounded her medicines. Being interested in bird life, she took me to see a pair of eagles nesting in a large tree on the banks of Salt Creek. Many an hour I sat in the woods listening to her telling stories out of her youth. She had the strength of character of the pioneer women—buoyant and uncomplaining. Her outlook on life was commanding and yet generous. Her interpretations, with her advice, became indispensable to me. She helped me through many a difficulty, and I owed her much.

Another friendly hand was extended by our neighbor, Allan Hendricks of Indianapolis, who had built a lodge farther down on the Belmont road on Bracken Hill, overlooking Salt Creek Valley. He had purchased the land in early summer shortly after the painter had finished his building operations on the hill. The Hendricks lodge was completed during our first year. Meanwhile, he lived in a tent on the Parks place and took his meals with Mrs. Parks. They became very fond of him, and Mr. Parks always referred to him as his son. He was a gentleman in every sense of the word. All the men at the country store accepted him "as very common." They spoke of him in generous terms. To us he became a marvelous friend.

Being so isolated and difficult of access we did not expect visitors other than those of the natives who continued to come throughout the year. We were very much surprised at the large number of people who came to see us from the surrounding towns and cities. It was a colorful autumn and dry. Although the roads were rough and steep, they were not impassable. Just what the impressions of the city inhabitants were, was not always clear. As a rule they had come out of curiosity. We had to wait for a later time to learn how most of them believed the isolation of the place outweighed any benefits the painter could derive by living here, even though the country admittedly was indescribably beautiful.

September had now passed. We were living the glorious days of October intensively. The painter had arranged for two exhibitions of his new Brown County landscapes, one to be held in Indianapolis from November 27 to December 7, the other at the St. Louis Museum opening on December 19. This meant that much more time must be devoted by him to his work. So

106

with this began the "painter's day," which was adhered to, not only through-out this fall but throughout all the painting days of other years spent in Brown County. The time for meals was made variable so as not to interfere with the exact hours needed to catch certain color and light effects which he was painting. And as he said: "There is always a vigor and a freshness in the things done at once—and, too, it is the impression of one mood—so difficult to hold and give in a work that drags through many days."

Mr. Steele believed that during a work season no landscape painter should be in bed after four o'clock in the morning. So breakfast always came early—more nearly at five o'clock than six. Dinner at midday came long before the hour of noon. After dinner came a short period of relaxation, generally con-sisting of some reading, music, or a short time spent together out-of-doors. Then followed the afternoon and evening hours of painting. Ofttimes, when the evening subject was a distance from the house, I carried the evening meal to him and we ate it from a mossy stone or bank.

I marveled at his capacity for work. I marveled at his skill. In his painting he carried on four main subjects a day, not including the various prelim-inary sketches gotten ready for the work of coming days. I came to real-ize how rare was the gift with which he had been born. It was like an inner flame that kept his whole being—mind, body, and soul—ever alive to the shifting scenes about him. Nature he would always speak of as the great teacher and "of the proper balance of sentiment and objective realization as the ideal." Again he said: "Is it not wisdom to get from each thing its essence of beauty—its peculiar quality? To always keep sensitive and get from each change in nature, that which is characteristic—for nature does not often sing out of tune. It is only our own narrowness makes it seem so."

More and more came the conviction that the painter, through the fineness of his character, the depth of his mind, and quality of his work would leave a definite impress upon the future. Fortunately I had always drawn and used colors. I had had excellent teachers. I had had opportunities for travel. I was taught to love the outdoors. Thus I was able to bring a sympathetic under-standing to those ideals which the painter had accepted as an essential part of his art. In this we were comrades.

Despite all our enthusiasms about the locality being a veritable paradise of painting ground, the painter acknowledged that it did present certain difficulties during the first year in the matter of composition, in placing his subject material on the canvas. The countryside was very heavily wooded.

There was a lack of simplicity because of the crowded growth. "There is a dignity in space," the painter would often say. He thought it would become necessary to cut into this growth of trees in order to open up more vistas. With that we began to envisage a landscape plan that would not disregard the natural beauty, but rather enhance it, by a certain amount of clearing—making for open spaces and an ordered arrangement of planting of shrubs and flowers. We both grew enthusiastic over the possibilities of developing a landscape composition. Nothing more than a few large trees were cut during the first year. We had to wait for the next year to see a beginning.

Autumn moved rapidly. Canvases were now accumulating within the studio room. They were in various stages of drying. Last touches were being made to prepare them for the coming exhibitions. The days for assembling the work were limited. The painter's time for doing this should have been free from interruptions and interferences. Much to our regret it was not.

The time had arrived when we needed an open fire in the fireplace. As I have said, the large room had been primarily designed to serve as a studio for the painter. Again the unforeseen was to happen. In the hill cabins the old fireplace had long ago been replaced by the sheet-iron wood stove. Again we were presenting a novelty that was destined to provide ample reason for a return visit of the natives to the house. On their way back and forth to the country store, it was very pleasant to stop for a rest and chat, sitting before a roaring fire.

I tried to guard the working hours of the painter as much as I could, but that was not always possible. In fact, I became very unhappy as a result of some of the visiting hours. Tobacco chewing was indulged in, by both men and boys. The women smoked their corncob pipes. The visitors seemed unconscious of the impropriety of spitting their streams of tobacco juice into the open fire. Doing so, they often stained both hearth and firedogs with the juice. Once—when it had been done and it looked too indecent to pass it by, I turned to the painter and said that there must be a way to solve this problem. "I know," he replied, "we are up against a difficult situation. What can you do, when the practice is even carried on during services at church, by both minister and men? We must not lose their goodwill."

"Yes, I realize that—but couldn't we plan to build a separate room for a studio that would be less accessible? We could build one at the other end of the house. It would be away from the driveway."

"Yes, I have thought of that, too. I think we will try to build one, when we come back next year—that is, providing the sales from the coming exhibitions justify the expenditures."

"Can we go further?" I queried, pointing to the kitchen.

"Of course," came the answer.

At the end of the season, the painter did not feel wholly satisfied with the landscape work he had done. He felt that he had not completely expressed himself. He had not lived long enough with his subjects. The quality of the subject matter, too, differed from that that had gone before. He felt there had been uncontrollable conditions to affect his work. These were sufficient reasons that he must not be denied better working conditions.

The painter had not come to Brown County to establish a reputation. This had been done long before. As early as 1893—at the Columbian Exposition— one of his landscapes had received a No. 1 rank, an honor accorded to only one of the nine hundred pictures placed on exhibition. The picture chosen was an Indiana landscape, and the jury was surprised when the name of T. C. Steele was announced and it was found to be the work of an artist comparatively unknown.[30]

He is quoted as saying at this time (1893) "that he believed the work of the art school is over when it has taught the pupil a correct technique—that is to draw and paint. The technique once mastered, the soul of the artist will refuse to be entirely bound by its limitations and will declare itself in its own way. It will even modify the technique, which becomes by the force of his originality, the outgrowth of his temperament."

In 1898 he was recognized, the acknowledged leading artist of the state, and one of the notable painters of the West. "The simple, natural beauty of Indiana woods and fields had never been interpreted. This task—with others —Mr. Steele undertook," were the words of a critic.

Again the painter is quoted as saying at this time "that landscape painting offers the most distinctive form of American art. . . . Critics acknowledge that there is truly a note in American landscape. Portrait painting is more or less similar the world over, but this is not true of natural scenery. . . . Landscape painting depends necessarily on temperament and interpretation. . . . As in the writing of a novel, there is no real realism; a landscape, while it may be essentially true to the scene depicted, always mirrors more or less the artist's own consciousness."

[30] The two paintings that Steele exhibited at the Chicago World's Columbian Exposition were "On the Muscatatuck" and "September," shown in Fig. 26 and Plate III.

For the first exhibitions of Brown County paintings the painter had chosen thirty-three canvases. We both knew that this first show would attract considerable attention. It would probably cause much discussion, not only among the laymen fond of art, but also among artists. Our artist friends had not believed that this untamed wilderness to which we had come would offer suitable material for the painter's work. Our friends, in general, accustomed to associating all cultural efforts with closely knit communities, believed the painter's work would suffer from lack of proper stimulating environment.

Both of these beliefs might have proved true had we not been schooled in a technique so thoroughly and deeply embedded and so distinctly an integral part of our lives that an environment such as this, even if it had been as different to the old as the night is to the day, could not have dulled our sensitiveness to the distinctive quality of our new world of beauty.

The exhibition at Indianapolis was well attended. Just as we thought, much interest was aroused by the fact that "Mr. Steele's picture material has come from the most primitive county of the State."

Speaking to a news reporter, the painter said that he had "bought this place not for agricultural purposes, but for its ravines and wooded hills." He added that "the present autumn has produced a richer display of tints in fresh foliage than for many a year. There are here fifteen to twenty different varieties of oaks, many hickories, but few maples. Here, too, is the sweet gum, which clothes itself in glory, with the on-coming of the early frost. It is the sassafras, which here grows to a tree of considerable size, that compels the artist's heartiest admiration with its wonderful reds—passing through flesh colors to crimsons and deepest reds, from which, as the season advances, it takes on tawny hues. So this pest of the farmer finds in the artist, a sympathetic friend. . . ."[31]

The reporter or rather critic speaks in his article of the painter's work as "luminous" in color, and "done with great delicacy yet with the sure hand of an artist."

The local artists spoke of a new note appearing in Mr. Steele's work—largely one of color; spoke of his treatment of the colors in the prevailing haze as possibly exaggerated, the purples used as too vivid, etc. He was warned against mannerisms. In reply the painter extended an invitation to come down and see and be convinced.

[31] Quoted in Indianapolis *News*, November 29, 1907, p. 15.

110

Fig. 37. California Hills near Redlands, 1902, 19 by 28 ins.
Private Collection

Fig. 38. California Mountains, 1902, 24 by 30 ins.
Private Collection

Fig. 39. Late Autumn on the Whitewater, 1903, 22 by 32 ins.
Hanover College, Hanover

Fig. 40. The Whitewater, 1904, 22 by 32 ins.
Private Collection

Fig. 41. Village Scene, 1905, 18 by 22 ins.
T. C. Steele State Historic Site, Indiana State Museum Collection

Fig. 42. The Return from Work, 1905, 20 by 28 ins.
Eleanor Evans Stout

Fig. 43. President William Lowe Bryan, 1907, 42 by 34 ins.
Indiana University, Bloomington

When the exhibition reached the St. Louis Museum, the painter was spoken of as "not an extremist in style or color. In subject and treatment he utilizes a considerable range. . . . His well-lighted, adequately painted landscapes are to be found in many collections and are familiar to frequenters of art exhibitions. . . . Mr. Steele has been an active factor in art advancement not alone through the medium of his brush and its influence upon other artists, but also as an enthusiastic laborer for the development of art appreciation." [32]

With the closing of this exhibition our first year in Brown County came to an end. Great gifts had been ours. They had come to us in various ways. How much had we achieved? In how much had we failed? All we were certain of was that the future held much that was precious in store for us. We had lived deeply. The memories of our hours together we knew would never die.

When the time for leaving the wilderness home for the city came, we wished it might have been postponed. The painter would have preferred to have stayed on, into the late autumn with its quiet, somber beauty. I, too, regretted our leaving. Yet I knew that there would be an expansive field of work awaiting me when we returned in the spring. For that reason I believed a change to city life would help me to work out some of the problems by allowing me to see them with a certain detachment. I was doing some wishful thinking.

In the world of my dreams was the beautiful home. Besides, I hoped that when I came back I would become helpful, in some form, to some of the "backward" neighbors without incurring resentment or effecting a discontent.

[32] Quoted from the exhibition catalogue. In 1896 Steele and J. Ottis Adams had had a joint exhibit at the St. Louis Museum of Fine Arts. Steele's canvases, numbering thirty-five, were mostly landscapes. In 1906 a special exhibit of western paintings was held in the St. Louis Museum. Indianapolis artists represented were Forsyth, Stark, and Steele, who showed ten landscapes. See below, p. 134.

3

IN THE LATE FALL OF 1907—just before Thanksgiving—we came back to Indianapolis to spend the winter. Since the painter's return from his studies in Europe in the eighties he had maintained a studio in the city. Our first winter there proved as happy a one for us as could have been desired; so much so that to dwell upon all the delightful experiences we shared with old friends, as well as new, would have made of it a story in itself. However, the intention of my writing from the beginning has been to confine myself to giving a view of the life in the hilltop home in its relation to the wilderness surroundings and its people. Then, too, I want to show that the problems of environment with which we were to become concerned, and to which we were to become committed, contributed much in defining a way of living for us.

When I came back from out of "the wilderness," I found myself so stimulated by city life that I felt that if I were to be withdrawn entirely from it I would suffer. This I explained by saying that city contacts were necessary to counteract certain depressing but unavoidable associations in the country.

Although we went much socially during the winter, there was also much work to be done. The painter not only carried on his portrait painting but was kept very busy with exhibitions, talks, and formal lectures. To me fell the work of establishing a small home for us whenever we were in the city. This I found all-absorbing. I had always had a passion for liking old things, and in my searching found them in the most unexpected places. As the old types of furniture in which I was especially interested were not generally sought for at that time, they were offered for sale at very low prices. Chairs, for instance, which I saw years later priced in the stores at $25.00 were identical to the ones I paid 75 cents for.

After a few years it was considered best to discontinue the home in the city. So all our acquisitions, including the old furniture, were sent to the country to be added to, or take the place of, the furnishings already there. Thus I was able to eliminate the temporary and less desirable pieces. The hilltop home now took on a decidedly old-time and mellowed atmosphere. Suffice it to say my home ideal was born. It emerged as one of unassuming simplicity and quiet character.

While I found the life and the sights and sounds of the city so exciting and exhilarating, I also found I could not forget the wilderness. And as the winter passed, with the February sunshine increasing in warmth and radiance, I could no longer suppress an intense longing for the open spaces and wooded hills. The painter was still busy with his portrait painting, and spoke of not being able to make the change from the city to the country until early summer. He had been glad to accept this work, for on the money earned depended the building of the new studio and the contemplated alterations to the house. He did, however, consent to a two weeks' interruption for a hurried trip into the country. During that time all the preliminaries necessary for the proposed new building could be arranged so as to avoid any delay in starting the work later when we came back to stay. As he said, by so doing he wished to forestall any possibility of the building operations interfering with his painting time.

It was in early spring, sometime in March, that we left the city for Nashville, going by train to Helmsburg and then on by "hack." The painter was anxious for the same carpenters to take charge of the new work. We felt relieved when Mr. Quick, the boss, accepted the job, promising to begin it sometime in June. And in a few days he came out to the house to discuss the new plans. According to his proposal, I was to take the responsibility of seeing that the materials were always at hand so that there would be no unnecessary loss of time. For, as he explained, "Mr. Steele is too busy painting to remember we need materials in order to build."

The painter would speak of our location as having great charm because its interests were inexhaustible. This was very true, and had "these interests" all been similar to the ones the painter had in mind, there would have been no doubt that we had come to live in a paradise on earth. But from a practical point of view our locality was not different from, but rather typical of, any isolated, backward community. In fact, undesirable conditions stood naked before us, which could not be ignored or excluded entirely from our lives. Not that I wished to do this. What I feared most was that I would begin to see them out of all proportion to the essential aesthetic experiences for which we had come into the country and that I would be disturbed by them. Knowing, too, that certain conditions should be altered, I would be made unhappy to see them continued without an effort on my part to effect a change. In time, it was experience that taught me that I must accept these wilderness problems as part of the existing conditions and deal with them when circumstances became right for me to do so, and that I must guard against becoming enslaved by the idea that they could be solved at once. Man-made

113

ways were not given to rapid changes. Nature's ways were very slow. With this, I concluded to assert my hold upon the beauty that existed about me, and let all else become a matter of time.

Bad roads were probably our most disturbing problem. We had no other outlet but over a road of gullies and shelves of rocks. Only in dry weather was it fairly passable. Not only did it make our coming and going uncomfortable, its disadvantages were real. It made transportation of goods difficult and increased our cost of living.

In driving over from Nashville on that March day of 1908 we realized as never before what a hindrance the bad roads were to the development of the county. During the previous fall I had taken occasion to discuss this matter of good roads with the natives, emphasizing the need for their betterment. Always I found them indifferent. A fear of higher taxation seemed to suppress all desire for them, I was told whenever I advocated improved roads along with better schools that my plans would result in increased taxation and thereby make living conditions harder than ever for them. I recognized that there might be some truth in this, but I also felt that this must be accepted as an avenue of escape from their poverty.

Later I was to write a road petition, asking the County Commissioners to place the highway running from the valley at Belmont to our gateway into the county system of graveled roads. The problem of taxation again made its influence felt, and I was refused certain signatures. The pleas to both state and county for better roads became a long story of argumentation. Each year it was renewed. Each year saw something gained. When the time arrived, however, for the people of the county to become owners of low-priced, secondhand automobiles, then, as if by magic, overnight the general attitude towards good roads was changed.

On this particular March day, upon our return from the city, we found the entrance way and the long driveway leading to the house in as bad a condition as that of the main highway. It has been appropriated by the natives as a better road for winter travel than the county dirt highway outside our property. Although well graded, it was a dirt road and could not hold up under the heavy loads of farm wagons nor under their method of locking wheels in going down hills. (Later I was to discover that the many gullies on the slopes leading from the house were nothing more than old road beds made through winter driving. It was customary when one roadway became impassable to use another way out.) We felt bad about this abuse of our property rights. In the end we came to accept that it would never be otherwise unless we had a way of showing our disapproval. So we faced reality and enclosed the immediate grounds with fencing and gates. This resulted in some resentment, but on the whole it curtailed a general abuse of the road during our absences.

Not until some years later, after a long severe winter of ice and rain, was the driveway to the house again found impassable. It was worse than it ever had been, with ruts three and four feet deep. The wooden gates had been chopped down. It was explained to me by the natives that it was an established custom in the neighborhood not to deny a neighbor the use of a property road during bad weather. By this time I had become firmly convinced that it was more than I could afford to keep up a road for county travel. So I bought steel gate posts and set them in concrete. The steel gates were kept locked. Although a drastic measure, it was sound. Eventually, under the pressure of those depending upon the outer road for travel, the county established a good gravel pike.

How well I remember that first day of our return. We had gotten over the roads and were glad for it. As the painter turned the house key, we looked ahead to the peace awaiting us within. I especially wanted to forget the disquietude that had been aroused in me by the road. As I stepped in, I was wholly unprepared to meet the disturbing bit of realism which was in store for us.

When we had closed the house in the fall, I had left it sweet and clean and in good order. In the meantime, during the winter, the field mice and squirrels had taken possession of all the rooms. In the kitchen, the pots and pans on the open shelves had been utilized to the fullest for their nuts and their nests. Nothing in the kitchen seemed fit for immediate use. During the previous summer in the remodeling of a closet we had neglected to close a narrow passage running up from the basement along the hand-hewn chimney stones on to the first floor. This proved an excellent entrance to our rooms for all the small wild animals of the forest who were seeking a shelter for the winter.

Unafraid, they continued with their nightly inroads until Mr. Quick, the carpenter, appeared with his tools to close up the passage. I was told by the natives that it was impossible to keep squirrels and mice out of a house—especially was that the case if the house was closed over a period of time. This I could not accept in its entirety. I did, however, decide to replace the open shelves in the kitchen with closed ones, possibly not so artistic, but at least more sanitary and mouse-proof.

During the two weeks' stay the plans for the new studio were discussed daily. After careful consideration it was decided to add a wing to the west side of the house which would fulfill the double purpose of housing the studio and serving as a storage room for painting materials. It was decided to build the studio first and let the remodeling of the house come later in the summer. The plans, too, for the new kitchen came under discussion, but the details were left to be decided upon after the completion of the studio. One thing at a time, said the boss carpenter.

That done, the painter and I turned our thoughts to other plans. He took up his landscape work and I turned my attention to a consideration of a plan for a garden setting for the house.

I did not expect to be able to make much of a beginning during this first year. In the first place, the ground around the house would be torn up by the teamsters hauling the materials for the building operations. Secondly, the carpenters would be utilizing much space. Yet I contended that as garden experiences had been a part of my life since early childhood, I could not be satisfied, even for one year, without a small garden plot. I selected a strip of ground bordering the north terrace which I believed would escape abuse by the builders. I had the ground dug by a son of the Parks family. I had brought with me a few packages of flower seeds from the city. These— with high expectations—I planted with care. Heretofore all gardens that I had tended had been on level ground, and I foresaw no trouble ahead in planting on a slope. To my consternation, when I returned from the city in June, I found little left of my first flower bed. The spring rains had washed it away, with the result that there was not a trace of a single plant. However, during my walks throughout the summer I would find in the thickets at the base of the hill miniature blossoming plants growing here and there. My seeds had traveled far. Instead of being disheartened by this failure, I came to look upon it as a fortunate occurrence. I was being taught at once that planting conditions in the hills would be very unlike those to which I had been accustomed.

Furthermore, it brought to my attention the reason for the extent of the erosion on our hilltop slopes. It made me realize, too, that this problem of controlling erosion would have to be mastered, or else before many years there would not be many feet of hill slope left for the house to stand on.

During the two weeks in March when I had laid out the first flower bed I had also made arrangements to start another type of gardening. During the winter I had decided to grow our own vegetables. The painter was not very enthusiastic about the idea, because of my inexperience. Nevertheless, he was willing to help select a plot of ground which might be used for vegetables. The neighborhood farmer who came to do the grubbing of the undergrowth, clear the ground, and plough it, intimated that the soil was not well adapted to the growing of vegetables. When asked why, he said that the top soil was too thin. Asked whether that could be remedied, he replied by saying that the application of stable manure would help. Readily he consented to sell me two loads from his stable. For this he asked 75 cents a load. Now, whether it was because the neighborhood thought I was paying a ridiculously high price for a load of manure or not, I was offered all, and more, than I ever expected I would be able to procure. For days, each time a wagon appeared coming up the driveway, it proved to be a farm wagon with another load of manure. The painter finally closed down on the sales. Fortunately, this did not happen until the whole garden spot had been well covered. With this we left it for the spring rains to accomplish the work of drawing it into the soil.

The two weeks' stay came to an end all too soon. It had been crowded with much thoughtful planning. More than this—there had come to the painter during this period the firm conviction that in using this locality with its wealth of material for his painting ground, he would have a permanent advantage over any other he had ever used. I could well understand his reasoning, for, I, too, had begun to accept the same idea regarding my own work. With this, all our work throughout that summer took on an added value. There remained no longer a question or hesitancy in our minds but that this home emerging out of a wilderness would provide the painter with the best possible conditions for his self-realization.

We built the new studio as a wing to the west end of the house. To it was attached a porch overlooking Salt Creek. Then the remodeling of the east end of the house was begun. One room was made out of the old kitchen and the adjoining open porch. This was accomplished by breaking out the east wall of the old kitchen and enclosing a part of the long porch. Two sides of the porch were framed with windows so as not to exclude the view into the forest. The outcome was a satisfactory dining room—twelve by eighteen feet.

The kitchen was developed from the south end of the open porch, with one small extension added at one end. A new kitchen chimney was built, and

117

after the room had been finished, Mr. Quick installed some low cabinets which made for an attractive effect. The results appealed to the painter and led to the painting of some kitchen interiors which he exhibited with other canvases. [See *Frontispiece*.] The kitchen and dining room, as then conceived, met our needs and have remained unchanged throughout the years.

Our building operations extended far into the autumn. Our household was disrupted even more than during the previous summer. There was nothing I could do about it until I had complete possession of the rooms. This would not come until after the carpenters had finished their work and the painter had taken his painting materials from out the crowded living room.

Various handicaps encountered the previous year remained unchanged and continued to make of housekeeping a complicated routine. Hauling water was still the order of each day. The problem of supplying the table daily with fresh vegetables had not been solved. The new garden had been somewhat disappointing. We had come late for the planting and the hot suns of July had brought the growing season to an early end.

One day I happened to be showing my vegetable garden experiment to our friend Dr. Alembert Brayton of Indianapolis—a botanist by nature. "Why do you experiment?" he asked, "why flounder when there are so many bulletins available on gardening and kindred subjects? They are issued, to be had free, by the Department of Agriculture of the Federal Government. Write, too, to the School of Agriculture of Purdue," he added. Needless to say, I followed his advice at once. A garden library was begun. It grew rapidly as I supplemented the bulletins with books and magazines on the subject.

I came to realize as never before that a garden—a successful one—does not simply happen. Accordingly, careful, intelligent planning became the rule before any actual garden work was begun. All available reading material on the subject was exhausted, and the working plan made to conform to that recommended as nearly as possible. Even then my enthusiasms got the better of me in trying to force a growth of plants and shrubs unfitted to the local conditions. It happened because of certain early associations in flower gardening that made me believe no garden of mine, no matter where, could be satisfying without the plants I had learned to love so dearly. Experience was to teach me otherwise. With all my acquired knowledge, neither flower nor vegetable gardening was ever to become an easy or a simple matter.

In all my gardening I could never lose sight of the fact that all my plant-

PLATE V

Catharine Merrill, 1898, 27 by 22 ins.
Butler University, Indianapolis

ing had to be done on steep hillsides. Ofttimes I stood aghast at apparently what seemed insurmountable difficulties, before any planting could be begun. With no restriction on the amount of land to be used my original plan covered a great area. With no assurance whatever that I would be able to see it completed, I believed it advisable to formulate a plan which would be all inclusive. As a result, no radical changes have ever been necessary. Year in, year out, efforts have been made towards further development whenever money and labor were available for it.

Since I profited from the items in my growing garden library, I concluded that such material, particularly the bulletins from the Department of Agriculture, should be brought to the attention of the farm homes around us. I had become thoroughly convinced that their methods of farming were so primitive because of their detachment from sources of information. I believed human beings were more or less alike. At least I thought of the average individual as susceptible to opportunities which would help him to escape from poverty and thus make living easier.

The hillsides were still being used for wheat growing and the wheat cradled by hand. So I sent for bulletins in great numbers to be used for general distribution. One morning I started out with horse and buggy, with visions of the excellent work I was to accomplish. I took great pains to explain the purpose I had in distributing the bulletins. Since they had been of great help to me, I believed that they would be of like help to the neighboring farmers. Nor did I hesitate to make plain that this which I was attempting to do was in reality work that the schools should be doing.

In the weeks that followed this going forth to open the way for a better understanding of the utilization of our poor farming land, I got by accident versions of the reactions to my efforts. When the men gathered at the country stores "to set and talk" and discuss it, they would slap their knees and howl about "how green that woman was." In part, what they said was true. I had to learn that "book-larnin" on farming methods was absolutely taboo out here; that the idea that any successful farming could be done "accordin to book" was a matter for ridicule. More than that, I had not realized that illiteracy was so widespread, nor aware that had the farmers been inclined to read the bulletins, the vocabulary of those who professed to be able to read was not sufficient to make the text intelligible enough to use it.

This did not keep me from going to the farm homes to ascertain for myself just what their reactions had been. In one case, the books were considered

119

useless and used to start fires. In another case, they had been utilized as a
padding for the rag carpet. In not a single case was there an acknowledg-
ment that made me feel repaid for my efforts.

It was because of my previous teaching experiences that it seemed the
most natural thing in the world for me to go to them and want to share with
them my newly acquired ideas concerning gardening and farming. Feeling
completely frustrated and humiliated by my failure, I drove back to tell the
painter that from then on I would remain the reformer reformed.

The first work for permanent landscaping was begun after the carpenters
had left—in the autumn of 1908. Walks had been built, made of wood, leading from the house to the two outdoor sheds. Alongside of these I outlined
some flower beds. After a few days of garden work, I saw myself compelled
to limit the work that fall to making a single bed. We found the topsoil on
the crest of the hill very shallow. The underlayers of soil consisted of heavy
clay and rock. It was a type of soil unfit to grow shrubs and plants. So I had
to resort to the tedious process of excavating down to the solid rock and
have the old soil hauled away. It was then replaced by soil found in the lower
slopes and hauled up the hill by wagon. To this was added decayed leaf mold
from the forests. This procedure had to be repeated with all plantings that
have become established on our hill land.

I am often amused at the statement made by visitors that the luxuriant
growth in my gardens is due to the excellent native soil. I confess I was
blessed in having so much forest humus available for my needs. More than
that, I was blessed to be so near the forests where nature was to show me her
way of growing things—through the heat of summer and dry periods of the
year. She had pointed a way which I had adopted; namely, to use a forest-
leaf mulch over my gardens. This not only held the topsoil from washing
away, but it also conserved the moisture. For I had no artificial system for
watering the garden. I also used quantities of stone for the same purposes.

By autumn it had become clear to me that I could not carry on a normal
household and at the same time direct all the work outdoors. I was in need
of indoors help. Since our home was in an isolated region, it was evident that
a girl too far away from her home would not remain contented in our household. I was compelled to seek help in the immediate neighborhood. In those
days girls in the capacity of servants were practically unknown thereabouts.
Daughters of the hill families went out to assist in the neighboring homes
only in cases of extreme illness or childbirth, and they were accepted as one

of the family. The remuneration was small, about a dollar a week. At other times, girls were used a great deal for work in the fields. The housework was left, as a rule, for the mother of the home. Cabin life had continued to be very simple. The school years were brief. Marriages came early. I recall two cases in which girls became brides at fourteen.

When I began to ask about "help" for my home, the answers were all discouraging. They saw little reason for my needing help. I did not seem to be sick, nor were we farming. At last a day came when there was an applicant at the door. She began her conversation by saying that she had "heerd I needed help," that she would not work for me, or anyone else, unless they were "too puny to do their own work." I could not admit that was the case, but tried to explain just how she could assist me. She stayed to give it a trial.

We soon found ourselves with a waiting list of applicants for work. Working for us meant higher wages than prevailed in the county where men often worked for 10 cents an hour ten hours a day.

Also gossip had it that we were very "queer." To see how much truth there was in this was another reason for the eagerness to work for us. Strange tales were carried by some we employed about our strange habits. How far? We were frequently to hear versions of tales as they were heard by friends around the dinner table at the Nashville inn. On one occasion a friend of ours who had stopped there for dinner was asked where he was going. When he replied that he was coming to see us, he was told that he "had better fill up on food, for at the Steeles there was little enough to eat. He had heerd that when you set down at Mrs. Steele's table, there was nothin on it but a bouquet of flowers." The informant further explained that "all the plates were piled up before Mr. Steele, so was all the food, and all the food you got was put on the plates by Mr. Steele, and you couldn't reach for a thing. This is what I heerd, and it must be so."

It was customary in their homes to have the table always "set," and eating was done very informally; you "reached" for whatever you wished.

Since our way of living was different, it was confusing and disturbing to the help who came to live with us. Realizing this, I tried to make the adjustment as easy as possible. Believing that the girl would not be comfortable eating with us, I started out with an arrangement to have her eat alone. When I found her outdoors on her knees praying "that I might see the light," I immediately sensed her hurt. She had reasoned that I thought her too inferior to join us at our table, and as she put it, "she was as good as we were—

even though she was poor." So I came to "see the light," and it became an established practice for the household to eat together—company or no company.

The girls who came into my employ with few exceptions had not been out of the county. Compulsory education had not been enforced. Teaching in the schools was very inadequate. Reading was not easy for most of them. Mother's way of doing work in the house had become the accepted way. The resentment on the part of the mothers to have their daughters accept "my way" became a definite obstacle in training them for intelligent service. One mother walked miles to tell me she hoped I would not "larn her daughter wrong." Another mother would so persistently ridicule "the ways" her daughter "picked up" in our household, that both daughter and I finally agreed it was too exhausting to both of us to try to work together.

Finally, there arrived a time when the neighborhood gossips came to have a change of mind and heart. Girls were leaving the household in better health. They were also becoming equipped with a training that made city jobs possible. At least they thought so. With this my school for home training became established. It is still going on, never having been closed.

But time had its effect. The community lost its interest in my peculiarities. In fact, they became commonplace, and new applicants came better informed of what to expect.

There was one disturbing factor regarding the "help" problem about which I seemed to be able to do little. The girls came to believe that it was but a matter of a few weeks' experience in my household to make them ready for a city job. As there was a steady demand for country girls, they took advantage of this to leave for higher remuneration and an escape from the boredom of the country. No matter what our previous arrangement had been, they discarded and ignored it, and accepted the first opportunity offered them. One year I lived through the experience of having nine different girls come and go.

"Outdoors help" like "inside help" was also a problem. During the first four years the Parks boys were at my disposal. Then this family decided to sell their home and move. Hearing that the prospective purchaser would not occupy the property throughout the year, and we would thus be deprived of a permanent caretaker, the painter decided to buy the property himself. This addition to our holdings was a boon to the painter. The forty acres extended his painting ground, giving him among other things superb valley views of both Salt Creek and Hunnicutt valleys. Within a short time he had built a studio on the highest hill overlooking their valleys. But I lost my outside help. It was "an unheard of thing" for a man to take orders from a woman, and in the eyes of the tenants who occupied the Parks cabin I was unqualified to give orders. This was made plain to me when my orders were ignored, and the painter and I had to devise a plan by which I would tell him what was to be done and he in turn would tell the tenant and thus save the latter the humiliation of "taking orders" from a woman.

To the whole neighborhood, especially to the men, it was an inexcusable waste of money and labor to grow flowers. As one of them said, the painter should not tolerate "such goins on." One day I was almost crumbling because of sharp criticisms indoors and out. The outdoor help had again informed me that it was inconsistent with his idea of "man's work" to be digging flower beds. This gave me a bright idea—I explained my reason for growing flowers was the same as his in growing corn and wheat. He sold his wheat and corn. My husband put my flowers into pictures and sold the pictures. This way we both were earning a living—only in a different way. He listened carefully and then said it explained much. I was to learn that this version came to be accepted "at the store."

Meanwhile, the painter was deeply engrossed in his work. He had the happy faculty for letting much which did not directly pertain to his own work go by unnoticed. So the neighborhood came to speak of him in gentle terms as "the contented man."

But one day—this in our second year on the hill—had the painter been seen by the neighborhood folks, he would not have qualified for that reputation. He had gone out to paint, but had returned after a short period. And it was a "paintable" morning, full of fine sunlight and color. As I looked at him, disturbed and white of face, I believed something serious had happened to him. It took some time to tell me. He related how, as he stood breathing in the great beauty of the morning, he began thinking of what his life would be like if necessity forced the disposal of this painting ground—that he had come to feel that he could not conceive of, or face, a future without it. As I saw him standing there, his whole being affected by the thought of it, for the moment I, too, was stunned. The idea that we would not be able to continue to afford living here had never entered my mind. So immediately I began with all kinds of subterfuges to dispel the mood and enumerate various practical things that I had learned to do. I ended by saying that we

123

would not let it happen. With a certain assurance he finally went back to his work.

Yet after he was gone, I, too, had my misgivings. The painter's kindness to others, his inability to deny assistance to the struggler, ofttimes put a strain upon him to meet his own obligations and brought financial worries. Furthermore, I was made to realize that it was imperative to begin at once to limit our spending. At least, this must be done in connection with our country living. But how? Up to the present time all development out-of-doors had been for the purpose of creating a beautiful setting for the house. Plans were now developed with the idea that it might be possible to have the gardens, with additional features, supplement the general income. I reasoned that, begun as an experiment, they might prove a way of making the place self-supporting.

That I was able to work out a feasible program is shown in some notes written after my sixth year on the hill—in October, 1913. We came in August of 1907 and had spent the winter months in the city.

I have come to the stage where I have decided to review the various efforts that I have made during these past six years which were concerned primarily with establishing an income from farm crops.

First, one hill slope, of about an acre, was planted in an orchard, comprising a variety of fruit trees. It was planned to enclose the orchard and have it become the poultry run of the future. Another hill slope was put into grapes, small fruits, and an asparagus bed. Also, a portion was to be used for the growing of table vegetables—although the slope was not the best suited for that purpose. The plot for vegetables would have to be relocated at a future time.

The first planting was done very carefully, according to bulletin directions. This happened in the preparation of a bed (16 by 120 feet) for the growing of asparagus. As most of the old soil had to be carted away and better soil substituted, the making of the bed proved very tedious. You can imagine the days it took to get this one bed ready. But I was planning for twenty years of productiveness instead of a few. Not only did every plant grow, but now, after five years, the bed has become quite productive, affording surplus for sale.

The grapes came next. Each hole for planting was carefully prepared. They, too, took good root, grew into strong plants, and now are supplying the family table. The same careful method was used in planting fruit trees. They are making, on the whole, a good growth. A very few trees have had to be replaced. A quince tree is bearing its first eight quinces, and there are a few stray apples and peaches. The small fruits have not done so well. I am planning to reset them on a lower slope.

Gardening seemed to come easier than chicken raising. . . . At first, because of inexperience, I seemed doomed to complete failure. I had never handled a hen in my life. Still, my chickens were doing about as well as those of my neighbors.

124

They were either taken by the hawks, or died, as I supposed, without cause. Finally, I concluded that as bulletins on garden subjects had proven helpful I would disregard the prevailing neighborhood methods and turn to bulletins available on this subject. These I sent for. A complete substitution of other methods followed "the old way." And the results? There are always eggs—not only a generous supply for the table but enough to put on the market to sell as quality eggs. I came to accept the fact that chicken raising can be made profitable even though the feeds are not raised on the place.

When we came here wild flowers grew in abundance everywhere: on the hill slopes, in the ravines, and on the banks along the roadways. There was a great variety of them. They had been left untouched to have their seeds spread by the winds and the birds. Seeing them in this natural state, bringing beauty through their successive stages, determined the plan which I chose for the garden picture that I had long visualized. I would "naturalize" flowers over my own hillsides. A day came when I set out, as a first experiment, a handful of Scotch daffodils. Now, at this writing, with over thirty years of further development, this bulb garden covers many of the hillsides. There are many varieties, blooming virtually by the thousands and thousands, contributing an unearthly and elusive beauty to the landscape, all enveloped in the soft atmosphere of springtime. The great forests about us came to serve as a background to this garden picture. They were full of dogwood and redbud which came into blossom at a time when the daffodils were waving over the hillsides.

There was much native growth in the forests which I believed usable for my garden planting. Experience taught me that to take forest planting from its natural environment brought more often failure than success. Some was adaptable, some not.

I carried on one very interesting experiment. This was the propagation of plants and shrubs and trees through the stages from seeds, seedlings or transplants, until they were ready for their permanent placements. At first I used this propagation method to keep down the outlay for garden material. Then it became so interesting that I could not think of using any other way. More than that, I found that plants so grown adapted more easily to their new environment. As a result, I have had a great satisfaction in seeing such a planting of six hundred evergreens grow into what are now sizable trees. The work entailed was hard, but if the heart is in it, the air is full of song.

I made, from the very start, the development of the garden plans run along lines supplementary to the character of the natural setting. Overplanting, with a disregard of the importance of the beauty already established, would detract rather than enhance our landscape scheme. When the painter came to speak of the underlying character of my work, I knew then I was not failing in my objective. But the joy in my work reached its highest peak when I found I had made flower and garden arrangements interesting enough to be placed on the painter's canvases.

4

THE SUMMER OF 1908 was coming to its close. The carpenters had finished putting the last touches to the studio, the new west wing of the house. The painter was busy moving his working materials from the living room into this new studio. I was filling the vacated places in the living room with articles brought in from the rear room, and the carpenters had begun with their work of remodeling this southeast section of the house.

A friend of ours—a musician of note—was standing by watching the painter and me at work. The painter, having come to the last load to be carried away, begged to be excused that he might put some order into the mass of painting materials that lay about in the new studio.

"Think it would interfere too much with your work if you gave me a little time?" our friend asked me. "Certainly not," I replied. "Then, let us get out of the mess and sit down somewhere outdoors."

We moved out onto the porch and he began. "Let me make myself clear. The fact that you choose to live in such complete isolation, withdrawn from the stimulation which comes from an interchange of opinion with those of your kind makes me fear for Steele's work. You know, as well as I, how delicately conceived this creative faculty is—how close the demarcation between the influences essential to giving it wings and those that hold it down to the counterpart of indifference. Therefore, it must be kept constantly susceptible to forces that give it form and not allowed to drift because of a monotonous existence. Your neighborhood might be interesting, but remember, too, it is primitive beyond belief. To drift with a leisurely outlook on life would be a natural thing to do. In fact, the influence of the whole situation is what disturbs me. I, too, feel its spell—one of peace and relaxation such as I have never known before. And," he went on to explain, "it will take a terrific effort on your part to hold on to your personal belief; for primitive influences can become very exacting. Thus, it might become easier, in order to smooth over the resentment felt towards you as a 'foreigner' to feel justified in leveling your aims, rather than fighting to uphold them."

"Your last sentence," I interrupted, "brings to my mind a recent conversation I had with a local schoolteacher. I had asked him why he did not teach the children in his schoolroom the long-accepted fact that the earth was round and not square. In answer, he explained that he could not interfere

127

with their religious beliefs. Their elders interpreted the sentence in the Bible, 'The angels stood at the four corners of the earth,' as proving that the earth was square. He told me that he met the situation by simply 'skipping' the page in the Geography where it was explained otherwise."

"No doubt," I went on to say, "I, too, like the schoolteacher, will be 'skipping a page,' when an issue gets beyond compromise. But do not let that disturb you. I think I am facing the situation in all sincerity. Although I am ready to admit that the things you spoke of are possible; yet I do not believe there need be a fear as to the future of the painter's work. As far as he is concerned, he will live here, outside of the influences that would be very disturbing to others. He has accustomed himself to withdraw, when necessary, from everything and anything not vital at the moment to his thoughts. If it does matter, he sees it—if not, it does not exist. Remember this: he comes here not as a beginner, but as one whose training has come over a hard road.

"Recently, unnoticed, I came to hear a part of a conversation between the painter and an artist friend. The friend made the statement that an artist's wife could not give an impersonal criticism because she believed everything a husband painted was good. To this the painter replied that he was fortunate in being able to benefit from my criticisms because of my Austrian heritage of a sensitiveness to fine composition and color. I am quite sure there is perfect understanding between us. You see we have a common goal. Already he is intoxicated by the quality of the beauty and the inexhaustibleness of the painting material on every hand. And I could never abide ugliness, no matter where or when.

"Our tastes are similar. We both love the outdoors intensely. We are fond of books and read extensively. The poets are especial friends. Together we are interested in the art movements in the state and beyond. There will be occasions for personal contacts with people engaged in other professions than our own.

"In time, I think, it will be generally accepted and proven that this venture was a wise one. Unless something unforeseen happens, this particular period in the painter's career will be spoken of as primarily his great landscape period.

"Furthermore," I continued, "to possess as his own a painting ground such as this must have been always a cherished dream of his, kept closely guarded in the recesses of his mind. I am told that he made an entry in his diary when he was barely twenty years old that he 'could not but wish for time and opportunity for the study of the landscape.' This gives me the conviction that here in this environment of beauty and silences, too, lies a meaning whereby the painter will come to a more thorough understanding of his true self, and, in the end, 'arrive,' as far as his landscape work is concerned.

"Before many weeks, when our remodeling is completed, we shall have a small room that I can set aside as a guest room. The only hospitality we can offer to our friends will be of the simplest type. I hope this will not deter them from coming and sharing with us the passion we feel for our independent way of life."

Before the friend departed we had made a bargain. He was to come frequently, as an interested house guest. So doing, he could approximate the result of my efforts, and determine whether I needed prodding or praising for the way I had set out to make or unmake the future of the two adventurous individuals.

I refer to the above conversation for the reason that it was so similar to others that happened during those first two years. Apparently I was to have not one, but two, taskmasters. There were the friends, skeptical of this detached, isolated home being able to serve the best interests of the painter, and me, too. On the other hand, there were the country folks, who looked at me as one of the city-bred "know-nothings." So to save myself from complete disgrace, it was up to me to prove to them that I knew what I was about. At least I had the faith to think so.

The painter could now withdraw with his painting materials into the new studio in the west wing. New work could be attempted without exasperating interruptions. The painting grounds were extensive, and the rough hill land covered considerable area. Finally there arose a need for distant shelters to serve as studios when inclement weather made it impossible to work in the open. Two temporary structures were built for that purpose. Shortly after the Parks property was acquired (1911), the painter built a well-lighted one-room studio on the top of the high hill overlooking the Schooner and Hunnicutt valleys. There were extensive views from these windows. They provided the subject material for many a canvas shown in various exhibitions. Also another one-room studio was erected on the bank of a winding stream that ran through deep ravines between high steep hills. Here many of the winter subjects were painted that are so splendid in their delineation of wintry snows and sunshine.

Then some years later, just before the opening of the First World War, came the "Dream Studio" of his life. The painter had always envisioned as a studio a large spacious high-windowed room that would give him the same lighting conditions that existed in public galleries used for exhibition purposes. The house studio did not fully meet this condition. The "Dream Studio" still stands. It is the only one of the four studios remaining and in use as an exhibition studio.

. . . the artist worships the beauty of the world, for his whole life's work is the endeavor to make permanent that which endures so short a time. The hours and the seasons, under the magic of light, weave and interweave the whole world of effect. Happy indeed is the artist if he can grasp and give again the beauty and significance of an hour, in this changeable miracle of nature, and make permanent upon his canvas the poignant charm of that which is so brief.

The above are the words of the painter. Suppose we scan the oncoming years. I think you will find the work shown in many, many exhibitions throughout the country, conceived by him during this Brown County period (1907–1926), based on a penetrating study of nature, and executed, as he often spoke of it, "as wrung out of one's soul," expressing a deep and inspirational chapter in his life. Throughout this period he was made the recipient of many honors—flowers and fruits to be plucked along the way. Alongside, hedged into the routine work, came thorny and prickly interruptions, too. But his nature was buoyant; and these did not matter. If meaningless, they could be relegated to the background.

The Indianapolis *News* of December 2, 1908, announced: "T. C. Steele's Latest Brown County Pictures from his Own Broad Estate of Landscape Glories on Exhibition at Lieber's." This exhibition ran from December 2 through December 9. The *News* article said that "the artist's friends who have seen this collection, presenting in its landscapes a greater variety of nature's varying moods than he has given in any previous exhibit, are warm in their praises of his work which began in the early spring and has just ended. . . . Mr. Steele has erected a bungalow on one of his several hills . . . to which he has appropriately given the name of the 'House of the Singing Winds.'"

The article quotes Mr. Steele as saying that artists who have tramped all over southern Indiana report that "they have found nothing to equal Brown County in artistic subjects. . . . the place I have chosen is certainly the most broken lot of acres in the county. I selected it because it was in the midst of innumerable beautiful subjects. . . . From my bungalow I can see fifteen miles up the valley. . . . It is rich in oaks of which there are twenty or more varieties, affording in the autumn a wide range of crimsons and purples. . . ."

The Indianapolis *News* of December 4, 1908, reported that

Will Vawter,[33] the well-known Indiana sketch artist and illustrator of Riley, has made several pen and ink drawings from the Brown county paintings of John Hafen [34] [of Salt Lake City], now on Exhibition at L. S. Ayres & Co.'s Store.

Since T. C. Steele, nearly two years ago, chose Brown county as a field rich in subjects for the landscape painter, many other artists, both of Indiana and elsewhere, have been attracted there to paint its scenery, and some of them its interesting people. A good-sized colony of artists were there this summer. . . .

Indianapolis is not the only city that is learning of the artistic side of Brown county. Several Chicago artists were among the county's summer visitors. One of them, Emory Albright,[35] has just won the prize at the Chicago Art Institute . . . for the best painting of the year by a Chicagoan. This was painted in Brown county and shows a small lad fishing with a little lass in the stern of the boat. It is called "The Enchanted Hour." [36]

In the spring of 1909 the painter entered Brown County canvases in the exhibition of the Society of Western Artists. This society was organized in 1896 "just after and under the influence of the Columbian Exhibition," and held an annual exhibition in Cincinnati, St. Louis, Chicago, Detroit, and Cleveland, as well as Indianapolis. In the exhibition of this year, held at the Herron Art Institute from March 31 to May 3, the Indiana artists, meaning the Hoosier Group, are rated as holding their own. Two of the most notable landscapes were the large canvases "Morning" and "A Vision of Morning," by Steele. A critic wrote, "In the first, a beautiful morning radiancy softened by the atmosphere of early autumn glows through a glade. The other, also of

[33] Born in Boone County, Virginia, in 1871, Will Vawter grew up in Greenfield, Indiana. A favorite of Riley's, he became an illustrator of the poet's works. He also contributed drawings to the Indianapolis *News* and *Sentinel* and the Cincinnati *Gazette*, illustrated children's books, and made drawings for *Judge* and the old *Life* magazines. He lived in Brown County from 1908 until his death in 1941.

[34] A Mormon, John Hafen came to Brown County in 1908 from his home in Springville, Utah. He was then in his sixties. He had three seasons of painting in Brown County before his death in 1910.

[35] Born in Monroe, Wisconsin, in 1862, Adam Emory Albright studied at the Art Institute of Chicago, the Pennsylvania Academy of Fine Arts, and in Munich and Paris. A Chicago resident, he spent the summer of 1908 in a primitive cabin near Nashville. His specialty was child life and an exhibit of his "Pictures of Country Children" was held at the John Herron Art Institute in 1902. He died in 1957.

[36] This was the Twenty-first Annual Exhibition of Oil Paintings and Sculpture by American Artists, October 20-November 29, 1908, and the prize was the Cahn prize of $100.

spare autumn woods, seems to be earlier in the day with the mists still hanging heavy in the background, but is probably later in the season. There is a stateliness about such pictures as these, that gives the feeling that 'the one of the dim old forest, seems the best of all.'"

That winter the public was also informed through the newspapers of the talks given by T. C. Steele on Sunday afternoons at the Herron Art Institute on the current exhibitions. As chairman of the Fine Arts Committee of the Institute [37] his comprehensive understanding of the works included in the shows made these talks very popular. He always drew a large audience. It was generally accepted that his interpretations of the "other fellow's work" were never opinionated but based on a generous outlook. "The first thing in art to be considered," he said, "as well as the last, is truth. Different men may have different impressions, and consequently there follows different work from different artists."

This service to the Art Institute was given freely and gladly during the winters of many years.

We have come to December, 1909, when the painter opened an exhibition of new canvases at Sander and Recker's gallery in Indianapolis. [38] Of this exhibition William Henry Fox, director of the Herron Art Institute, [39] writes: "In the forty examples that compose this collection, the impression of the love of nature, and the searching analysis of the elements which compose its beauty must be manifest to every visitor who sees them. Never has Mr. Steele given such evidence of his artistic productiveness and inexhaustible power for producing work of high average merit; their variety is another of the striking features of this collection." [40]

There were other reviews in the local papers. But I want to quote from the one by Roderic S. Mumford in the Indianapolis *Star* at length: [41]

[37] Steele served on the Fine Arts Committee of the Indianapolis Art Association until his death. He was also vice-president of the Association from 1896 to 1908 and a member of the Art School Committee for many years.

[38] This gallery was in the store of the Sander & Recker Furniture Company (Gustave A. Recker, president, and Carl G. Sander, vice-president), 219–23 East Washington Street.

[39] A native of Philadelphia and graduate of the University of Pennsylvania, William Henry Fox (1858–1952) was director of the John Herron Art Institute from 1905 to 1910. He had served as secretary of the Department of Art and of the International Art Jury Awards of the St. Louis Exposition in 1904, and left Herron to serve in a similar capacity for the International Exposition of Art and History held in Rome in 1911. From 1913 to 1934 he was director of the Brooklyn (N.Y.) Museum.

[40] Indianapolis *News,* November 27, 1909, p. 8.

[41] Issue of December 1, 1909, p. 6.

The artist comes up to the city with the pictures he has been painting all through spring, summer and fall, each one a record of nature in some one of her thousand moods. He has returned from out of doors with the bright pictures that the eye sees, suddenly arrested in their variations of color and light and fixed forever on canvas. It is as if they were caught by a thinking camera before the great Magician, on whose palette are spread the rainbow and the mists, and the dissolutions of morning and evening, can shift his colors. And the artist who thus comes back from the country seems verily like a gleaner returning with his sheaves.

Is this too fanciful a vein? It seems all that and more. To some persons imagination is given, to others, the eye that sees truly, and to still others the hand that records what the eye sees. In a very few men these qualities are blended so that when they paint nature you see it all there before you, only somehow glorified, as if nature had put on the robes of a high office, to be painted on this occasion by one who knew her well.

. . . But pictures outlive men, and if you are transcendentalist enough, you can almost imagine that the great picture in the time that it lives on earth gains a soul. Or if you do not care to believe that, you may safely trust that it finds a place in the hearts of men.

Something of this you will feel when you look on the pictures T. C. Steele has brought up from his studio in the Indiana hill country. At Sander & Recker's are the results of some of the most profitable months this artist has ever given to his work. Mr. Steele has been at his work long, and is well at the forefront of the Indiana group of artists. He is also well up among the first artists of the country. During the years he has been painting he has produced some notable things.

But when the public views his latest pictures . . . it will be strange if it does not declare that the artist has struck a more sympathetic note than ever before.

It is hard to say in so many words just what the addition is. Perhaps it cannot so be defined. There is more color in these Brown County studies, but the new note is not the increased mastery of color. There seems to be more luminosity in Mr. Steele's late oils, and more air and distance. Besides, with all the richness of color present, there is harmony, no note of sharp color out of tune, whether the bright flame of sumach along a roadside or the red garment of a figure trudging up toward the crest of a hill.

The critic might find these landscapes exhibit a finer technique in gradation of tones; he might find or think he finds one thing or another, but perhaps the truth of it all could be summed up by saying that Mr. Steele had gone closer than ever to the heart of nature. . . .

In December of this same year (1909) the painter was awarded the $500 Chicago Fine Arts Building Prize given for the best entry in the annual exhibition of the Society of Western Artists. The Steele painting which won the award was entitled "A March Morning," a 35 by 45-inch canvas. When told of the award and questioned by a newspaper reporter about the canvas, he said, "I painted the picture last March. It represents a broken country with a roadway running over the top of a Brown county ridge, and the view is on my Brown county farm. . . an admirable farm for landscape purposes, and pictures are the only crop it produces." [42]

The St. Louis *Republican* of December 26, spoke enthusiastically about the award, saying that it would "meet with almost universal commendation, as the place of Mr. Steele's pictures and Mr. Steele himself, in Western art is important and appreciated." The critic continued:

Mr. Steele represents the West not merely as a native of it, but as an artist who finds in it his themes and his inspiration. His paintings are intimate and sympathetic portrayals of nature. . . . Mr. Steele's work is familiar to St. Louisans. . . . The first characteristic exhibition in the new art building in Forest Park was of selected pictures by Western painters, held in December 1906 . . . in which there was a good showing of the Hoosier Group, led by Mr. Steele, with ten strong pictures. . . . Two or three of Mr. Steele's pictures remained from that exhibition in private St. Louis collections. . . .[43]

One of the notable things about Mr. Steele is that he was an early leader, a pioneer among those Western art students, who, after enjoying the educational advantages afforded by the great art centers, have returned to the West, to live and work permanently, to identify themselves with its hopes and advancement. To these artists, the development of art in the West is lastingly indebted. Associated with Mr. Steele as students, were several men, whose names will be prominent in the history of Art in the West, Frank Duveneck, sculptor, painter, etcher, Frederick Warren Freer, Meakin, Adams, Forsyth and others, from whose return from abroad, to paint and teach, an epoch in the Art History of the Middle West may be dated.[44] The influence of all these workers, as teachers and examples for the younger generation of art students, is abundantly manifested in this fourteenth annual exhibition of the society.

During this same winter beginning with February, 1910, a retrospective exhibition of seventy canvases was held by the painter in the main gallery of the Herron Art Institute.[45] Referring to the work and life of Mr. Steele,

[42] Quoted in the Indianapolis *News*, December 20, 1909, p. 2. The prize was contributed by the Corporation of the Fine Arts Building, Chicago. This was the second time that it had been won by an Indiana artist, J. Ottis Adams having received it in 1907.

[43] The ten Steele canvases shown in this 1906 exhibition were landscapes. In reviewing this show a St. Louis critic observed that "behind the work of certain of the 'Hoosier School' artists—present examples Messrs. Steele, Forsyth, Stark, and with a distinction, geographical, Mr. [L. H.] Meakin, of Cincinnati,—one seems to sense the expression of a fear that if they don't 'hang together' they may not be able to 'hang separately'—yet their work is valuable, and closer study discloses an individuality for each. . . . Steele remains the strongest of this group, with a virtuosity that keeps his freedom close to Nature." *Reedy's Mirror* (St. Louis), December 20, 1906, p. 71.

[44] J. Ottis Adams and William Forsyth were, of course, members of the Hoosier Group. Duveneck and Lewis Henry Meakin were from Cincinnati and Freer from Chicago.

[45] The catalogue of this exhibition lists seventy-three paintings, including two early portraits, one painted in 1873 and another in 1878, eleven canvases from Steele's Munich period, 1880–1885, eleven painted between 1885 and 1906, and the rest, done between 1907 and 1909, were Brown County scenes.

PLATE VI

Brookville, 1904, 22 by 32 ins.
Private Collection

Mr. Fox, the director of the Institute, wrote in the Indianapolis *News:* [46]

For the month of February a retrospective display of the works of T. C. Steele will be made in the main gallery. About seventy of Mr. Steele's canvases will be on the walls, covering the art activity of this distinguished painter since his Munich days of "the eighties." Some few of his paintings preceding that period will be included. It must be of interest to every Indianian, and indeed to all Americans of the west and the east who feel a pride in the growth of a native school of painting, and who can appreciate Mr. Steele's influence, potent and widespread, yet quietly and modestly exerted, that it is proposed to honor him by assembling his representative life work in the institution which he has done so much to build up. Not all of the best pictures he has painted during his long career are procurable. They are scattered about in various parts of the country. . . .

The Exhibition will show how Mr. Steele's art has developed through different periods, and how strongly he has himself been influenced by his environment. His life in Germany will be reflected in his Munich pictures, and the generalized differences of his surroundings at Vernon, Brookville, and in Brown county, will also be notably set out in this collection. Apart from his landscapes, and his studies of the familiar life of his own people, a number of Mr. Steele's portraits will also be shown. The list is a long one, including many notable persons among his acquaintances, and including also individuals of all ages. . . .

Mr. Steele is constantly referred to as the dean of Indiana painters, and the seniority that term implies refers more to his quietly established leadership in the development of a popular interest in the fine arts in this part of the country than to the long period of Mr. Steele's great service to the people.

The retrospective exhibition of Augustus Saint-Gaudens [47] which had been the great attraction at Herron during the month of January was continued through February. W. H. Fox, writing of the two artists—Steele and Saint-Gaudens—said: [48]

Mr. Steele has gone the way of the best painters of our time. His emancipation from academic preciseness of the earlier day he has shared with all representative artists, whose works interpret nature in the present prevailing spirit. It is the same spirit that animated the great Saint-Gaudens, whose inspiration was, as he himself said, "energy and directness, the freshness and promise of it all." This is essentially true of Mr. Steele's work.

An editorial in the Indianapolis *News* of February 9, 1910, is worthy of quotation:

In passing from the works of Saint-Gaudens to those of our fellow townsman, T. C. Steele, also displayed in a way representative of his whole career as an artist,

[46] Indianapolis *News,* January 29, 1910, p. 13, c. 3.
[47] The Irish-born sculptor in America who died in 1907.
[48] Indianapolis *News,* February 5, 1910, p. 24.

135

we renew and enlarge our acquaintance with a man whose aims and character are made clearer by the presence of the Saint-Gaudens sculpture. However great may be the difference in kind of work and degree of actual final achievement, there are similarities between these men in manly strength and sincerity, combined with delicacy of perception and poetic vision. Here, too, is a man of all gentleness yet firmness of purpose, true at once to what seems worthy to those without and those within the special world of art—beloved of both. Saint-Gaudens sought to know all the world could teach him about his art, but returned from Europe and its 'art atmosphere' to work sturdily in his adopted land, a true American, seeing things in the American way, but also in the universal way. Similarly, Mr. Steele learned in Europe only a better way of expressing Indiana and has done for Indiana something of the same thing that Saint-Gaudens has done for America as a pioneer making us understand of our selves and of others, showing that art with the beauty that art reveals is not a thing of a special place but of everywhere that the right spirit seeks it. He also is a man whom it is good to know and good to have among us.

We hear and know much of the peculiarities of the "artistic temperament," and it would be foolish to deny ourselves the pleasure and insight that may be gained from works of art that may not at once appeal to us as natural, normal or even sincere; but it is very refreshing to meet with art and artists that at once seem to stand on a level with ourselves and yet carry our perceptions far beyond their ordinary discernment. So the Art Institute now offers a peculiarly agreeable means of becoming acquainted with art.

The exhibition of the Society of Western Artists, showing the work of eighty-seven artists with two hundred canvases, among them the prize picture, "A March Morning," by T. C. Steele, was on view at the Herron Art Institute during the month of March, 1910, after a long tour of other cities. There were other exhibitions at other places that featured Steele canvases.[49] On March 1 the painter spoke to the Nature Study Club in Indianapolis on "How an artist looks at Nature."

The Boston, Massachusetts, *Evening Transcript* of May 4, 1910, mentioned that the current number of the magazine *Handicraft* carried a reprint of "a very readable article" by T. C. Steele on "The Mark of the Tool," which had appeared in *Modern Art* some years before. "As the editor of Handicraft points out," said the *Transcript*, "this article, aside from its literary charm, is notable for its expression, by a painter with a high rank, of his appreciation of the dignity, value and necessity of the handicrafts."[50]

[49] Two of Steele's paintings, listed as "Midsummer" and simply "Landscape," were shown in the Fifth Annual Exhibit of Selected American Paintings at the St. Louis Museum in 1910 and two others, "The Tranquil Hour" and "Morning in the Ravine" later in the season at the Seventeenth Annual Exhibit of American Art at the Cincinnati Art Museum.

[50] Steele had first presented "The Mark of the Tool" as a lecture before the Contemporary Club of Indianapolis on January 31, 1894.

A few weeks later we were back again among our "misty hills." Not for long, for the painter had agreed to go to Terre Haute to paint a portrait of Dr. William Wood Parsons,[51] the president of the State Normal School. By May 31 he had left for Terre Haute, difficult as it was to tear himself away from the landscape work already begun. I remained at home, for I had expectations of a first flowering season from my newly established gardens. I wrote him with great enthusiasm of counting nearly eight hundred blossoms in the iris beds bordering the driveway. Also I found occasional peonies in blossom and some phlox, too. And he answered that if there were blossoms left he would paint them when he got back. And I remembered that he had not painted "flowers" for many a year, and I looked forward to a "new note" to be added to the great variety of subjects shown in his exhibitions.

He spoke, also, in his letters from Terre Haute of Dr. Parsons as a man "agreeable and direct, with decided character, especially in the eyes, which are his best feature." When the portrait was finished, he regarded it as a strong picture and said that it was liked by the president's friends and associates. The portrait was a full-size, three-quarter view, and was presented to the school by the alumni association in celebration of Dr. Parsons' twenty-fifth anniversary as president of the school.

The frontispiece of the Indiana University senior class annual, *The Arbutus*, for 1910, is a reproduction of a painting, "A Brown County Valley," by T. C. Steele. The painter also made true his intention of painting a "flower canvas," for in the autumn exhibit of the year's work there was "an interesting flower painting, 'The Zinnias.'"[52]

During the summer we were again at work, adding two more features to the house. On the east side our carpenter, Mr. Quick, built a pergola attached to the house.[53] The natives found it "queer," saying it reminded them of a railroad trestle. On the west side the small porch was replaced by a much larger one.

I cannot let the year of 1910 pass without mentioning that the painter was

[51] A member of the first class to graduate from the State Normal School at Terre Haute (1872), William Wood Parsons (1850–1925), taught for a few years in public schools and then returned to teach in his alma mater. He became president of the State Normal School (presently Indiana State University) in 1885 and served until 1921.

[52] This was also shown in the exhibition of the Society of Western Artists which was held in Indianapolis December 4 to 25, 1910. It was the first of several Steele canvases to feature this flower.

[53] Steele had a canvas in the Indiana Artists exhibit at Herron Art Institute in 1914 entitled "The Pergola."

represented in the International Exhibition held at Buenos Aires, which opened June 12 and closed September 1.[54]

Aside from local exhibitions in Indianapolis and other towns throughout the state during 1911, the painter received wide publicity for his exhibition and lectures at the University of Missouri. In his gallery talks there he said that the appreciation of the outdoors was a modern thing, and that it was only recently that color and light in nature had been appreciated to their full extent. "Landscape pictures," he said, "should represent moods of nature; for the outdoors is never the same at different periods of the day or seasons of the year. . . . When I paint a picture,—I do all I can possibly do to get the spirit of the subject when I am most interested in it. . . ."

Some of the canvases were retained, to be included in the permanent collection of the University.[55]

During the same winter of 1911–12 my collection of shawls was on exhibit at the Herron Art Institute, in the Sculpture Court and overflowing into one of the adjoining galleries.[56]

By now we had come to realize that our schedule throughout the year must be kept flexible, that we could not plan definitely, according to certain months of the calendar year but rather be governed by the work being done by the painter. Consequently, our time was divided irregularly between the country and the city. When the landscape work was pressing for attention, we accepted country life in all its fullness. When there were portrait commissions, and there were some each year, we stayed close to the city studio. The painter tried to arrange to fill these commissions as much as possible during the period of his exhibitions. This was not always possible, since often they had to be carried out at a time agreeable to the sitter and sometimes out of the city.

Although he was doing the thing he liked to do, yet one could not help

[54] The catalogue of works shown in the United States Section Exposicion Internacional de Arte del Centenario Buenos Aires and the Exposicion Internacional de Bellas Artes Santiago, 1910, lists Steele's entry as "In the Valley." Other Indiana artists represented were J. Ottis Adams, William Forsyth, and Otto Stark.

[55] Steele's lectures at the University were reported in the Columbia *Missourian,* and two of his landscapes are now hanging in administrative offices of the University.

[56] Among Mrs. Steele's papers deposited in the Indiana State Library there is a letter of November 22, 1911, from Milton Matter, acting director of the John Herron Art Institute, asking permission to keep the shawls on exhibition for a while. "So many people have admired them," he wrote, "and I have dreaded so much the bareness of the walls that would result from taking them down . . . ." As a collector of, and lecturer on, Persian, Indian, and Paisley shawls Mrs. Steele gained a broad recognition.

being amazed at the inherent energy he possessed to meet the variety of tasks that each day brought.

Unquestionably he was of the stuff of those persons of whom Thomas Carlyle wrote in his *Heroes, and Hero-Worship:* "And yet, I say, there is an irrepressible tendency in every man to develop himself according to the magnitude which nature has made him of; to speak out, to act out, what nature has laid in him. This is proper, fit, inevitable; nay it is a duty and even the summary of duties for a man. The meaning of life here on earth might be defined as consisting in this: To unfold your *self*, to work what thing you have the faculty for. It is a necessity for the human being, the first law of our existence." Thus so—with an honesty of purpose, the painter kept forever searching for a realization of his own mission of things.

I came to love life as never before. Daily I saw it enriched not only through my companionship with my husband and my intimate contact with nature, but through people, too. My friendships became precious. The country home became the mecca of friends and acquaintances. The lines of Emerson came frequently to mind: "This morning I awoke with a profound Thanksgiving for all my friends, both old and new." There was the unalterable friendship of our near neighbor, Allan Hendricks, and the rare friends in the University group: the William Lowe Bryans, the Alfred M. Brookses, the J. W. Piercys,[57] and others. In the Indianapolis group were the Dr. Alembert Braytons, the Clarence Forsyths, the Carl Liebers, the Evans Woollens,[58] and others. At nearby Nashville was the group of painters. Some of these became residents, others came for a season. There was Gustave Baumann, the Will Vawters, Ada Shulz,[59] the Fred Hetheringtons,[60] and others. They came, singly and in groups, in spite of the difficulty of transportation. We thought of these friendships as blessed because these people fitted so wholeheartedly into our

[57] In 1911 Joseph William Piercy became head of the Journalism Department of Indiana University. A native of Cloverdale, Indiana, and a graduate of DePauw University, he had worked as a reporter for various papers and in the editorial department of the Indianapolis *News* from 1890 to 1907 and had taught at the University of Washington. .

[58] Founder (1912) and chairman of the board of the Fletcher Trust Company, Evans Woollen, Sr. (1864–1942) served as president of the Art Association of Indianapolis from 1907 to 1941.

[59] Ada Walter Shulz, wife of Adolph R. Shulz, was born in Terre Haute in 1870 and studied in the Chicago Institute of Art and in Paris. She lived in Brown County after 1907, becoming known particularly as a painter of mothers and children.

[60] While very successful as head of Hetherington & Berner, Inc., a structural iron firm, and the inventor of a method of asphalt paving, Frederick A. Hetherington (1859–1931) was also a gifted artist who illustrated Riley's poems and contributed art work to local periodicals. He also invented a portable camera on principles later adopted by Eastman Kodak. Before 1909 he had established a part-time home in Brown County north of Nashville.

atmosphere of quiet detachment. Heart spoke to heart, and there was silent understanding. Also valuable were the interruptions they brought to the ever-increasing strenuousness of our way of life.

We have come to the year 1912. The painter had a letter from Professor George Breed Zug, instructor in art at the University of Chicago,[61] asking for photographs of late landscapes done in Brown County. Professor Zug was preparing a series of illustrated lectures. He stated that in his estimate T. C. Steele was one of the "foremost landscape painters in America today." Referring to one of the Brown County landscapes, he remarks that Steele "had caught God's own sunlight." "In addition to understanding his art," said Professor Zug, "Mr. Steele is a painter—a craftsman and gets beautiful, noble and satisfying results." He spoke of another canvas "as the acme of simplicity. . . . The broad expanse of sky, the far-away stretch of earth, was the poetry of nature and it took a master's touch to attain such results."

The painter had been one of the speakers at the ceremonies attending the laying of the cornerstone of the Herron Art Institute in 1905. Regarding the future of the Institute he said: [62]

We shall secure and present in properly lighted galleries the best of contemporary art. These exhibitions will be constantly changing and will be not only a source of enjoyment but a school for the people. The appreciation of the best in art comes only from seeing the best. Art criticism and lectures in art have their place. They give information and awaken interest, but the message of a work of art, that which is vital and gives it its quality, comes only from the work itself. So it is not too much to claim that these constantly recurring exhibitions will become the art school of the people. . . .

As chairman of the Fine Arts Committee of the Institute, the painter was able to carry out the intention of encouraging wide interest in the current exhibitions and bringing to the public the best available.

In April, 1912, the fifth annual show of Indiana artists was held as one of the exhibitions.[63] The following is from the art column in the April 25 issue of the Indianapolis *News:*

At the east end of the main gallery . . . are two large winter scenes by T. C.

[61] A graduate of Amherst College, Zug studied at Harvard and in Berlin, Paris, and Rome from 1893 to 1903, and was a member of the faculty of the University of Chicago from 1903 to 1913. He later taught at Dartmouth College.

[62] Quoted in the Indianapolis *News,* November 25, 1905, p. 2.

[63] The first exhibition by Indiana artists sponsored by the Art Association of Indianapolis was held in the spring of 1908. In it Steele had shown four landscapes and a portrait of his daughter. He exhibited regularly in these shows and served as a member of the jury.

Steele—"New Fallen Snow" and "Winter Sunlight" which draw attention both of reason of their size, and because of the new winter venture of the well-known artist. One feels in them the tang of reality as well of the beauty of the wood and the little stream. They have a purplish tinge which is said to be more noticeable in the gallery than where they were seen separately.

Note that the public was becoming conscious of "the purple haze" appearing in the Steele canvases, but as yet was not ready to accept the fact that it appeared in the pictures because it was characteristic of the Brown County region.

The winter studies referred to are the first to emerge from the little hut built in the ravine purposely for the study and painting of winter subjects.[64] The column in the *News* continues:

Another large picture by Mr. Steele on the north wall of the main gallery seems more unusual for him than winter landscapes. It is a still life called "Wild Roses," in which the roses are the main flowers in a blue octagonal vase. To Mr. Steele's admirers he is best liked for making familiar Indiana landscapes even more dear to them and in this picture he has taken a bit of Indiana early summer landscape— the wild rose—indoors and put it in a vase. His fellow artists have their own technical reasons for admiring the way he has done these flowers and also speak in special admiration of his "October Landscape" in the west gallery because of its tone and range of color.

During the year the painter had done a number of flower studies. This brought about a revived interest among artists in flower and still-life studies, and from then on one found similar studies appearing again in their own exhibits. In other words, he had set a vogue for flower painting.

Also this year we decided to discontinue keeping a town house since we occupied it over so short a period in midwinter. This would reduce our city expenses and also give me a period free from household management. Besides, it left the way open to be at the country home during parts of the winter if it was deemed advisable.

The new little hut-studio in the ravine recently built was to provide a comfortable place for midwinter painting. It followed then that on a morning in early February of 1912, with temperatures hovering near the zero mark, we left the city for some deep winter experiences in the country. When we arrived at the hilltop home there were only the tracks of the furred ani-

---

[64] "Winter Sunlight" was purchased by the Art Association of Indianapolis for the John Herron Art Institute. Steele's entry in the Art Association's Twenty-seventh Annual Exhibition, held December 31, 1911, to January 29, 1912, was entitled "The First Snow."

mals in the snow to give evidence of life. All else was still and profound. I was given opportunity to enjoy an aspect of winter such as I had never experienced before. Here stood winter in all its purity. Daily I saw the fleeting moods etched by the driving snows upon the great panorama of hills and valleys, and on the brook in the deep ravine. Daily I saw them take form in compositions on the canvases of the painter. No more perfect provision could have been made for an undisturbed study of the glory and beauty of winter than that now at the painter's command.[65] When these canvases came to be exhibited, artist critics were so impressed that they suggested the painter concentrate exclusively upon the painting of winter subjects. This, of course, would have been contrary to his belief. To him, his landscape painting represented moods of nature, and these he found equally beautiful throughout all seasons of the year. Even was this true of summer, which so many painters pronounce uninteresting.

By leaving the city in midwinter, the painter forfeited the time used for portrait painting. It became necessary for him to return to the city in late spring. By June he had completed his last portrait commission, but at the end of July he went to Columbus, Indiana, to paint the portrait of Professor Wertz,[66] long connected with the city schools.

Portrait painting continued throughout his life, a part of his routine plan of work each year. Although he thought of "landscape painting as the most distinctive form of American art," he also felt that the intimate associations with notable men brought about through his portrait work were of value and experience in keeping him living in a world that would have been closed had he devoted his time exclusively to landscape painting.

In January of the next year (1913) we went to Chicago to attend a banquet given by resident artists at which the painter was a guest speaker. He was again represented in the February exhibition at the Chicago Art Institute, with four Brown County landscapes. The stay in Chicago was limited to a few days; there was a portrait to be painted and he hurried back to his studio in Indianapolis.

In late autumn he spent a week at Nashville, investigating the painting

---

[65] One of the two paintings by Steele in the Twenty-eighth Annual Exhibition of Oil Paintings by American Artists at the John Herron Art Institute, December 17, 1912, to February 3, 1913, was a winter scene, "Woods in Winter." "Winter Sunlight" was shown at the Annual Exhibition of American Art at the Cincinnati Art Museum in the spring of 1912. "Winter Sunlight" and "Winter Landscape" appeared in the Society of Western Artists exhibition in 1913.

[66] Samuel Wertz, who served as principal of the Columbus High School for thirty years.

Fig. 44. Winter in the Ravine, 1912, 34 by 32 ins.
Greater Lafayette Museum of Art

Fig. 45. The Red Cloud, 1913, 30 by 45 ins.
Heirs of Brandt T. Steele

Fig. 46. The Yellow Shawl
(Selma N. Steele),
1913, 24 by 20 ins.
T. C. Steele State Historic Site,
Indiana State Museum Collection

Fig. 47. The Hill Country, 1913, 30 by 45 ins.
Dr. and Mrs. John Shively

Fig. 48. The Wheat Field, 1914, 30 by 45 ins.
Indiana University, Bloomington

Fig. 49. Country Road in Summer, 1914, 30 by 45 ins.
Hanus J. and Kirsten Grosz

Fig. 50. Belmont Road, 1914, 30 by 45 ins.
Private Collection

Fig. 51. Studio in Autumn, 1915, 22 by 32 ins.
Private Collection

opportunities then so sought for by nonresident artists. He found the old bridge an interesting subject, but, on the whole, concluded that he had a greater variety of subjects at his command on his own painting ground.

The next winter months, in fact the whole of 1914, proved very momentous. No recognition was more coveted by an artist of this period than being chosen as an associate of the National Academy of Design of New York. This honor was conferred upon Mr. Steele in 1913, on condition that he furnish a portrait of himself. All persons qualifying for membership in the Academy were required to do this. The portrait was expected to be of the highest excellence, for it was to be placed in the gallery with the portraits of those already so honored with membership in the Academy. It is said that this collection of portraits is one of the "choicest in the land." To meet his obligation, the painter went to Boston and asked his old friend Frank Tompkins,[67] a portrait painter of note, to paint his portrait for the "Immortal Gallery," as the artists termed it.

By February 17, 1914, the painter was registered as a guest of the Boston Art Club and giving daily sittings for his portrait in the studio of his friend. "He was painted in his characteristic abandon," and the result was a portrait full of "character, finely modelled and painted with freedom." The artists of the local art colony, on their visits to the Tompkins studio, pronounced it one of the very best painted by the artist, which was saying much, for as a portrait painter he had an acknowledged reputation.

This put Mr. Steele in a quandary, for he liked the portrait exceedingly well and disliked the idea of parting with it. It finally ended by him suggesting that Mr. Tompkins paint a second portrait. The first one painted was a full-front head, the second a profile. In a letter to me he said, "They are not at all alike in pose, lighting or mood, yet both are good and interesting pictures." This made the choice even more difficult, for some of the local group of artists thought the full view the most sympathetic, while others decided upon the profile study. The general opinion was "that they were the best heads painted in Boston, for many a day." Because of this difference of opinion, he decided to send both portraits home, "to give us an opportunity to choose the one we want to keep."

---

[67] Born in Hector, New York, Frank H. Tompkins (1847–1922) studied at the Art Students' League in New York, the Cincinnati School of Design, and, like Steele, under Loefftz at the Royal Academy of Munich.

During this stay in Boston he met many artists and saw their work in their studios and current exhibitions. On the last day before he left a group of twenty artists and other professionals were invited to the Tompkins studio to view the portraits. Steele was charmed with the city, its atmosphere of mellowness, its architecture, its streets, and the museum. Of the artist group, he spoke of John J. Enneking [68] as the most picturesque—a genius in his way.

He left Boston with regret, and wrote, "The things I will remember longest, and which have been of most value to me, are the Sargent water colors at the museum. One cannot imagine more direct, vivid presentation of subject and effect. It is all of the Art of the Sargent portrait turned to landscape." He went on to say that he had seen nothing "to discourage him. . . . have run across a few things which will be profitable for me to study—some things to clarify my ideas, and make me more definite in my aims."

On the 17th of March he reached New York City, of which he wrote: "I can realize how its people might become so attached to it, as to be unhappy anywhere else." He saw its galleries, museums, etc., with William Henry Fox, his friend and the former director of the Herron Art Institute but then the director of the Brooklyn Museum. He found a still larger collection of Sargent water colors at the Brooklyn Museum. He saw interesting exhibitions, although he mentioned the inroad of "futurists paintings." Again he met prominent men in the artist group and took luncheon with Mr. and Mrs. John Alexander [69] at their apartment in the city. John Alexander had been a student in the Munich studios of Benczur and Loefftz where Mr. Steele had also studied. Both also had worked with the Boston landscape painter Frank Currier. In his letter Mr. Steele spoke of the hours they had together, and also mentioned "that they have a country place, too, which they are developing."

When the two portraits of Mr. Steele arrived in Indianapolis they were placed on exhibition at the H. Lieber Galleries. [70] On April 6, 1914, the following letter was received from the National Academy of Design:

---

[68] A native of Ohio and a pupil of Bonnât and Daubigny in Paris and Lehr in Munich, Enneking (1841–1916) won recognition as a landscape painter.

[69] John White Alexander (1856–1915) was a portrait and mural painter of considerable note. Born in Allegheny, Pennsylvania, he studied in Europe from 1877 to 1879—Paris, Munich, and Florence—and then settled in New York. He won many honors both in America and Europe and his works hang in museums over the country. He served as president of the National Academy of Design from 1909 until his death.

[70] The full-front portrait was sent to the National Academy (see Fig. 66) and the profile portrait was retained by the Steeles. It is now in the T. C. Steele Memorial in Brown County.

Mr. T. C. Steele, A.N.A.
Belmont, Indiana
Dear Sir:
Your portrait has been presented to the Council, and you have been declared a
duly qualified Associate of the National Academy of Design.

Yours very truly

[Signed]   Harry W. Watrous [71]

During the month of April he was exhibiting with a group of western
painters from Chicago, Cincinnati, St. Louis, and Richmond, Indiana, at the
National Arts Club Galleries on 19th Street in New York City. The group
was described as being not only "highly capable craftsmen, but they have
something distinctly worth the while to tell, and they are quite abreast of the
times in a technical way. Incidentally, they have many admirable and enter-
taining motifs. . . . T. C. Steele is represented by four landscapes. . . .
He discloses a fine vision in several of his pictures—his 'Red Cloud' escaping
any banality in rose tints—always a stumbling block with the painters—and
having poetic suggestiveness." [72]

After the painter's return from his trip East, he painted in his Indianapolis
studio a portrait of Harry S. New for the Marion Club. [73] It was regarded as
an excellent likeness.

I must not neglect to mention the painter's study of Henri Bergson's theory
of art and his lecture on the subject in January, 1914, before the Portfolio
Club of Indianapolis. Let me quote from a review by an art critic, a member
of the club:

Bergson's theory, as explained by Mr. Steele, is that the artist is needed to interpret Nature and truth more directly and fully, through his especial fitness to
recognize and respond more quickly to beauty and truth. Mankind, according to
Mr. Steele, through the humdrum of earning a living—is likely to get out of relationship with the natural and the beautiful, or may fail to develop and foster the
original ability of appreciation.

Thereby, he believes, a need is created for the artist who is an interpreter by
endowment, and sees into the heart of the beautiful with a perception unhindered
by utilitarian obligations.

[71] A genre painter, well known for small figures very highly finished, Harry Willson Watrous
(1857–1940) served as corresponding secretary of the National Academy of Design from 1898
to 1920 and as president in 1933. Born in San Francisco, he studied with Bonnât, Boulanger,
and Lefebvre in Paris, and then lived in New York.

[72] See Fig. 45.

[73] An ardent Republican, Harry S. New (1858–1937) was editor and publisher of the Indi-
anapolis *Journal*, from 1878 to 1903, was elected to the Indiana Senate in 1896 and to the United
States Senate in 1916, and was postmaster general in the Harding and Coolidge cabinets. The
Marion Club was a Republican organization.

The function of the artist is to lift the veil which dimly shrouds mankind's true vision of the beautiful, and to present the truth and beauty in a strong direct effort, said Mr. Steele. If he hits the mark mankind will respond to the effort, because of its universality of feeling. . . .

In regard to the year's landscape work being shown in the local exhibitions, there was an opinion that there was "a vivacious note" in Mr. Steele's canvases, and that "more than ever before [he] seems interested in transient effects of lighting." "One notices the growing tendency of the artist to introduce figures and animals in his compositions and we must acknowledge the added element of 'human interest' in the pictures."

Yet the year is not done. In November four large wall decorations done during the summer were hung in the sculpture court of the Herron Art Institute to be on view to the public before being placed permanently at the City Hospital. The subject used for the canvases was the four seasons.[74] They were highly coloristic and accepted by authorities as paintings that would some day be taken from the hospital and made more accessible to the art-loving people of the city.

Let me quote from a letter written to me on December 14, by Alfred Brooks, of Indiana University, after a study of these four canvases. These lines, more than any others written at the time, show the deep impact the paintings made on those who viewed them.

To my mind there must be a mystical sort of union between the painter and nature, akin to the mystical sort of union that existed between St. Francis and Poverty. The only real priest of nature is the artist and his works always seem entrances as it were to her temple and shrine—entrances, portals by which we ordinary mortals can ever hope to approach the divinity within. And four such beautiful portals, such as your husband has built in his four seasons, are to my mind extremely rare. As pictures they have about them something of that sacred tranquilizing view which all great pictures have, reality and something more—ah that precious more.[75]

[74] More than a dozen Indiana artists under the supervision of William Forsyth painted a series of murals for two units of the Indianapolis City Hospital (presently the Marion County General Hospital) which were built out of a bequest from Alfred Burdsal. Steele's paintings depicting the four seasons were placed in the main ward in the "B" wing where they may be seen today.

[75] Alfred M. Brooks contributed an article entitled "The Art and Work of Theodore Steele," to *The American Magazine of Art* (VIII, No. 10, August, 1917, pp. 401–6), in which he discussed the "Four Seasons" canvases. Reproductions of the four paintings and also one entitled "The Oaks" (1915) accompany the article. Of the "Four Seasons" Brooks wrote: "They are representations plus art. They alone should go far towards proving to anyone who doubts it, that representation, an imperative end, is not the chief end of art. On the side of representation it would be difficult to better the anatomy of Steele's trees, for example . . . [or] the knife edges of the sheets of frozen snow which overhang his cold brook. . . . or the anatomy of the 'Summer'

In making arrangements for carrying out the commission from the City Hospital the painter found the existing Brown County studio wholly inadequate. The room was not spacious enough for the wooden framework on which the canvases had to be placed and stretched. Thus, for the second time, the living room came to serve as a studio. Once more we concluded that we would take up building and erect a larger studio just as soon as our finances permitted.

During the fall of 1914 there was one more obligation that the painter had to meet before he could turn his thoughts to his outdoor work. On October 25, he was in Chicago serving on a jury for selections and awards[76] of which Douglas Volk[77] was chairman of the committee. There was a very large group of canvases from over the country, and he enjoyed the routine work of making decisions regarding their merits. He met many artists of reputation, among them Waugh, Ochtman, Wendt, and Buehr.[78] In a letter he mentioned that most of the landscape painters painted their landscapes indoors, from memory and studies. This was contrary to his method of working and interpreting all his landscapes under the inspiration and presence of the moods of nature as he felt them and saw them out-of-doors.

There is one more item worthy of mention. On December 1, he went to Cincinnati to serve as a member on the jury of selection for the Department of Fine Arts of the Panama-Pacific International Exposition which held its meeting in the galleries of the Cincinnati Art Museum in Eden Park.[79]

The year 1914 was ending. It had proven a fuller, more varied and inter-

hills. . . . But these are things which many men can do, though few can do them better, and not many half so well.

"When, however, it comes to the larger considerations of design—feeling but not crowding his pictorial areas with sustained passages of interest, and lovely echoes of light and shade, made to play over, and to accentuate, rather than conceal, the highly representative character of the details which make up the purely pictorial nature of the subjects, these 'Seasons' are masterly and, decoratively, masterful. They bespeak the inherent bigness and breadth of the scenes they represent so faithfully. They have detail. . . . They have design. . . . Finally, they breathe the inmost spirit of each season, and they represent the artist's mood; the reaction of a poet to the ceaseless yet quiet hum of a July noon; to the rustling blaze of October; to the stillness of winter; to the promise which the annual return of spring makes and keeps."

[76] Steele was a member of the jury for the Twenty-seventh Annual Exhibition of American Oil Painting and Sculpture held at the Art Institute of Chicago from November 3 to December 6, 1914.

[77] Painter and teacher, Douglas Volk (1856–1935) was born in Pittsfield, Massachusetts, and studied in Paris. He was an instructor at the National Academy of Design and Cooper Union.

[78] Frederick J. Waugh of Montclair, New Jersey, Leonard Ochtman of Cos Cob, Connecticut, William Wendt of Los Angeles and Chicago, and Karl Albert Buehr of Chicago.

[79] Steele was a member of the advisory committee for the Middle West headed by Frank Duveneck. William Forsyth also served on this committee.

esting one than any that had preceded it. And then at its close twilight fell as I faced the first great sorrow of my life, the death of my father.[80]

The next year, 1915, brought the usual number of local exhibitions in which the painter was represented, and more than that, three of his Brown County landscapes were shown in San Francisco at the Panama-Pacific International Exposition.[81] Referring to the work shown at this exhibition a writer in a special newspaper contribution, says:

Mr. Steele, as a leading landscape painter of Indiana, and as an Associate of the National Academy of Design, may be legitimately included among those painters whose note is distinctly American. . . . The simple, natural beauty of Indiana woods and fields, broken occasionally by hills and streams, had never been interpreted. This task—Mr. Steele among others—undertook. It was the sunshine, and its buoyant, cheerful influence on the native landscape, which appealed strongly to the artist. More than anything else, Mr. Steele is now known for the sunlight in his pictures. . . . Although sunshine is sunshine the world over, its effects on the individual vary. It is the sunshine that makes Mr. Steele's art notable. In all his work there is to be found a characteristic western brightness and a versatility of happy expression. . . .

Among the portraits done that year were two life-size, half-length portraits of Dr. Robert W. Long and Mrs. Long of Indianapolis.[82] The portraits were to be placed in the Robert W. Long Hospital, a gift of Dr. and Mrs. Long to the Indiana University School of Medicine.

The year's activities for 1916 began for the painter with an exhibition of fifteen canvases from Brown County held at the Propylaeum at Indianapolis beginning January 11 and ending February 8, under the auspices of the Woman's Department Club. A reception and tea with a musical program marked the opening of the exhibit. The newspaper reviews were numerous. The following is quoted from one of them: [83]

[80] Ludwig (Louis) Neubacher. Steele painted a posthumous portrait of his father-in-law in 1915 which was shown in the Steele Memorial Exhibition in 1926. The portrait was described as an "almost profile view of an elderly man of marked German type." It now hangs in the T. C. Steele Memorial in Brown County.

[81] The three landscapes were "The Hill Country" (see Fig. 47), "November Afternoon," and "The Poplars." The exhibition ran from February 20 to December 4.

[82] Born in New Maysville, Putnam County, Indiana, Robert W. Long graduated from Franklin College, studied with his father, a doctor, then attended Rush Medical School and graduated from Jefferson Medical College in Philadelphia. He began his medical practice in Irvington, then an Indianapolis suburb, and later moved to Indianapolis. The financial gift from Dr. and Mrs. Long to Indiana University made possible the construction of the Robert Long Hospital at the Indiana University Medical Center in Indianapolis. The portraits are now on the sun porch of Ward AB on the first floor of the hospital.

[83] Indianapolis *Star*, January 10, 1916, p. 16.

Mr. Steele always is a seeker after truth, and while his style might be called conventional in the light of present day extremists, he portrays nature in its simple beauty, which after all, is real art and which will live long after the gaudy disagreeably brilliant school has been forgotten.

Here, for a moment, let us look into the written words of the painter and get at his interpretation of the nature of art:

Yet the medium ever remains but a necessary detail that should never be compared with Art itself, for Art must come out of Nature. And the price exacted from Life for admitting workers into an intimacy, is that they express her vividly, emotionally, heart-breakingly perhaps, but truly at any cost. This is Art Creative.

In connection with Indiana's centennial celebration the painter was selected by Governor Ralston to paint portraits of four of Indiana's epochal governors: William Henry Harrison, the first territorial governor, Jonathan Jennings, the first state governor, Oliver P. Morton, the state's war governor, and Thomas A. Hendricks, a peace governor. These portraits were to be hung as part of a permanent collection in the Governor's offices in the State House.[84]

On March 18, Governor Ralston visited the Steele studio and expressed himself much pleased with the finished portraits, especially with the portrait "of the gentle, yet courageous Hendricks whom he, as a young man, beginning the study of law, had for a friend. Members of the Hendricks family . . . have expressed their admiration for the Steele portrait." [85]

Mr. Steele had known both Morton and Hendricks. In fact, he said that Morton had discussed with him about a year before his death the painting of his portrait which he wished to give to Hanover College. For some reason the portrait was not painted. Others who knew Morton and Hendricks conceded that the portraits of them were forceful in character.

Previously the painter had done portraits of Governors Hovey, Chase, Matthews, Porter, and Gray.[86] He had also painted President Benjamin

---

[84] The Indiana Historical Society owns another portrait of Thomas A. Hendricks by Steele probably painted between 1885 and 1890. It was among the paintings shown in the Steele Memorial Exhibition at the John Herron Institute in 1926.

[85] Indianapolis *News,* May 20, 1916, p. 17; Indianapolis *Star,* May 18, 1916, p. 17.

[86] The portraits of Governors Albert G. Porter (1881–1885), Isaac P. Gray (1880–1881, 1885–1889), Alvin P. Hovey (1889–1891), Ira Joy Chase (1891–1893), and Claude Matthews (1893–1897) were all painted from life. They are part of the state's official collection of portraits of its governors and hang in the State House. The Hovey and Porter portraits were shown in the Memorial Exhibition in 1926. See Fig. 20.

Harrison's portrait,[87] and Vice-President Fairbanks',[88] and Senator Albert J. Beveridge's.[89]

During the early part of May, 1916, printed leaflets began to appear on the campus of Indiana University, announcing that there would be a T. C. Steele exhibit in connection with the statehood centennial pageant to be given by Indiana University and the city of Bloomington. The paintings were hung in the West Parlor and in the Y. W. C. A. room in the Student Building. On the opening day of the exhibition, May 16, it was announced through the *Indiana Daily Student* (the campus newspaper) that with this exhibition "Brown County has been transported to the Student Building by T. C. Steele, A. N. A., one of the leading landscape artists of the United States. . . . The list of the exhibit includes, besides splendid samples of landscapes of every sort, a few pictures of flowers and a portrait or two."

From the pen of Alfred M. Brooks of the Art Department, through whose suggestion the painter had been invited to exhibit during the pageant, came the following article printed in the *Daily Student* of May 16. It is but one example of the many expressions of appreciation both in print and made verbally by students and faculty:

That Mr. T. C. Steele is a distinguished landscape painter needs no proof. The many honors which have come to him outside Indiana as well as in are known. The present exhibition, in connection with the pageant, is a special centennial token in his honor. And too, it honors Bloomington and the University by being here. It will give us all pleasure.

That Mr. Steele's pictures are lovely everyone knows who has seen them, but the present chance to see them is unique. Such an opportunity has not occurred before and it is doubtful if it ever will again. I mean the opportunity to see and study so many examples of his art in one place at one time.

Mr. Steele has done a thing probably unique in the history of landscape painting. For years he has been living peacefully on his Brown County hill, recording sympathetically, canvas on canvas, the year's cycle in its endless change; spring

[87] The first Steele portrait of President Harrison was executed in 1896. Commissioned by John Wanamaker of Philadelphia, it now hangs in the Benjamin Harrison Memorial Home in Indianapolis. In 1900 Steele painted a second portrait of Harrison which is in the University Club in Indianapolis (see Fig. 33), and a third hangs in the Officers' Club at Fort Benjamin Harrison on permanent loan from the Indiana Chapter of the Sons of the American Revolution.

[88] Charles Warren Fairbanks (1852–1918), a lawyer and a Republican, served as United States Senator from Indiana from 1897 to 1905 and as Vice-President of the United States from 1905 to 1909.

[89] The portrait of Senator Beveridge was painted in 1903. It was loaned by John C. Shaffer, of Chicago, for Steele's Retrospective Exhibition in 1910. Beveridge, lawyer, orator, a Republican and Progressive in politics, and a distinguished historian, served in the United States Senate from 1899 to 1911.

PLATE VII

The Clearing, 1910, 30 by 45 ins.
Katherine Woollen Fitts

and summer, autumn and winter, and not only the seasons but the weather; snow, rain, hail, mist, sunshine and cloud, heat and cold, darkness and light. Nature's true portrait, in a single beautiful spot, whether waking up or going to sleep, whether smiling or frowning, is depicted in a fashion unequaled upon these splendid canvases.

Mr. Steele's greatness and that of every artist who is great lies in this simple fact. Living in the same world as the rest of us, in Brown county which we all know, he has gained,

> "clear sight
> Of a new world,—a world, too, that
> was fit
> To be transmitted, and to other eyes
> made visible;"

These "other eyes" are our own, together with the eyes of all who are fortunate enough to see the Steele paintings while they are here.

This Steele exhibition was held over and continued during commencement week, ending on June 14. It had been the first time that the painter had had a "one man's show" in Bloomington, although a few Steele canvases were owned by local families. It was a comprehensive exhibition—the painter's ideas of nature given and enclosed in simple form. The attendance was large throughout. This did not indicate to the painter that the students viewing the exhibit had had much association with pictures. As I recall this came to mark the beginning of an interest on our part to assist more vitally and give impulse to a better understanding of art expression among the students attending the University. More of this a little later.

Shortly before commencement week I had been told of a secret which must be kept as a surprise to the painter. At the same time I was to arrange that he would be present at the final ceremonies of the presentation of diplomas to the students. In due time a formal invitation came to him. He conceded that it was kind of the president to ask him, but other than that he made no comment. The final day arrived, a beautiful morning on the campus, a morning fit to give solemnity to any outdoor ceremony: the blue skies of June, the morning sunshine, and birds flitting about among the old forest trees and breaking into song, the upturned eyes of the many watching the proceedings on the platform, and I, spellbound among them all awaiting the great moment to arrive when the president would confer the degree of LL. D. upon the painter. When finally the presentation by President Bryan came, in words so beautiful that I was in tears, the painter, too, showed plainly how deeply he was moved by the honor bestowed upon him. Later he told me how difficult it had been to grasp the idea that this recognition had come to him. His unassuming nature would always have it so.[90]

The ceremony remained with me as the most solemnly beautiful one that I had ever been privileged to see. Everything concerned with it carried an atmosphere of ritualism.

The following editorial appeared in the Indianapolis *News* of June 17, 1916:

The conferral of the degree of doctor of laws on Theodore C. Steele, by Indiana University is an unusual but a fitting recognition of an exponent of the fine arts. President Bryan's beautiful tribute to Mr. Steele was not in advance of the high esteem in which he is held by the people of Indiana as an artist, a citizen and modest gentleman of fine and scholarly tastes. The Indiana school of artists, no less than her men of letters, hold high rank in this country only because of merit. No one can think of Mr. Steele in connection with a publicity bureau. He shrinks from public praise, but his work glows because of its honest merit. Mr. Steele may recoil when his friends "Doctor" him, but it is well that his rich deserts have been recognized in his lifetime.

At the close of the commencement period, the largest canvas in the group was retained by the Men's Faculty Club, to be placed in their club rooms on the campus. This purchase became the first of a collection of Steeles acquired by the University.[91]

Again at home, after this marvelous experience at the University, we decided to take up immediately the building of the large studio. With the World War on and the future very uncertain, it hardly seemed justifiable for us to be incurring heavy expenditures at this time. On the other hand, we argued, the painter could meet with a saving by dispensing with the all-year-round studio kept in the city—the new studio would make ample provision for the storage of long-accumulated paintings and materials kept in

---

[90] The University was very conservative in the number of honorary degrees it bestowed during this period. It had awarded one to James Whitcomb Riley in 1907, as noted earlier. Two years later David Starr Jordan was so honored. No other honorary degrees were granted until 1916 when Steele was the sole recipient. The artist had received an honorary Master of Arts degree from Wabash College in 1900.

[91] Steele canvases hang in various buildings on the Indiana University campus, including the Auditorium, the Union, and the Administration buildings. In addition to the portraits of President Bryan and Dr. Woodburn already mentioned, there are likenesses of Elisha Ballantine, James D. Maxwell, Theophilus A. Wylie, Daniel Kirkwood, David Starr Jordan, and Joseph Swain. Other canvases are "The Cloister Kitchen," painted in Munich, various campus scenes, landscapes, and still lifes. See Figs. 43, 48, 52, 54, 58, and 63. There are six Steele canvases, five landscapes and a still life, in the Dailey Family Memorial Collection of Hoosier Art at the University.

the city. Portraits could be done under more favorable conditions of lighting out in the country. If, however, they could not be done conveniently out here, a room for that purpose could be rented over a short winter period in the city.

Also, there was a great need for more living space in the house. The present studio, which had been added during our second year on the hill, would easily lend itself to such remodeling.

More than this, the proposed plan of placing the studio—detached—in a forest setting would make it the first large privately owned studio in the Middle West, open free to the public. As such, we believed, it could be made an instrument—silent in its influence—in developing an interest in, and a habit of, attending exhibitions of the fine arts, no matter where. Moreover, seeing the actual places that were the interpreted subjects of the painter, a consciousness could be awakened to the beauty existing in nature and in other things. As the painter would define it, "appreciation, both in nature and art, was the art of seeing beautifully."

With the cobwebs brushed aside, we entered wholeheartedly into the painter's dream of building a studio—spacious and splendidly lighted. It was nine weeks before the new building was completed and the remodeling of the west wing finished. Once done, we forgot the long, hot trying days of the summer, and were glad we had had the strength of our convictions to set out upon another new adventure. We had not long to wait to test the usefulness or the failure to be encountered in this new field.

In spite of the inaccessibility of our location, the studio and the home continued to be the mecca of visitors—not only from nearby communities but far distant places. Brown County was becoming known the country over for its scenic beauty.

The trek of visitors to the studio increased with the years, from simple farm people who were attracted to the gold frames around the pictures as much as to the pictures themselves, to the people of note not only of this country but from abroad. And the students attending the University came, and they in large numbers.

During the autumn of 1916, by a mutual arrangement between the painter and Professor Brooks, the former agreed to lend a number of small canvases to be used as a traveling exhibition, to be sent out by the Art Department of the University over the state.

The year ended with the usual number of exhibitions held locally and through other parts of the state.[92] Also there was a commission for a portrait to be done during December. John C. Shaffer, of Chicago,[93] had asked for a copy of the Steele portrait of James Whitcomb Riley done from life some years earlier. It had been enthusiastically accepted as an excellent example of portrait painting.[94]

No previous winter had found us so impatient to shorten our stay in the city and get back to the country. The reason—the home could no longer be separated in thought from the new studio.

We had no illusion as to the extent we had overreached financially in doing all that we had done in new construction and reconstruction. We knew we were facing, with war conditions of 1917—worse rather than better times —an unstable future. This was always more true in such a period of an artist's income than of others. Did not Carlyle say: "Man is properly speaking based upon Hope, he has no other possession but Hope; this world of his is emphatically the Place of Hope"? So we accepted this as our best criterion and dedicated our year to working out our plans.

As a workshop the studio had proven ideal in every respect—in spaciousness and lighting. To bring it alive as an exhibition room, for the groups of canvases to be shown on walls and easels, was another matter. We felt that the color of walls and general arrangement must bring a distinctive atmosphere and give character to the room if we were to expect an open response on the part of the public.

The grounds adjoining the studio and house had been badly torn up by

---

[92] On January 7, 1917, a joint exhibit by Steele and Simon P. Baus (see note 96, below) was opened at the Propylaeum under the auspices of the Woman's Department Club. Eleven Steele landscapes and flower still lifes were included and also Baus's three-quarter-length portrait of Steele. The Indianapolis *News* of January 17, 1917, remarked that the pose in the portrait was characteristic of Steele and the head was like the sitter to a remarkable degree. This portrait is now in the T. C. Steele Memorial in Brown County.

[93] Newspaper publisher and successful as a grain dealer and developer of municipal transportation systems, John C. Shaffer (1853–1943) lived briefly in Richmond, Indiana, and Indianapolis, and after 1892 in Chicago. He was born in Baltimore, Maryland. His wide newspaper holdings included the Indianapolis *Star*, the Muncie *Star*, and the Chicago *Evening Post*. A strong supporter of the Chicago opera and symphony orchestra, he was also a promoter of the Hoosier Art Patrons and the Hoosier Salon.

[94] Steele painted several portraits of Riley. The earliest was done in 1878 when the poet was only twenty-nine years old. It is now in the possession of a niece of Riley's, Lesley Payne of Indianapolis. A second portrait was painted in 1891. The property of the Indianapolis Literary Club it now hangs in School 9 in Indianapolis. In 1902 Steele painted a portrait of Riley for the Bobbs-Merrill Company. It was purchased in 1936 by J. K. Lilly and now hangs in the Lilly Library at Indiana University. A copy of this portrait, dated 1916, is in the State Museum. At the request of John C. Shaffer, in 1912 Steele made a copy of the 1891 portrait and in 1917 made a second copy. One of these now hangs in the Riley Hospital for Children in Indianapolis.

the teamsters bringing the building materials. An entirely new garden between the studio and house became necessary.

It was amazing how quickly the news traveled about our new studio being open to the public. We were reminded of the first year of our coming into the country, when large families came in their farm wagons to inspect the house. The same curiosity was repeated in regard to the contents of the studio. It came to be just another window through which to look into another world. The painter thought well of their oft-repeated statement that "the pictures looked natural, and they liked them." In reply he told them that "he painted so simply that they would be easy to look at."

Many of a different type came—among them artists. And descriptive articles about the new studio began to appear in print. Among those was one which appeared in the autumn of 1917 in the *Daily Student* published at Indiana University.[95] I quote in part:

When the fall was at its height of color, there was a splendid opportunity for seeing Brown County and for seeing Mr. Steele's home, "The House of the Singing Winds" and his studio which is the envy of all artists.

His house is truly the house of an artist. One enters a long, beautiful living room with its fireplace which bears the inscription: "Every morning I take off my hat to the beauty of the world." The walls are hung with his paintings, most of which are Brown County scenes and some of which are copies of old masters which he made while he was studying in Munich—notably Titian and Rembrandt. One also notices the Paisley shawls in the room. . . . It is Mrs. Steele who has planted the shrubs and made the flower gardens which are so beautiful in the summer—an environment to inspire any artist.

After resting for a while in the living room, one visits the studio, which is one of the largest and finest in the country and which Mr. Steele himself planned. It is a thing which all artists want, but few have the environment for. Its most notable features are its spaciousness and its splendid light. Almost the entire north wall is glass. When one enters the number of canvases is impressive. But at this point, one ceases to describe, for no one can describe all that is in a canvas. In Mr. Steele's own words we know what is in his pictures:

"The highest aim of art," he says, "is interpretation rather than realism. Of course, one must present truth, but the highest thing is interpretation."

On December 17, 1917, we were back in Indianapolis, to open an exhibition of twenty-four canvases of the year's work at the H. Lieber Galleries. There were the usual newspaper notices, all enthusiastic about more and new landscape material represented in the exhibition.

[95] Issue of November 10, 1917.

For winter studio use the painter had found a room in a building next to the Circle Theater on Monument Circle. From the windows in this room, and from the balcony outside, he found interesting painting material. There was the Monument, Christ Church, and street life around the Circle north into Meridian Street. The outcome from this was the painting of an interesting group of canvases architectural in pattern and subject, showing the Soldiers' and Sailors' Monument shrouded in a sunlit effect of ice and snow and Christ Church on the Circle under wintry snowy effects of sunshine and mists [see Plate VIII and Fig 56]. A photograph of "The Monument" was used on the outside cover of the bulletin issued by the Herron Art Institute, announcing the March exhibit of Indiana artists. Part of this new Monument Circle group was shown for the first time at this exhibition.[96]

During the winter period the painter had given sittings for a portrait to Simon P. Baus, a portrait painter of the city. This portrait was given a prominent place in the March exhibition and received favorable comment from art critics. After the exhibition it was brought to the country. We thought so well of the portrait that we hung it in the living room where it still remains.

Aside from carrying on his own extensive output of work, the painter had met unflinchingly the various demands made by interested groups for loan collections accompanied by talks or lectures to assist in a better understanding of and insight into the paintings shown. Then in the summer of 1918 came the unexpected. I was convalescing from a hospital experience that I had had during the winter. Now, for the first time in his life, the painter was compelled to withdraw from active duties. Never before had he known a time when he could not paint. Whether as a result of exposure to extreme cold and icy winds during the painting of the "Circle Group" of canvases or because of an infection located in his teeth, the painter became very ill with rheumatic fever. No doubt both had contributed to undermine his health. The rheumatic condition was confined to his shoulders and arms.

It was very difficult for him to accept this illness as just a passing phase. The reason was simple. Helpless in arms and hands, he could not paint. There came months of pain and suffering, at first in bed under protest, then a long period of sanitarium treatments. Naturally he was depressed much of the time—until friends came to believe that he was to be disabled permanently.

[96] The catalogue for this exhibition, which was held from March 10 to April 7, 1918, not only carried a picture of "Soldiers Monument, Midwinter," but also a portrait of Steele by Simon P. Baus. Another Circle painting, "Christ Church, the Deep Snow," was included among the total of five Steele canvases exhibited.

Finally it became urgent that something be done to lift him from out of this mood of despair. So I opened and prepared a studio for him on Monument Circle, placed canvases on the walls, and made the room otherwise attractive —which gave him an opportunity to renew his contact with artists and friends in a studio environment. A change for the better was apparent at once.[97]

Shortly after, six sonnets, "Lines to T. C. Steele, Painter," were printed anonymously in an Indianapolis paper. The author, W. J. Greenwood, of Indianapolis—unknown to us—we found had been long a silent admirer of the painter and his work. This, too, helped to bring about a different attitude on the part of the painter on his outlook for the future.[98]

Personally I carried no other thought than that it was merely a matter of time until he would be restored to normal health. As soon as the spring suns came to warm the earth, I dismantled the "Circle" studio and we turned to nature for a complete cure. By August, 1919, he was painting again, feeling splendid, with no longer a need to avoid doing any of the many things he loved doing.

There were many visitors to the studio—about five hundred during the open weather. In October we entertained the Nature Study Club.

Aside from the many canvases painted on the place, the painter went to the Indiana University campus to paint a picture of the proposed "Pageant Grounds" that could be used as a poster for the centennial of the University in 1920. The picture became the property of the University and now hangs in the Administration Building.

The year 1920 brought a number of outstanding happenings. We were astonished to find the country studio on the way to becoming a profitable salesroom. We had the honor of including Hamlin Garland, the novelist,[99]

[97] The Indianapolis *News* of December 22, 1918, carried a story about Steele's Circle studio, featuring the city scenes on view there, including "Christ Church in a Rainstorm" and "The Monument on a Snowy Day."

[98] Printed in the Indianapolis *News*, October 19, 1918, p. 19, and signed "G."

[99] For a previous reference to Garland (1860–1940), an early exponent of American realism and "chronicler of the Middle Border," see above, p. 40. Garland had given a lecture at Indiana University on November 20, and gone to Brown County with Steele to spend the night. In his volume *My Friendly Contemporaries* (1932, pp. 317–19) Garland recalled this visit: "As he [Steele] displayed the work in his studio, I honored him for the devotion to his state. I said to him, 'The work you have done is beautiful and absolutely American.'" Then Garland continued, "'There is something large and brave in this man's action,' I made record at the time. . . 'In his quiet way he is a master—as true to the Mid-West as Gardner Symons and Willard Metcalf were to their Eastern hills and streams. He is a lone pioneer, toiling on without adequate recompense and growing old in his toil. His hand is tremulous, but it has not lost its cunning.' On my way to the railway I thought of this fine old artist going back to his brush, eager to catch some part of the ineffable beauty of the morning while his brave wife washed the breakfast dishes!"

among our house guests of the year. During his visit he told the painter that "he had made no mistake in the choice of his painting ground," and "that he had never seen a more interesting bit of country."

In December the painter had a "one man" show at the Herron Art Institute. He took over the two eastern galleries with his forty-three canvases—all Brown County studies. We put a great deal of effort in the preparation of this exhibition, purchasing new frames, unpretentious, simple in size and pattern, the same throughout for all the canvases placed in the large gallery. This was for the purpose of bringing unity to the room. In the general run of exhibitions, the eye is frequently disturbed and the attention distracted by the jumble of frames used, with their variation in size, pattern, and color. This we wished to avoid. The consistency of the plan was demonstrated in the comments on the extraordinary beauty of the gallery.

A local editorial was typical of the character of the response of those who attended the exhibition:

This month the special exhibition is made up of the paintings of T. C. Steele, Indiana's leading artist. They are pictures that must afford a peculiar satisfaction to all local visitors, for they are not only works of art in themselves, showing the deft touch of the skilled hand, the mastery of color, the imaginative power of the true artist, but they portray familiar scenes. He has painted what he saw about him—Indiana hills and valleys, bits of streams and pastures, picturesque woods and lanes, humble homes by the way-side—all places such as we may see any day, but invested with a special charm by the magic of his brush. He has celebrated his own State, not caring to wander afar for grander or more striking landscape. Because of this Indiana holds him and his pictures in especial esteem.

Another writer, Bessie Hendricks, in speaking of the exhibition, said in part: "His beautiful interpretations of Brown County scenes have brought many visitors to the galleries and will linger long in the memories of those who have seen them. The artist has caught the mood of the season and the place of each of his subjects from the time of apple blossoms and redbud on to the end of the year." [100]

"Brown County to many a Hoosier," says the Herron Art Institute's *Bulletin* for May, 1921, "now seems instantly connected with thoughts of Mr. Steele and his paintings, and this exhibit but increased such a habit of association. This inspiring region was shown under all atmospheres and in all seasons with the characteristic treatment which make a Steele painting, especially of this region, so much enjoyed and sought after."

[100] Indianapolis *News,* December 25, 1920, p. 13.

Fig. 52. Rainy Day, Schooner Valley, 1915, 30 by 45 ins.
Indiana University, Bloomington

ig. 53. Indiana Hills, 1915, 30 by 40 ins.
ollection of the Lyndon Baines Johnson Library and Museum, Austin, Texas

Fig. 54. Peonies, 1917, 25 by 30 ins.
Indiana University, Bloomington

Fig. 55. The Big Oak, 1917, 34 by 42 ins.
T. C. Steele State Historic Site, Indiana State Museum Collection

Fig. 56. A Snowy Day on the Monument, 1918, 24 by 36 ins.
T. C. Steele State Historic Site, Indiana State Museum Collection

Fig. 57. Edge of the Field, 1914, 29½ by 44¼ ins.
Ball State University Art Gallery, Muncie,
Permanent loan from the Frank C. Ball Collection, Ball Brothers Foundation L29.079

Fig. 58. When Skies Are Blue, 1920, 30 by 40 ins.
Indiana University, Bloomington

Fig. 59. Hazy Day, 1920, 30 by 40 ins.
Private Collection

At the close of the exhibit at the Art Institute the collection was taken to the Indianapolis Public Library where it was exhibited during January, 1921. Referring to this Kate Milner Rabb wrote in her feature column "The Hoosier Listening Post": "The Library's usefulness to the community in having such an exhibit where it can be viewed by hundreds, who otherwise would never see it, can not be too much emphasized. . . ." In a previous column she had commented: "How many pilgrimages have been made via Bloomington to the Brown County Hill-top of our much loved artist. And what a subject for reflection is the fact, that this county, once despised as the most backward county in the State, has become a resort for artists and beauty lovers." [101]

In this connection it is hard to resist including the entire article entitled "The House of the Singing Winds," written by Alfred M. Brooks, which appeared in the February, 1920, issue of *The American Magazine of Art*— a magazine published by the American Federation of Arts in Washington. It was an interpretation—how he saw and felt the influence of the house. Here is the closing line: "This is a house where art and life, art which is 'the nearest thing to life,' are both at home."

During the winter of 1921 Wayman Adams painted "The Jury," a portrait study (full length) of the "Hoosier Group of Painters"—T. C. Steele, J. Ottis Adams, Otto Stark, and Will Forsyth. The painting was acquired by the Herron Art Institute and now forms a part of its permanent collection.

The painter and I also gave sittings for portrait studies to Simon P. Baus who had painted a full-length portrait of Mr. Steele in 1918. [102]

When the automobile came to disrupt comfortable driving by horse on our country roads, the painter held tenaciously to the idea that we, as artist-folk, never would be financially able to own a car. But somehow the miracle happened. A few years before, when the large outdoor storage house was being built, I proposed that instead of a small entrance door, we put in large double doors in case the time came when we should want to use it as a garage. The painter would hear none of it. So before the car—during the summer of 1921—the large door space had to be cut into the building. Then the Ford was bought and I became its chauffeur. The purchase of the car brought on a renewed incentive for me to keep on with my relentless agitation for decent roads into and throughout the county.

[101] Indianapolis *Star,* January 10, 1921, p. 6.

[102] The 1921 portrait of Steele by Baus was purchased by the Art Association of Indianapolis and is in the permanent collection of the John Herron Art Museum. Another portrait of Steele by Simon Baus is in the Dailey Family Memorial Collection of Hoosier Art at Indiana University.

A need for a better road to the studio was becoming essential. The number of visitors could now be counted into the thousands. Large groups from clubs over the state visited the place. And the Bloomington *Evening World* in October, 1921, reported that "the studio of T. C. Steele, the well known Indianapolis artist, two miles south of Belmont, was visited by scores of people. . . . All were delighted with the wonderful display of paintings in the studio. Mr. Steele has done more to advertise Brown County than any other person and the people there are just waking up to the fact. . . ." [103]

As the years passed, our winters in the city were shortened. We found we had achieved more than we had ever expected from what we had accepted at first as an untried experiment in an isolated locality. This held even true to our last venture—the erection of the large studio. The interest in the studio had widened by leaps and bounds. From being a mere studio-home, our place was rapidly taking on all the aspects of a public institution. As a result, the work entailed in meeting these newer demands increased out of all proportion to the amount of "help" at our command.

At last, on our return to the country in the spring of 1922, after a particularly strenuous period in the city, the painter agreed with me that we must break away during the coming winter months from the routine we had so tenaciously clung to, for so many years. We accepted the invitation from an artist friend of New Orleans to join him the following winter just as soon as the preliminary work attending the current exhibitions had been taken care of.

My dream of seeing New Orleans was of short duration. I clung to it even after I realized that another invitation which "would be taking the painter to broad fields of activities at Indiana University," would in the end be considered by him as desirable of acceptance. The question that was involved was not of the opportunity to be afforded the painter for laying a foundation for a more general, keener appreciation of the arts on the campus, but whether it was best for him to add more to his already innumerable interests. In my opinion, it would become but another phase of our lifework in progress and functioning on our hilltop home.

Dr. William Lowe Bryan, president of the University, had asked the painter to the campus as honorary professor for the coming year. Alfred M.

---

[103] Issue of October 24, 1921, p. 1. According to the Indianapolis *News* (October 7, 1922), nearly two thousand persons had visited the Steele studio in 1921. The following summer the Bloomington road was under construction and fewer people found their way to the "House of the Singing Winds."

Brooks, of the Art Department, was leaving the University to take a position at Swarthmore College. There were to be no stipulated duties attached to the professorship other than that the painter be in residence six months of the year.

This was the way it was put by the art critic Lena M. McCauley, of Chicago: "Indiana University invited T. C. Steele to fill a chair of the Fine Arts. His personal influence to beauty in the Fine Arts was all that was asked of him, and he responded by saying that his mission was to lead students 'to see the Beautiful in nature and in life.'"

On the surface, accepting the invitation seemed simple enough. The painter, unhampered by a specified school routine, could continue to devote the major part of his time to his painting. This was true enough, yet to do this, it became imperative that a studio-room be created which would both serve as a workshop and afford the students a place where contacts could be had with the painter. In the end, we decided to go into the project wholeheartedly. We would create an artistic room, such a one as might become a forerunner to greater expressiveness of beauty on the campus. We suggested for this purpose a wooden portable to be placed among the trees where the Union Building now stands. Had we been allowed this privilege, we would have created with the thought of making it a permanent studio, which would exert a continuing influence after the painter's connection had been severed.

Our idea was not accepted, and we chose one end of the top floor of the University Library for the studio. This was before the new wing had been added. As we had no furnishings that could be spared from the place in the country to use in the University studio, I spent a week shopping for furniture and rugs.

Finally we were in residence in Bloomington. The studio was opened to the students and the public. A student visitor explained it thus: [104]

Mrs. Steele has arranged the studio so beautifully with old furniture and window plants, Turkish rugs and specimens of her collection of colorful shawls, that it is a delightful place to be in. It also is a temptation to pick up the book which Mr. Steele evidently has just been reading to see if there is anything in a book on art which the ordinary mind can understand. If Mr. Steele is painting when you visit the studio, he continues to paint, and you may either wander about looking at the canvases on the walls or watch him work.

However, I caught the artist the other day in one of his perhaps less-inspired moments—at any rate he was not unwilling to leave his easel and speak to me and

[104] Quoted from an article by Vera Sangernebo in the Indianapolis *Star,* April 22, 1923, p. 7.

161

the students who had come with me. One visitor happened to say he thought one landscape painting looked "so natural."

"So many people seem to think," said the artist, . . . "that the landscape artist merely makes an exact copy of what he sees in nature. Not at all! The artist is not so much a student of the face of Nature, as of her moods. And while he is painting, he unconsciously emphasizes those of her features which at the time seem more related to the particular mood in which he finds her."

"Do you mean to tell me," I asked, pointing to a picture on the wall which showed the dome of the observatory on the campus surrounded by leafless trees on a misty morning, "that that is not the exact production of the picture you saw when you looked from this window?"

"Indeed it is not," said Mr. Steele. "I have emphasized that dome out of all proportion to its actual perspective. It is that wet and silvery dome which is the keynote of the picture, and tells the observer that the morning was a misty and poetical one. If it had been a hot, sunny midday, the dome in my picture would have shrunk accordingly and the blueness and expanse of the sky would have been emphasized. On a windy day it would have been the surrounding trees. . . .

"Here is an experiment I made last fall," he said. "These three pictures are of the same subject, but each one was painted at a different time of day. Note how different the pictures are, particularly in color. Note especially the difference in the skies. . . . I think you always will find that the sky is the most expressive part of a landscape picture. From the sky come the different lights and atmospheric changes. . . . And from this you can tell whether nature is angry and cold, or warm and friendly.

"An artist finds that he must first of all be able to feel in order to paint, and in order really to appreciate and enjoy the picture the observer also must feel the mood which inspired it."

The student continued by saying that

when Mr. Steele stops his painting to speak to the students informally in this way, they learn many interesting facts in an entirely painless fashion. During the pleasant days of the spring . . . the artist plans to do most of his painting outside on the campus. The students will not be permitted to paint with him, but they may watch his work. . . .

Members of the faculty of the University and even residents of Bloomington who have no connection with the University also are profiting by having Mr. and Mrs. Steele in their midst. Occasionally Mr. Steele abandons his studio for an afternoon, in order that some club may meet there, and on Sunday afternoons Mrs. Steele has been giving a series of teas for members of the faculty. . . .

The above is a student's grasp of the underlying meaning of the Steele studio on the campus. When we came to establish the studio there, we had an idea that it would not be continued more than the one year. No one could realize better than I that with an established studio-home in the country demanding a prodigious amount of supervision, there was need for a curtailment—rather than for an increase—in our interests. However, instead of the one year, we maintained the studio on the campus through four successive years, up to the painter's death in July, 1926. Reasons for this came logically. The painter was sympathetic with, and very happy as part of, the life on the campus. He would have missed it had he been deprived of it. He found many interesting subjects on and around the campus to paint. In fact, the last landscapes he did were done on the campus. He came to hold the esteem of all—from the president of the University down through the faculty, the student body, and the townspeople. The respect for his contributions to the community was attested by the many honors that were conferred upon him during these four years.

During the first year, in April, 1923, the Indiana Union, the men's organization on the campus, acquired seven Brown County landscapes. To these the painter added a landscape painted on the campus. In May of the same year the painter was made an honorary member of the Bloomington Rotary Club. During the month of March, 1925, the Hoosier Salon had its initial opening in Chicago.[105] The painter was prevailed upon to assist in the venture by sending canvases to be exhibited and also by representing the University as speaker on the opening evening. The first Hoosier Salon proved its potential as a means of publicizing Indiana painters and sculptors. The painter also attended the Salon of 1926, when he was again a speaker on the preview program.

At the time of the first Hoosier Salon, the Indiana University alumni of Chicago honored the painter by giving him a luncheon in Marshall Field's Wedgewood Room. It was a large gathering of alumni, friends, and artists, a very beautiful and touching occasion. President Bryan and James Adams, an alumnus, spoke in glowing terms of the association of the painter with the University. Adams, who had been a student on the campus during the past two years and who came to be included as an intimate to our circle of friends, described the painter's philosophy as "beautiful, sincere, and real."

---

[105] The first Hoosier Salon was held in the gallery of Marshall Field & Company in Chicago, March 9 to 19, 1925, under the auspices of the Daughters of Indiana, The Earlham Alumni Association of Chicago, and members of the Indiana Society of Chicago. The second Salon was sponsored by the Daughters of Indiana. Salons were thereafter held annually in Chicago under the auspices of the Hoosier Salon Patrons' Association until 1941, when they were transferred to Indianapolis.

Steele was represented by four paintings in the first Salon (1925), three in the second (1926), and three in the third (1927) which was held after his death. At the Indiana University luncheon held during the third Salon the program was in the nature of a memorial to Steele.

To this, the painter responded, developing the thought that he believed "the function of a university was not how to make a living, but how to live." At the end there was the presentation to the painter of a gift of a one hundred dollar gold piece by the Alumni Association. This was given with the stipulation "that something for the studio be bought with it."

We both loved being surrounded with beautiful things. We had been adding unusual things to our studio whenever it became possible. Would not they who visited the studio enjoy them equally with us? So we had no scruples about spending this money. We shopped for days, ending up by spending all and more. It was worth it. We decided on a seventeenth-century Spanish chest and copper bowl. Both these treasures are a part of the Brown County studio.

During this University period the Brown County studio and home was kept ready for our return at any time during weekends or vacations. Thus it was possible for the painter to carry on his landscape painting in the country. He had not discontinued giving his "one man" show each year in Indianapolis, and he contributed freely to other current exhibitions. Some of his best canvases were created during this period, including three outstanding portraits.

He had also continued his lectures and talks away from the campus. In December, 1925, he was asked to come to Fort Wayne to speak on the occasion of the opening of an exhibition of Brown County artists in the Fort Wayne Art School and Museum. The address was printed in leaflet form by the school.[106]

Our stay of a few days in Fort Wayne was a marvelous one—we met with fine hospitality. We spent our last night in the home of Dr. Miles J. Porter. He and the painter were old friends, and they sat up talking into the wee hours of the morning. We started at a very early hour the next day for Terre Haute, where we were to be guests in the home of Dr. J. H. Weinstein.

Life had been too strenuous for the painter. In Terre Haute he suffered a severe heart attack. It was during the night, and fortunately Dr. Weinstein was at hand to give immediate help. He recovered, and, curiously, he was never even to suspect how close had been the call. But I was told the full

[106] Steele's lecture on "Hoosier Painters" marked the opening of the fourth annual exhibition of Brown County artists in Fort Wayne, sponsored by the Art School and Museum and the Fort Wayne Women's Club. The lecture was also printed in full in the Fort Wayne *Journal-Gazette*, December 8, 1925, p. 2. Steele's pictures in the exhibition included three flower subjects, four autumn landscapes, and one winter scene.

164

truth. I was instructed to watch over all his activities and prevail upon him to rest at definite periods during the day. The doctors had ordered him to stop smoking and limit the amount of coffee he drank.

It was well that before this we had established ourselves in the Anibal Cottage [107] in Bloomington adjoining the campus on the east. We were comfortable there with our rooms on one floor. One room had good northern light, and there I arranged a studio. The winter was a snowy one, and I prevailed upon the painter during this snowy period to use the cottage studio, while I attended to the University studio. So far, so good.

The Hoosier Salon was announcing its second opening at Chicago. To try to persuade the painter not to attend, I said I was not interested. He was so disappointed at our not going that I consented. He came through, but my anxiety, day and night, permitted me no sense of enjoyment in being there.

As the spring came on, the painter's strength returned. I felt encouraged. He went out painting on the campus.

He had a very beautiful exhibit in Indianapolis at the H. Lieber Company, beginning May 3, and he spent some days in the city during that time. Some of the "campus" canvases were included in this collection. The consensus of opinion was that it was one of the loveliest of his shows. The Indianapolis *News* of May 6, observed: "The pictures give the impression that the artist is at peace with himself and the world and that he has launched himself into a new vital phase of production." [108]

We continued in Bloomington into May. Occasionally we went into the country. The flower gardens had never been more beautiful. Here Mr. Steele decided to paint peonies out-of-doors—a bit of garden—and paint a peony arrangement indoors. This latter remains as his last unfinished effort, on an easel in the Brown County studio. It is as he left it. [109] The day before Commencement at the University he became ill. He went back into Bloomington. On Commencement Day Dr. Charles P. Emerson and Dr. Willis D. Gatch ordered him upon examination to go to Long Hospital in Indianapolis for observation. We went up the next day. I was soon to learn the worst. X-ray showed a closing of the gall duct. Dr. Gatch assured me there was no help. I

---

[107] Claude E. Anibal was an associate professor of Spanish in the University in 1923.

[108] This exhibit consisted of nineteen canvases, one still life and the rest landscapes. Twelve were painted in 1925, one each in 1912, 1923, and 1926, and four were undated.

[109] This canvas was shown in the Memorial Exhibit at the John Herron Art Institute. It was listed as "Last Work of the Artist (Unfinished). . . . The beginning of a flower picture—iris and peonies growing amid greenery." The unfinished canvas is still on exhibit at the Steele Memorial.

could not accept it, so I telephoned Dr. Weinstein, president of the Terre Haute Clinic, to ask whether I could bring the painter there and put him under his care. The next day we left for Terre Haute. I was relieved to be with friends who I knew would practically do the impossible to save him. It could not be done.

On July 4, we came back to the hills. Dr. Harold Pierce of the clinic brought us home. We both thought the return to nature would work miracles. I placed a couch hammock under the trees. Here he saw his friends and I read to him. On the 17th the students of the summer session of the University were scheduled to visit the studio-home. I suggested that we postpone the visit until later. He would not consent to this, and on the morning of that day prepared to be up to meet them. When the hour for their coming arrived, he decided to see a few at a time in his room. I think he enjoyed this visit. He had been previously told that the University yearbook, *The Arbutus*, for the coming year would be dedicated to him.

I am sure that he held to the belief that he would be able to use the new studio which the University was incorporating for him into the new wing of the Library. It was to be finished by the next fall. It was not until Friday, the day before he died, that he realized that he was desperately ill. A few days before I had read to him an article entitled "Religion and Life—How Shall We Think of God?" by Harry Emerson Fosdick, which appeared in *Harpers* for July, 1926. He had asked for a second reading. And when I came to the following paragraph, he asked me to read it again. It was the one, he said, that he had pondered over.

In man at his best, then Reality receives its clearest revelation—that is the faith of all high religion. The place where man vitally finds God, deals with God, discovers the qualities of God and learns to think religiously about God is not primarily among the stars but within his own experiences of goodness, truth, and beauty, and the truest images of God are therefore to be found in man's spiritual life.

He lapsed into unconsciousness late the next day and died at eight o'clock in the evening of July 24, 1926. And I recall some words of his, spoken at a time when I was going through deep sorrow—"Don't you know there are some things one cannot reason out?"

At a simple ceremony, and hundreds attending, his ashes were placed in a forest of great oak trees.

All that I have written is very inadequate of all which could have been said.

He lived deep enough to inspire all from the most humble to the most high —to a sweeter and finer outlook upon life. His philosophy of life is told in his own words: "What God thinks of beauty we know from the fact that he has made it so universal."

February 26, 1941

IN MEMORIAM

Under the skies and trees, the grasses waving,
   The singing winds in requiem melody
Break on that farther shore in tender laving
   The age-old thought of immortality.
And as they bring the master to his homing
   Who gives today his ashes to their care,
At early morn or in the day's sweet gloaming
   The hills he loved will guard his slumbers there,
While those to whom he passed the torch of beauty
   Must ever joy to feel its glorious flame,
Making of art a consecrated duty
   As they its gospel lovingly proclaim.

EMMA B. KING

EPILOGUE

"NO ARTIST PAINTS the thing as it is, but only its reflection in his soul, so that the mind and character of the painter are really portrayed. That accounts for the loveliness, purity and veracity of Steele's work." These were the words of the Reverend Frank C. S. Wicks spoken at the memorial service for Theodore C. Steele on September 12, 1926, in All Souls Unitarian Church in Indianapolis. Funeral services had been held in the city on July 26, and the painter's ashes were buried in a grave among the white oak trees on the slope of the hill below the House of the Singing Winds. At the burial service Meta Lieber, wife of Carl Lieber, sang the "Wanderer's Night Song," the Goethe poem set to music by Schubert:

> O'er the hills' summits there's rest.
> Hardly a breath of air stirs in the trees;
> Hushed is the song of birds:
> Hushed in the woodland far—
> Wait awhile, wait awhile,
> Ere long—thou, too, shalt rest.

In December a Memorial Exhibition of 183 of Steele's paintings and sketches was held in the John Herron Art Institute. Included were canvases covering his entire painting career from 1869 to 1926, illustrating "the development of Steele's artistry from youth to death and the great diversity of his reactions to beauty as seen under various conditions and in different places. . . ."

There have been many other recognitions of the painter and his work. The week of December 9, 1929, was proclaimed T. C. Steele Memorial Week and observed throughout the state by schools, libraries, clubs, and business places. In 1962 Indianapolis Public School No. 98 was dedicated to his memory and named the T. C. Steele School. Two years later, in September, 1964, a fourteen and a half-mile hiking trail was opened through the Brown County hills that he knew and painted and called the T. C. Steele Memorial Trail.

171

But the most important of all is the State T. C. Steele Memorial in Brown County. After the painter's death Mrs. Steele continued to develop the Brown County studio-home as a "Sanctuary of the Future," which would be to others the "ever-unfailing source of inspiration" that it had been to the painter. Then in the spring of 1945, she offered it all—over two hundred acres of land, the house, the large studio, and other buildings, valued at $18,000, and over three hundred paintings and sketches valued at more than $100,000—to the State of Indiana, to be maintained as a memorial to the painter. The offer was accepted, and the buildings and grounds and art collection were placed under the direction of the State Department of Conservation, now the Department of Natural Resources.

A few months after completing arrangements for this gift to the people of Indiana Mrs. Steele died, on August 28, 1945, and her ashes were buried on the hillside beside those of her husband.

THE WORK

THE WORK

BY WILBUR D. PEAT

LIKE MOST YOUNG PEOPLE endowed with an aptitude for drawing and an insatiable desire to make art their life's work, Theodore C. Steele revealed at an early age his intention to become a painter. In an interview with a reporter in the Indianapolis *News* in December, 1924, he remarked, "I have been interested in painting ever since I was a boy. In the school at Waveland, Indiana, I was put in charge of a class in drawing. I was only thirteen years old, and didn't know much about drawing, but at that I knew more than anybody else. After graduation I went to the Royal Academy at Munich and studied there five years."

Steele telescoped a number of years and a host of experiences into that last statement, because between his graduation from the Waveland Institute in 1868 and his departure twelve years later for Munich he had married, had spent a short time in Chicago and Cincinnati picking up what instruction he could in the way of painting, had painted professionally for three years in Battle Creek, opened a studio in Indianapolis, and participated in various art activities in the capital city, including the organization of the town's first art association. When he left for Munich in 1880 he had two sons and a daughter. He also had the reputation of being one of the leading members of the local art colony.

Returning to his earliest artistic efforts and to his initial attempts to make his work known, it appears certain that the first public showings of his paintings were in the annual state and county fairs. However, report that at the age of thirteen he was winning prizes at the fairs has not been confirmed; but, on the other hand, it is a matter of record that in the State Fair of 1867, when he was twenty, he received an award of five dollars for the best portrait painting in oil in the amateur class.

According to a statement made many years later by the artist's son Brandt, Steele's skill in drawing portraits had so increased by 1867 that he was able to sell a few. But he found that he was in competition with portrait photographers. Having an opportunity to buy the equipment of an itinerant photographer who became bankrupt in Waveland, Steele undertook photographic portraiture for awhile and also experimented with the method of enlarging photographs onto canvas by means of a pantograph, thus producing a drawing that served as the basis of an oil painting. Judging by entries in his journal, he also made enlarged photographic prints of people which he tinted. However, his true artistic instinct and better mastery of brushes and paints led him in a few years to abandon the camera's aid.

It is difficult to account for young Steele's rapid development as a painter in those formative years between 1865 and 1870. His lessons in art at the Waveland Institute could not have been very rewarding. What examples of good portrait painting, originals or reproductions, he might have seen in that small town, or even in neighboring Greencastle, could not have done much to inspire him or aid in his technical development. It is reported that with the money he received from the sale of his photographic equipment he went to Chicago in the hope of getting some instruction. One evidence of the Chicago sojourn is a painting in the T. C. Steele Memorial Collection in Brown County which bears the following notation: "'A Revolutionary Bell,' a copy of a Gilbert Stuart painted in Chicago under instruction of Mr. St. John, 1868." This St. John was very likely Josephus Allen St. John who, with his artist wife, Susan Hely St. John, had a studio in Crosby's Opera House at this period. Mrs. St. John was a student of G. P. A. Healy, an artist whose work seems to have influenced Steele.

Then he went to Cincinnati. There he came under the tutelage of one of the best portrait painters of that time, according to Brandt Steele, and he did so well that he won the top prize in the school exhibition. The name of his instructor is not known. If we knew the year of his stay in the Queen City, we could come close to an informed guess. If it was in 1869, he doubtless attended the McMicken School of Art and Design, which opened that January with Thomas S. Noble, noted painter and teacher from New York, in charge. On the other hand, he might have studied with J. Insco Williams in his Academy of Art, because Williams, not unknown in Indiana art circles, was certainly one of the leading portrait painters in Cincinnati at the time.

Opportunities to paint portraits drew Steele to Battle Creek, Michigan, in March, 1870. His first commissions there, based on his journal, were likenesses of George Peters and his wife, for which he received twenty and twenty-five dollars, respectively. In addition to about thirty portraits in oil, his journal lists a dozen colored photographs and about half a dozen still-life studies painted at Battle Creek. Three or four landscapes are also listed, indicating that the painter was becoming interested in outdoor subjects at this time.

Evidently at Battle Creek Steele had access to original portraits or color reproductions of paintings by earlier masters to study and copy. In his journal he speaks of the "peculiar effect of color in my copy of Stewart's [Stuart's] portrait," and refers to a copy of Lawrence as well as to colors used by Reynolds and others. He does not mention Healy, but copies of Healy's portraits by him were shown in early exhibitions, which helps to confirm the observation that Healy's work had a marked influence in the development of Steele's portrait style.

The above reference to landscapes and the speculation that Steele was beginning to take an interest in outdoor subjects, give the following journal entry special significance. It was written in Battle Creek on July 30, 1870:

Just returned from a walk under the trees. The day is lovely. Resembles a day in early autumn more than one in summer. The sky is full of purplish haze and the dim clouds are almost motionless. While there is not much haze in the air the light and shade has the peculiar indecision or indistinctness that with the golden sunshine is the charm of autumn. . . . While I lounged under the shadow of a beautiful elm and studied the light and shade, or rather drank it in, and the glorious colors that composed the beautiful dreamy landscape . . . I could not but wish for time and opportunity to devote to the study of landscape art.

He went on to say that his efforts up to that time had been confined almost entirely to portraiture and that he questioned whether he should devote himself to it so exclusively. He resolved that at the earliest opportunity he would commence to make landscape compositions, but in the meantime "studies are to be made from nature and the mind trained to closer observation of the effects of light."

Fifteen years will elapse before landscape painting will become an important part of his output.

By 1873 Steele and his family were in Indianapolis where he was to cast his lot with the dozen or so artists who were trying to make a living there. The best of the resident painters were Jacob Cox, Barton S. Hays, James F. Gookins, William R. Freeman, Frank E. Scott, Thomas B. Glessing, and James M. Dennis, the last two preparing to leave the city before the end of the year.

It was not the best time for anyone to start a career in a new town. What patronage there had been for the arts in the late sixties and early seventies was rapidly disappearing because of the financial panic of 1873, and luxuries such as works of art were not easily marketed. It was during these hard times that James Whitcomb Riley and Steele are supposed to have joined forces in painting signs and the earliest Riley portrait dates from this period. Steele painted Riley several times from life and in addition he made replicas of at least two of the original poses.

The earliest newspaper account of Steele and his work in Indianapolis appeared in the Indianapolis *Saturday Herald,* February 20, 1875. After telling of his visit to Cox's studio, the reporter wrote:

> Our next stopping place is at the room of Mr. T. C. Steele, in the gallery of Salter and Judd, No. 45 East Washington street. The gentleman is at present absent from the city, but we were courteously allowed to inspect his works by one of his pupils, and in justice to him we are led to say they give promise of unusual artistic talent, but are very deficient in the language of color. Under favorable auspices, Mr. Steele would rapidly develop into a real artist. His room gives indication of industry and study; his pictures—we refer more especially to his portraits—are painted with a boldness which is refreshing, and which, as in the head of Cervantes, suggest something of Healy, but his backgrounds are dead and unaccessory, and his drapery is stiff and flat. His free use of the brush and color give spirit to his work, and in time, when his chaotic feeling and force are reduced to artistic order, Mr. Steele will produce works which will live. Judging by what we have heard of him, he is a young man of modest manners and unpretentious appearance, well liked for his sterling worth and noble qualities of mind.

Few of Steele's paintings of the mid-seventies are known. He painted himself, members of his family (Fig. 3), and occasional commissioned portraits, one of the best being the likeness of George Rauch (Fig. 4).

In 1874 he sent sixteen paintings to the Indiana Exposition, Indiana State Fair, which was the first major public showing of his work. Except for one still-life composition they were all portraits, and all have disappeared, with the possible exception of a study of Thomas Lakin, which may be the one now owned by the Herron Museum of Art (Fig. 1) and a self-portrait which may be the one in the T. C. Steele Memorial Collection in Brown County (Fig. 2).

In the summer of 1876 Steele and Charles Nicoli, local wood engraver, decided to go to the Philadelphia Centennial Exposition to see the international collection of works of art. The two days spent in the galleries gave the visitors from Indianapolis a great thrill and no doubt added to their store of technical knowledge.

The following May another long account of Steele's work appeared in the Indianapolis *Saturday Herald,* which is of interest because it shows that he was doing more work out-of-doors:

The Work

In friendly contiguity to the door of Mr. Love's studio [in the Bradshaw Block] is another, which, being of glass, is pretty certain to afford a view of a tall romantic-looking fellow hard at work at the easel. . . . [Mr. Steele's] studio is a pretty large room, and the walls only contain a fixed number of square feet, and in despair the pictures have given up the effort to find places, and lie in heaps on tables and under them, in corners and on chairs—everywhere—delicate, ethereal little sketches, in cool gray and neutral tints, with a carefulness and fidelity in detail which bears out the artist's assertion that his work has been more and more toward a strict and accurate following of nature. Mr. Steele never fails to improve any little vacation he may get from portrait painting by a stroll into the suburbs or country, and as he is a rapid worker his collection increases almost daily. The trunk of a beech tree, a little sketch of corn stubble with the shocks still standing, a winter foreground of snow and dry grass and weeds, with a thousand other like things, all executed with a lightness and airy sparkle much resembling water color effect. Here is a little study still unfinished, looking up Wabash alley from the canal, with a distant view of Christ church and other buildings about the Circle. It is an early morning effect, entirely executed before most of us have begun to suspect the presence of another day.

As the decade drew to a close things began to happen on the Indianapolis art scene. In January, 1877, an organization was formed by the artists to stimulate public interest and to bring the painters of the city together to work toward a common cause. It was called the Indianapolis Art Association, and the leaders in its formation were John Love (who had only recently returned to Indianapolis from Paris where he had been studying art for five years) and T. C. Steele. One of the regulations they adopted was to limit the membership to male artists, a regulation that aroused the ire of many local residents, including a reporter on the *Saturday Herald*, who wrote a sarcastic and scathing article in the issue of January 27, captioned "High Jinks in High Art."

The Association immediately staged an exhibition of paintings in its gallery in the Bates Block. In addition to work by its seven members it invited one woman painter to show her work—Lotta Guffin. Steele showed seven paintings in addition to several study heads; a portrait of B. F. Taylor, two landscapes—"Sunset" and "Dawn"; and compositions entitled "Boy and Cat," "Rabbit and Bird," "Quails," and "Corn."

In the fall of that year the Art Association extended its activity by founding the Indiana School of Art, and held classes on the upper floor of the Fletcher and Sharpe's Block. James F. Gookins was made director and John Love was assistant. The two men were not compatible in their ideas and after a year or so the school closed. Reportedly, Steele took some lessons in the school, perhaps under Gookins, who was fairly accomplished as a portrait painter and draughtsman, and he also went sketching out-of-doors with John Love who was a very competent landscapist.

The next major project of the Art Association was the holding of a second exhibition in May of 1878. This was not confined to the works of artist members only. Most resident painters were invited to submit work, and a number of canvases by eastern painters were included. Ten paintings by Steele were shown—all portraits.

It was in the following year that steps were taken by local citizens which allowed Steele to go abroad for further study. The Royal Academy of Munich was his choice. Why Munich? Before answering the question it might be of interest to deviate a little and review the subject of the European art centers which have been selected by young American artists since the middle of the eighteenth century. First it was London, of course, with trips to Rome to study the works of the great Italian masters first hand. Then in the classic revival era (after 1800), and with the English influence subsiding, Rome became the strongest magnet. Then it was Paris; then with the rise of a strong landscape movement in America, Barbizon became the mecca for young men who felt the urge to work and live in the hamlets and forests made famous by Corot and Millet and their contemporaries. At about the same time there was a surge toward Düsseldorf. Several things contributed to this. The anecdotal painters of Germany became very popular among collectors in America —so much so that an art firm was established in New York called the Düsseldorf Gallery. Exhibitions were held in different cities in which canvases by artists associated with the Düsseldorf school were shown, and these stirred up considerable excitement among the younger painters. The trek of American students to Germany began with Bierstadt (who, incidentally, was born in Düsseldorf) and Leutze, who went and stayed.

And then it was Munich. For the young and courageous artists of the next generation the Düsseldorf method seemed technically labored and overly sentimental—even old-fashioned. The professors at the Royal Academy, Munich, on the other hand, were quickly becoming known through exhibitions and publications and their teaching methods were regarded as most up-to-date. They stressed artistic qualities in their compositions, placing less emphasis on sentimental anecdotes. Brilliant brushwork and rich orchestration had become the new ideal.

As early as 1862, eighteen years before Steele sailed for Europe, David Neal enrolled in the Munich Academy (Königlishe Akademie de bildenden

Künste). Eight years later Duveneck, Currier, Shirlaw, and Indiana-born Gookins went, with Chase arriving in 1872. They were followed by others, and by 1880 a sizable American colony had formed in the old and charming Bavarian capital.

Reportedly, Frank Duveneck had strongly recommended Munich to Steele as the place to study. This may be so. Steele might have met him in Cincinnati in 1874 or early in 1875 when he was back from Munich for a short period of time. But Steele could not have been unaware of Munich's new position in the art world, and he must have known about the recent successes of those Americans who had been there, which would have been reason enough for him to select the Royal Academy as his destination. Probably the man who exerted the strongest influence was James F. Gookins who had been living in Indianapolis since he returned from Munich in 1873.

Munich had several advantages over other European cities beyond the instruction given at the Academy. According to William Forsyth, in his pamphlet *Art in Indiana,* there were several reasons why art students went to Munich, not the least being the fact that at that time and for long afterward it was the cheapest capital in Europe in which to live and study. The Academy was "easier of access" to foreigners than, for instance, the École des Beaux-Arts in Paris, being the most liberal government-controlled art school abroad. Munich, too, was one of the most important art centers in Europe, with a great art museum, the Alte Pinokothek, and exhibition galleries and libraries—not to mention its music halls and opera house.

The painters living and teaching in Munich were regarded as the strongest and most progressive in Germany. The leaders were Karl von Piloty, Alexander Wagner, Wilhelm Leibl, and Wilhelm Dietz. Their rich, dark tones and unctuous brushwork became the essence of the new movement. Some Americans, particularly Duveneck, Currier, and Shirlaw, who studied with two or more of them, carried the technique to great heights of brilliancy and dash. When Steele arrived at the Academy in the fall of 1880, most of those professors were still around (Piloty was director of the school), but the teachers he chose were Ludwig von Loefftz, who became director in 1893, and Gyula (Julius) Benczur.

For the first year Steele studied life drawing under Benczur, and a large group of his charcoal studies made at the time was brought back to America, and, fortunately, saved. In the next school year, 1881–82, he studied with Loefftz, and he continued working under the latter's tutelage until the close of the school year in the spring of 1884. During the last year at Munich Steele did not attend classes but worked by himself on figure compositions and land-scapes.

During the first year abroad the Steele family lived in the city of Munich. For the next four years they lived in Schleissheim, a small village about six miles north of the town. Frank Currier, although no longer attending classes at the Academy, was living at Schleissheim part of the time, and during sum-mer months he was of great assistance to Steele in outdoor sketching. Land-scape painting was not taught at the school. Whatever aids Steele received in this line of endeavor he got from Currier. One of their favorite sketching places was Dachau and the swampy moor to the south. Steele made several studies there during the last years of his Munich sojourn, one of the best of which is "Late Afternoon, Dachau Moor" (Fig. 15).

Other sites and towns were, of course, sketched and painted: quaint Schleissheim houses (Fig. 8), the road between Schleissheim and Munich lined with old gnarled linden trees (Fig. 6), the old cloister at Mittenheim (Fig. 12), and Schliersee in the Bavarian Alps, to mention only a few.

Although some of the German artists were painting landscapes at that time, the tendency was to portray peasants, market vendors or people engaged in menial tasks, with landscape or buildings serving as backdrops. In other words, the human interest or anecdotal element still seemed important. The practice was to make drawings and sketches of the elements to be included in a painting and then to compose and execute the picture in one's studio. While Steele showed a tendency to break away from this practice—which made for, in his words, "too much studio look"—and to capture the truer atmospheric effects and colors of a scene bathed in natural light, he nevertheless worked in the tradition as long as he was in Germany. Human figures and farm ani-mals are invariably seen in his finished paintings—a practice which certainly did not diminish the value of his work in the eyes of his friends and clients when he sent canvases back to be exhibited and offered for sale in Indianapo-lis.

Head and figure paintings made in his last year at the Academy are among Steele's most attractive canvases. The four reproduced in this book (Figs. 7, 9, 10, and 14) show the artist's mastery of drawing and sensitive rendering of character or personality. It is of interest to note that they all have one thing in common; namely, the placing of the model between the studio's source of light and the painter's easel, throwing most of the face in shadow and illumi-

PLATE VIII

Christ Church, the Deep Snow, 1918, 30 by 40 ins.
T. C. Steele State Historic Site, Indiana State Museum Collection

nating the profile of the face and arms. This backlighting, as photographers term it, presents many interesting problems, among others that of reproducing correctly the colors and tones on the shadowy side of the face and body. Incidentally "The Boatman," which is obviously a studio production (Fig. 10), won a silver medal at the Academy's exhibition; and the Bavarian government's offer to buy it was turned down by the artist.

The same method of illumination was used by Steele in some of his outdoor studies, too. In the Dachau moor canvas, for instance (Fig. 15), the observer is facing the overcast sky from which the light is emanating, the objects in the composition casting their shadows toward him. The same backlighting was used in the Pleasant Run picture (Plate I), which was one of the first landscapes Steele made after returning to Indiana.

The first paintings which Steele sent home from Munich arrived in May, 1883, and the Indianapolis *News* on May 29, reported that the pictures realized the early hopes of Steele's Indianapolis friends. Exercising his critical judgment, the reporter commented that the pictures "show he has true artistic perception, is most accurate in his treatment, and utterly ignores any false or meretricious aids in producing effects at the sacrifice of truth."

Almost a year later, on March 10, 1884, the *News* announced that the latest pictures by Steele had arrived from Munich and that they were on view at Lieber's. "Haying on the Koenigsfeld" was singled out as being particularly appealing with its dark broken sky, pearl gray tones, and white fleecy clouds.

In April, 1885, an exhibition of thirty paintings by Steele and William Forsyth was shown at English's Hall—the second floor of the old Plymouth Church which adjoined the north end of English's Hotel just north of the Circle on Meridian Street. It was given the title "Ye Hoosier Colony in München." Forsyth had arrived in Munich in the spring of 1882 and had entered the Royal Academy in January, 1883; thus he had been over there about three years when the canvases were shipped to Indianapolis. Steele and his family, on the other hand, were preparing to return to the States in the early summer of 1885.

The exhibition, under the sponsorship of the Art Association of Indianapolis, was accompanied by an elaborate and unique catalogue, illustrated by means of engravings made from pen-and-ink drawings by members of the Bohe Club (Bohe standing for Bohemian). Steele's painting "The Boatman" was undoubtedly the most imposing of his group of seventeen canvases.

183

Some of his pictures that were in the 1883 show at Lieber's were displayed again, but the majority were new to the Indianapolis audience.

One might reasonably wonder why the exhibition was limited to two men. Did the Indiana "colony" in Munich consist of Steele and Forsyth only, in the spring of 1885? Records show that it did not. Samuel Richards, who had gone over with the Indiana contingent in 1880, was still there, as was J. Ottis Adams. Why their paintings were not included will likely remain a mystery. One probable explanation is that neither artist had anything to send for the exhibition. Richards was apparently spending all his time on large historical compositions, and Adams was doing little beyond life drawings in the Academy's classroom. There is no indication that he, like Steele, was going around the countryside sketching.

Not long after "Ye Hoosier Colony in München" exhibition closed Steele and his family returned to Indianapolis and settled in the Tinker homestead or Talbot Place, located on the north side of Seventh Street (now Sixteenth Street) east of Pennsylvania. It was a stately two-storied brick residence with an attractive cast-iron porch, situated on a large wooded lot. Here the family lived until 1901 when the Art Association of Indianapolis bought the property for the purpose of building there an art museum and school. At the back of the old residence the artist built a small studio in which he worked and where he occasionally held exhibitions of his paintings—which, according to the historian Jacob P. Dunn, was the first building erected for this purpose in the city.

Little had happened in the way of art activities in Indianapolis during the five years Steele was abroad. Most of the artists with whom he had associated in the seventies had left the city or had died. The most accomplished resident painters were Richard Gruelle and Sue M. Ketcham. Jacob Cox, seventy-five years old, was not very active. However, with the return to the state of J. O. Adams, William Forsyth, and Otto Stark in the ensuing years, a new fraternity of kindred souls was formed that was to last for a number of years.

Unquestionably the most significant cultural event to take place in the city during Steele's absence was the founding of the Art Association of Indianapolis (not to be confused with the Indianapolis Art Association of 1877). This was in 1883. In later years Steele would be taking an active part in its affairs, as a member of its board of directors, as vice-president (1896–1908), and as a member of its committee on accessions.

So far as affecting the community at large the Art Association's most important projects were the local and international exhibitions of paintings and other works of art which its committees arranged annually. These varied in content and, since the Association had no gallery of its own, they were displayed in different buildings.

Exhibitions in which Steele participated during the decade after his return to Indianapolis were the Association's Third Annual of April and May, 1886, in which he was represented by four canvases; a show, sponsored by the Association, held at Pfafflin's Hall in November, 1886, in which one hundred and fifty of his paintings and sketches were displayed; the Fourth Annual and all succeeding annual exhibitions of the Art Association, in each of which four or more of his canvases were hung; an exhibition titled "Old Vernon, Hill and Stream," which was held at Lieber's gallery and which included nineteen pictures by him; and the "Exhibit of Summer Work of T. C. Steele, William Forsyth, R. B. Gruelle and Otto Stark," shown at the Denison Hotel during November, 1894, sponsored by the Art Association. In all, more than three hundred paintings and sketches by Steele were on public view during that period of about ten years.

The last of these exhibitions was of considerable significance to the artists, as matters turned out. Hamlin Garland saw it and was so impressed by the quality of the work that he arranged to have it taken to Chicago and displayed at the Central Art Association galleries in the Auditorium Tower during December. J. Ottis Adams was added to the list, bringing the number of exhibitors to five. On the basis of this, the exhibition was given the title "Five Hoosier Painters."

The catalogue issued by the Central Art Association is of considerable interest because it contains a discussion supposedly taking place in the exhibition rooms between three persons: a sculptor, a painter, and a novelist (Lorado Taft, Charles F. Brown, and Hamlin Garland), who dub themselves the Critical Triumvirate. Their remarks about the paintings, informal and spontaneous, are enlightening because they constitute the first critical judgments passed on Indiana paintings by out-of-state critics.

The preface to the catalogue, addressed to Art Lovers of Chicago, stated:

The Central Art Association takes peculiar pleasure in presenting, as its first special exhibit, the work of five "Hoosier" painters, for aside from their inherent excellence as artists, the history of their development has special significance. It exemplifies all the difficulties in the way of original western art and foreshadows its ultimate victory.

185

These men were isolated from their fellow-artists, they were surrounded by apparently the most unpromising material, yet they set themselves to their thankless task right manfully—and this exhibition demonstrates the power of the artist's eye to find floods of color, graceful forms and interesting compositions everywhere.

These artists have helped the people of Indiana to see the beauty in their own quiet landscape. They have not only found interesting things to paint in things near at hand; they have made these chosen scenes interesting to others. Therein lies their significance.

As the opening remarks and bantering are gotten out of the way the members of the Triumvirate get down to the business at hand. Their initial fear that work by the different Indiana painters might look alike ("only a lot of big Steele's and little Steele's," as one of the men put it) was allayed when they saw the exhibition in its entirety and found that "the versatility of some of them is astonishing, the individual note is always strong." The Sculptor observed that he failed to find a single picture that looked as if it had been founded on another man's work: "They have personalities, those Indianapolis fellows. I want to know them. Steele seems the biggest man of the lot. Who knows him?"

The Novelist replied that he had met him, that he was a middle-aged man of evident refinement, and that the garden pictures in the exhibition were probably all views of his home in Indianapolis.

The Conservative Painter remarked that "it's refreshing to see men working by themselves and producing such fresh vital work. They are of the few who are doing the right thing. They are painting their own fields as they see them, with a real affection." And then the Sculptor observed that the members of the World's Fair jury of admission (presumably for the Chicago Columbian Exposition of 1893) were enthusiastic over Steele's work, saying that they had discovered a "strong" man in Indianapolis. A remark made by the Novelist following this revealed that in 1893 there was a showing in New York of Steele's paintings: "The New York fellows liked his exhibit at the Academy of Design last winter."

More of their remarks might be quoted here but the above are sufficient to show that as early as 1894 the landscape painters of Indiana had made an enviable name for themselves beyond the borders of the state, and that T. C. Steele was regarded as the strongest and most deserving of praise.

Except for two portrait studies of a "Young Lady" and a "Young Man" all of his fourteen entries in the Chicago exhibit were landscapes, painted either around Indianapolis or in the Muscatatuck Valley at Vernon. The "Bloom of the Grape," originally labelled "Muscatatuck Valley," painted near Vernon (Plate IV), was one of the group.

Another series of annual exhibitions in which Steele participated was that of the Society of Western Artists. The Society was organized in 1896 for the purpose of holding shows in midwestern cities of paintings by midwestern artists. The original membership included three artists from each of the following communities: Chicago, Cleveland, Detroit, St. Louis, Cincinnati, and Indianapolis. The three local members were Steele, Forsyth, and Adams. Other artists were added to the roster in subsequent years.

The exhibitions went on circuit each year to the above cities, usually being shown in Indianapolis in January, February, or March. After the Fifth Annual, these displays became the regular annual exhibitions of the Art Association of Indianapolis, and were so designated. The last of the Society's annuals was in 1914, and in the nineteen shows Steele exhibited more than sixty canvases. It might be mentioned here that he was president of the Society in 1899.

In a review of the Third Annual that appeared in *Brush and Pencil* in December, 1898, John H. Vanderpoel of New York wrote:

If there is anything distinctive in the character of the present exhibition the public may soon learn for itself. But if the organization (which has weathered safely its period of infancy) desires to meet the test of time it must disclose in its art a vital quality akin to the force which has given character to the people of the West. It must breathe of our great prairies, with their lofty dome of wind-swept clouds; of its blue lakes and placid rivers; its hillsides and valleys in all their moods of color and form. It must show regard for the tradition in which figures the Indian of history and the pioneer settler of early days. It should touch upon the poetry of rural life. That this feeling finds appreciative response among the members of the society, I need but to refer to such men as T. C. Steele of Indianapolis, who has fathered the "Hoosier School of Painters." There is a virility in his work that is of the soil. Forceful in technique, harmonious in colors and unconventional in composition.

High praise indeed, and especially significant in having come from one of the leading writers and critics of the day.

In the Fourteenth Annual of the Western Artists Association, in 1909, Steele was awarded the $500 Fine Arts Building Prize contributed by the Corporation of the Fine Arts Building in Chicago.

Before leaving the subject of exhibitions in which Steele's work was shown during the decade and a half after his return from Munich, it should be mentioned that he was successful in having his work included in several large eastern shows. In May, 1886, he had three canvases in the exhibition of the Society of American Artists at the Metropolitan Museum of Art in New York. In 1888 he exhibited two canvases in the Pennsylvania Academy of the Fine Arts Annual: "On the Moor near Schleissheim" and "Meridian Street, Thawing Weather." In the 1900 Pennsylvania Academy Annual he showed "A Winter Morning."

Paintings by Steele were shown regularly in the Annual Exhibitions of American Art at the Cincinnati Art Museum from 1895 to 1914 and also in 1916, 1917, 1918, 1922, and 1923. In 1899 his painting "A Winter Morning" was hung in the annual exhibition in the Carnegie Galleries in Pittsburgh and was regarded by the New York *Times* critic as among the most striking offers. At the Columbian Exposition in Chicago in 1893 two of his landscapes passed the jury: "On the Muscatatuck" (Fig. 26) and "September" (Plate III). In the same year his painting "The Boatman" (Fig. 10) was on view in the Chicago Society of Artists exhibition; and at about the same time, as mentioned above, there was a display of his work at the National Academy of Design in New York.

The Saint Louis Museum of Fine Arts (as it was then called) hung an exhibition of paintings by Steele and Adams in 1896. In the list of thirty-five canvases by Steele there appears again "The Boatman," "The Bloom of the Grape," and "September." In 1900 "The Bloom of the Grape" was awarded honorable mention at the Paris Universal Exposition. It is worthy of note, too, that Steele served as a member of the jury of selection of American paintings for the Paris Exposition.

Before continuing the subject of exhibitions and enumerating the awards and honors that came to Steele after 1900, it will not be amiss to discuss the sources of his landscape compositions.

Studying the titles and dates of his pictures in exhibition catalogues between 1885 and 1907, one learns that he has explored a variety of places in and out of the state in search of satisfying subject matter. The immediate neighborhood around Talbot Place offered him material for several canvases (Fig. 24); in going a few blocks north to Fall Creek (Fig. 16) or south to Pleasant Run (Plate I), he found other motifs. In the western part of the state, in Montgomery County and the Shades, he added still other themes (Fig. 21).

His first trip to what was to become one of his favorite painting spots, Vernon and the Muscatatuck River valley, was in 1886, and he returned there repeatedly for about eight years (Figs. 19, 26, and Plate IV). William Forsyth frequently accompanied him on those outings. In 1887 Steele visited friends at Ludlow, Vermont, where several striking canvases were painted (Plate II); and he visited Hanover on the Ohio River, essentially to paint a scene requested by John H. Holliday (Fig. 25). These were, of course, summer sketching trips, because in the winter he stayed in Indianapolis, working in his studios, conducting art classes, getting pictures ready for exhibitions, and painting portraits when commissions came his way.

Continuing the recitation of his sketching areas, we find that he painted along the Mississinewa River with his fellow artist J. Ottis Adams in 1895. In 1896 he and Adams began their yearly visits to the Whitewater Valley in Franklin County, first living in Metamora and then at Brookville (Figs. 34, 39, and 40, and Plate VI). He built a studio wagon in 1896, which he found useful in getting around the countryside. Then in 1898 Steele and Adams acquired the house which they called the Hermitage on the outskirts of Brook-ville on the east fork of the Whitewater. This remained the summer home for the two families for many years.

In the summer of 1899 Steele went to Tennessee, largely in the hope that it would improve his wife's health. The mountains offered new material and new effects, and among the canvases that record that trip is "Tennessee Mountains" (Fig. 32).

Two other painting areas outside Indiana should be mentioned before con-cluding the survey of the sources of his pictorial compositions; namely, west-ern Oregon and southern California, where he spent the summers of 1902 and 1903. The scenery that he found in both areas was strikingly different from anything he knew in or around Indiana, and instead of being baffled or dis-turbed by its strangeness he executed some exceptionally handsome canvases (Figs. 35, 36, 37, and 38).

In a letter dated September 28, 1902, to Carl Lieber from Redlands, Cali-fornia, Steele wrote:

And when it comes to trying to get something out of this world by my art, out of the sea of which I knew nothing and of these southwestern mountains, unlike any I have ever seen, I found I had tremendous work on my hands, and I have allowed everything else to go by default. . . . After two weeks spent in the mountains . . . we went to the Oregon coast, and from the very first I experienced a fascination for its wonderful beauty that I scarcely felt before. We were there a month and it was a month of tremendous work for me, and I can only account for the amount of work I could do by the tonic air of this coast. I brought away fifteen canvases. . . . I am satisfied that I never did a better thing than in breaking away from my Indiana work for awhile. . . . What about an exhibition the last week in November? Try and arrange it for me if your dates are not all taken. . . . I think I can promise you the best exhibition I have ever had. . . .

In a report on his 1903 trip to the same places, the artist wrote almost apologetically—as though to minimize his previous outbursts of praise for western scenery: "In conclusion let me say . . . that as a lover of my state and a believer in the beauty of its scenery, that I will love none the less but perhaps appreciate the more its charm of woodland hill and field, because I have lived awhile where long waves of the Pacific break on the Oregon coast, or felt the fire and color of the southern sun in the land of the orange and olive and fig tree."

What must have been a pleasant and rewarding experience for him was his duties in the fall of 1903 as a member of the jury of awards for paintings that had been selected for display in the Louisiana Purchase Exposition at St. Louis in 1904. (He had already been on the jury of selection in New York.) His experiences were recorded in a manuscript which he titled "The Art Juries of the Louisiana Purchase Exposition." It was a large jury, composed of both European and American artists. Among the Americans were Joseph Pennell, Duveneck, and Chase, the last "our former fellow townsman . . . quietly appreciative, looking first for the good in a picture, and with an almost infallible judgment as to quality of a picture on the side of its technical expression as a painting. . . ."

According to an article in the Indianapolis *News* of January 4, 1908, and reprinted in the *Indiana Magazine of History* (Vol. IX, 1913), "At the St. Louis exposition in 1904, Indiana artists had the best exhibit made by any Western State. Of the pictures offered for exhibition in the Palace of Fine Arts nineteen works by Indiana artists were accepted; . . . Besides the nineteen in the Palace of Fine Arts, seventy-eight pictures by native Indiana artists adorned the walls of the Indiana Building during the entire period of the exposition."

Four of Steele's canvases, "Low Tide on the Oregon Coast," "The Old Mill," "November Morning," and "The Old Sycamores," were hung in the Palace of Fine Arts.

Two years after the fair, and again in 1907, the people of St. Louis had further opportunities to get better acquainted with the work of some of the Indiana men, even beyond what they had seen in the circuit exhibitions of the Society of Western Artists. In December, 1906, the St. Louis Museum of Fine Arts arranged an exhibit which they called the First Annual Exhibition

Fig. 60. Autumn Landscape, 1922, 30 by 34 ins.
Private Collection

Fig. 61. Brown County Farm, 1922, 22 by 32 ins.
Reproduced from 1966 photograph

Fig. 62. Early Spring Afternoon, 1923, 20 by 28 ins.
Private Collection

Fig. 63. Morning on the Jordan, 1923, 24 by 30 ins.
Indiana University, Bloomington

Fig. 64. God's Acre on Campus, 1926, 22 by 32 ins.
T. C. Steele State Historic Site, Indiana State Museum Collection

Fig. 65. Early Morning—Winter, 1926, 20 by 28 ins.
Theodore L. Steele

Fig. 66. Portrait of Theodore C. Steele by Frank H. Tompkins, 1913
National Academy of Design, New York City

The Work

of Selected Paintings by Western Artists. Fifteen men from Chicago, Cincinnati, St. Louis, and Indianapolis participated, the Hoosiers being T. C. Steele, William Forsyth, and Otto Stark. Steele showed ten paintings, and above their listing in the catalogue was a biographical note:

> Of the school of Hoosier painters congregated around Indianapolis, Mr. Theodore C. Steele is dean and leader. Students of the Munich School of Painting—several were at the Royal Academy contemporaneously—these Indiana men have widely deviated from the teachings of the Munich masters, in that they follow the French landscape painters in the interpretation of light. All work directly from Nature, out of doors, using both a peculiar technique and a peculiar tonality in their interpretations of Nature.
>
> Not an extremist in style or color, Mr. Steele utilizes a considerable range, both in subject and treatment. His well lighted, adequately painted landscapes are to be found in many collections and are familiar to frequenters of art exhibitions.

The second exhibition in St. Louis, that of December, 1907, held at the Museum of Fine Arts, too, was a one-man show. It was titled "A Special Collection of Paintings by Theodore C. Steele," and consisted entirely of landscape compositions, many of which were his first Brown County canvases. The catalogue carried a biographical statement not unlike the one above, and thirty-three titles were listed.

Meanwhile, in January, 1905, Steele was represented in an exhibition by members of the Society of Western Artists at the National Academy of Design in New York, with a painting titled "A Street in the Old Town of Brookville, Noon." In February of that same year Pratt Institute in Brooklyn, New York, had a one-man show of landscapes by Steele. Twenty-nine paintings were hung, including scenes in the Whitewater Valley, Oregon, and California. The catalogue stated: "Mr. Steele's style is fresh and vigorous. His transcripts of nature show keen appreciation for beauty combined with power of discrimination and individual interpretation. His treatment is broad, free and simple." While no portraits were included in the show, the critical note stated that "his portraits partake of these [same] qualities, placing his work with the best of the school."

In 1908 the first of a series of annual exhibitions of the work of Indiana artists was held at the John Herron Art Institute, giving the resident men and women an opportunity each year to compete for spaces on the gallery walls and for prizes. Steele was well represented in all of them, except two, until the year of his death.

The last time he apparently submitted work to any of the large eastern shows was in 1906 when his canvas "In the Valley" was shown at the 101st Annual of the Pennsylvania Academy. Then in 1910 Steele was represented in the Buenos Aires, Argentina, International Exhibition of Fine Arts, along with Adams and Forsyth, the latter being awarded a bronze medal. Steele's entry was his canvas "In the Valley." And then in 1915 he was represented by three paintings at the Panama-Pacific Exposition in San Francisco, for which event he also served as a juror. The Steele canvases there were: "The Hill Country," "November Afternoon," and "The Poplars."

To enumerate all of the other exhibitions in Indianapolis and elsewhere in which his canvases were shown would be tedious. The major ones include a retrospective showing of his work at the John Herron Art Institute in 1910, another one-man show there in 1920, and the Memorial Exhibition in 1926.

In 1925, a year before his death, his friend William Henry Fox, director of the Brooklyn Museum, arranged an important show titled "Paintings in Oil by American and European Artists," in which fourteen Indiana painters, including Steele, of course, showed their work. Steele's acquaintance with Fox went back about twenty years when the latter was director of the Herron Art Institute.

In view of the quality of his work and the high regard in which it is held, it seems surprising that Steele was not awarded more prizes in the various exhibitions. However, this was not so much due to lack of appreciation as to the fact that the majority of the shows were invitational and awards were not made. This was the case with the annual exhibitions sponsored by the Art Association of Indianapolis, beginning in 1883; and it also applies to the Society of Western Artists shows from 1897 to 1914, with the exception of the Fine Arts Building Prize, awarded when the show was in Chicago—the prize which Steele won in 1909, as mentioned before. Reference should be made, however, to the Mary R. T. Foulke prize of $50.00 which was awarded to Steele in 1906 for "The Cloud," judged to be the "most meritorious" painting by an Indiana artist in this annual show of the Richmond (Indiana) Art Association.

In none of the Indiana artists' exhibitions held at the Herron Art Institute after 1908 did he win a prize, probably because he served on the juries annually until 1922, with the exception of two years. The Hoosier Salon competitions, with their long lists of prizes, were not inaugurated in Chicago until 1925, and Steele won the $200 Mrs. Edward Rector Prize in the second exhibit—the year he died.

The Work

Perhaps what he regarded as the highest honor bestowed on him was his election to the National Academy of Design, as an Associate Member, in 1913, to which was added the pleasure of having his portrait painted for the Academy by his friend and former Munich comrade Frank H. Tompkins (Fig. 66). There were also the honorary degrees—the Master of Arts awarded by Wabash College in 1900 and the Doctor of Laws conferred in 1916 by Indiana University.

Another important facet of Steele's career after returning to Indianapolis from Bavaria was teaching. No art school was in operation in Indianapolis at the time, the one established by the Art Association in 1884 having survived only a year. Sue M. Ketcham, who, with Charles M. McDonald, had taught in it, teamed up with Steele soon after the latter was settled in his new home and they started a new school in the old Plymouth Church, where the previous one had expired. This was late in September, 1885, according to the Indianapolis *News*, whose reporter commented that "prospects for a good school are encouraging." Evidently the venture was reasonably successful because it kept its doors open for several years. Miss Ketcham soon gave up her part in the operation and teaching, however, in order to devote all her time to painting and to organizing sketch and travel parties in various parts of America and Europe. In 1889 Steele opened the third art school, and after Forsyth returned from Munich he joined with Steele, though the latter continued as director of the school until 1891, when it came under the management of the Art Association as the Indiana School of Art, the third to bear that name. Classes were held on the top floor of the remodeled Beecher church, as it was popularly called, or Circle Hall, on the northwest segment of the Circle at Market Street. Steele and Forsyth were the regular instructors in painting and drawing and Mary Y. Robinson taught the children's classes. Clarence Forsyth had his music school on the floor below and the combined enterprise was known as the Metropolitan School of Music and Art.

To what extent Steele enjoyed teaching and operating an art school we do not know. He was doubtless a good and sympathetic instructor and mentor, but being so absorbed in his own work, he must have found the routine rather taxing. It should be pointed out, too, that during the first years after his return from Munich he was under great strain to pay off his debt to the men who advanced money for his foreign training. This he did either with portraits or landscapes. He was also under pressure to keep producing canvases for exhibitions and possible sale. He had a family to support and his only

193

source of income, except for what came in from art classes, was the sale of his paintings.

It would be of interest to us to know what he did in each case to satisfy his backers and pay off his debts. But no records exist. There is evidence enough, however, to lead to the conclusion that most of the men had their portraits, or those of a family member, painted; and in the cases of those persons who subscribed a second time, a landscape as well as a portrait apparently cancelled the obligation. According to notes written by Brandt Steele, his father painted in all twenty portraits in settlement of these debts.

His greatest indebtedness, morally, was to Herman Lieber, because of the latter's ceaseless efforts on the artist's behalf. Steele's portrait of him is one of the most successful of the artist's canvases, executed with restrained skill and strongly suggesting the warmth and sympathy that prevailed between painter and model (Fig. 17). According to the Indianapolis *Journal* that appeared on January 19, 1887, the portrait of Herman Lieber was just completed and had been placed on an easel at the Lieber gallery and shown to friends. "It is almost a full length, Mr. Lieber being presented seated in an easy and natural position . . . a copy of the Indianapolis Journal is open upon one knee. It is fine in drawing, color, atmosphere and all accessories . . . an admirable likeness." Steele painted a companion portrait of Lieber's wife, Marie Metzger Lieber, in 1889.

As there is not much information available today about the prices Steele asked for his paintings, it is of interest to learn in the same issue of the *Journal* that his canvas "On the Muscatatuck" was purchased by the Boston Art Club for five hundred dollars. This caused the reporter to remark: "Significant compliment to a western painter." This amount was much higher than the price tag on his average landscape but close to what he got for his commissioned portraits.

His sitters over the years included many of the best-known men and women in the state. Among them were Benjamin Harrison (Fig. 33) whom he painted twice and in different poses; five governors of Indiana: Albert G. Porter, Isaac P. Gray, Claude Matthews, Alvin P. Hovey (Fig. 20), and Ira J. Chase; and at least four college presidents: Joseph Swain, David Starr Jordan, William Lowe Bryan (Fig. 43), and W. W. Parsons—as well as a number of professors including Elisha Ballantine, James D. Maxwell, Elijah Fowler, John Lyle Campbell, and Simeon Smith.

Other notable persons whom he painted were James Whitcomb Riley,

Albert J. Beveridge, Thomas A. Hendricks, Charles W. Fairbanks, W. H. H. Miller, Isaac Elston, Dr. Nathaniel A. Hyde (Fig. 29), Dr. William N. Wishard, Col. Eli Lilly (Fig. 30), Catharine Merrill (Plate V), May Wright Sewall, John H. Holliday, Harry S. New, William W. Butler, and James E. Roberts.

In referring to different subjects painted by Steele—landscapes and portraits—mention should be made of a third category; namely, still-life compositions. In his later years particularly the artist evidently found pleasure and relaxation in making flower studies, and his fondness for flowers instilled into his depiction of them a special character. Whatever the species and whatever the compositional schemes, the resultant pictures had strength and conviction. Steele probably knew a great deal about flowers and plants but he did not assume the role of botanist when he painted them. He worked for striking effects and handsome color schemes rather than detailed description (Fig. 54).

Perhaps the most interesting aspect of Steele's work from the standpoint of the art historian is the evolution of his artistic vision and painting technique upon his return to America. The most obvious change that took place was the abandoning of the Munich manner for the French plein-air approach. In other words, the substitution of a lighter, more colorful palette for a brown, almost monochrome one.

That this change did not happen immediately after his arrival in Indianapolis is seen in one of his first important landscapes painted here in the fall of 1885; namely, "Pleasant Run" (Plate I). Like his Bavarian study, "Late Afternoon, Dachau Moor" (Fig. 15), which was probably painted in the late winter or early spring of the same year, it is basically a picture in browns, mostly burnt umber, with muted greens and only occasionally accents of other hues. The tonal values in both pictures are low-keyed, which suggest a tranquil, almost melancholy mood. Both give the impression of having been painted in studios rather than in outdoor light.

But it was not long before Steele began to shake off the bitumen habit— that is, the use of coal tar oils and brown pigments—and to introduce purer hues into his pictures in an attempt to capture the truer effects of light and color. Following the example of some of the French impressionists, he also worked toward a looser technique and a spottier application of color.

While still living in Munich, Steele and the other students had many opportunities to see French impressionist paintings in exhibitions there. Also, he doubtless read about the new plein-air theories in the then current magazines. And there is reason to believe that these theories, as well as their application in specific paintings, were topics of discussion among the artists.

It has been said that when Steele returned here he was surprised to see that there was far more color in nature than he had seen in Bavaria. One might reasonably wonder if this were not largely a matter of seeing with "new eyes." Certainly the more he saw of the work of Monet, Pissarro, and Sisley the more attuned were his mind and eyes to subtleties of color and atmospheric effects.

Soon after 1885 he began to abandon the dark underpainting or brown foundation upon which other colors were applied, and he put his colors directly on the canvas in lighter touches, and not infrequently—particularly in later years—with a palette knife. The first of his pictures to show the sharpest break with Munich's tradition was "Bloom of the Grape," painted in 1893 (Plate IV). It is a painting of atmosphere. In fact the title confirms this. The subtle colors, brought about by the enveloping, rather misty fall air, gives the whole scene a purplish cast that resembles the bloom on a grape.

At one time Steele wrote an essay on the trend of modern art, which not only confirmed the fact that he was becoming involved in the new impressionistic methods in his outdoor scenes, but showed that he had a sound comprehension of the theories. It is too long to transcribe here, but a few sentences may suffice to illustrate these points:

Another characteristic of the impressionists is found in their use of color. A greater sensitiveness to the violet tones and to the vibrations of color with its complementaries, is common in its followers, while the habit of painting in a mosaic, or patches of pure color, is practiced by many, though not by all. . . .

Whether grave defects can be found in the philosophy of impressionism or not, it must be conceded that by shifting the point of view from the detail to the general effect, from the actual things represented to their envelope of light and atmosphere, a new store of beauty has been opened to humanity and one almost unexplored before. . . .

The danger that is to be feared from impressionisms, lies in a possible lack of structural qualities, and the substitution of mere sensation for poetic and spiritual significance.

The first, which is technical, is to be corrected by a more thorough training in drawing, and the second by a better culture of the mind and heart of the artist. A full mind and a heart vibrating with the eternal harmony, will be more than a human camera.

Farther along in his essay he goes beyond an analysis of impressionism and enters the realm of the abstract—"pictures may be composed in which there will be neither subject nor form," meaning, in this case, the form of natural objects, not artistic or technical form. He went on to say:

It would not at present be a popular art, but I appeal to your own experience if you have not found many a great picture whose sole claim to distinction was the possession of just such a charm, for you went away from its presence and subject and form were quickly forgotten, but there lingered like a delicate perfume, the haunting memory of its color. The query is, would it not have been as great a work of art if the form and subject had never been painted, if the artist's work had been confined to that which interested him and interests you, the quality of its tone, the music of its color? Would it not be but carrying the impressionists' doctrine one step further and the further elimination of elements not necessary to the impression?

There is no evidence that Steele experimented with abstract or nonobjective painting, but he was not adverse to the idea.

Actually he never became a true impressionist, in the strict sense of the word, unless one can say that some of the canvases he painted late in life embody most of the tenets—forms dissolving in atmosphere, hues that are thought of in terms of the spectrum, pigment applied to canvas in daubs or interrupted strokes—and all done out-of-doors (Figs. 62 and 65). In short, the painting of light. None of the portraits he did can be classed as impressionistic in treatment.

Some writers and critics in the past have stressed the painter's poetic approach to his work. This is a valid observation. But poetic vision is a relative matter, and the degree that it is transfixed through subject matter or colors to canvas depends upon one's yardstick. While Steele was a poet at heart—and nowhere is it better revealed than in his prose writings—he was at the same time a painter of actuality, but one with fine sensitivity and a desire to make pictorial statements express something of his deeper feelings about his environment.

With the completion of his new home in Brown County in 1907 (it is not entirely correct to use the word "completion" here, because the residence underwent many changes, and it was several years before the large studio was built), and his marriage to Selma Neubacher in August of that year, the last and perhaps the best-known period of Steele's life began. It spanned his last nineteen years, years that were, by and large, very happy ones.

Summers only were spent there until the residence was made suitable for year-round living. When winter came they moved back to Indianapolis and he would begin painting in a studio in one of the office buildings in the downtown area. In 1922, after having been made honorary professor of paint-

197

ing at Indiana University, he and his wife spent winters in Bloomington, and many of the canvases painted during the last three or four years of his life were done there (Figs. 62, 63, and 64).

Not much more can be said about the character or quality of Steele's Brown County work beyond what has been said before. His style of painting did not change radically, although there was a tendency on his part to get lighter and more ethereal effects, as observed above. At times he seems to have wavered between firmly and rather tightly painted canvases and broadly brushed-in composition, using a palette knife to apply the paint as often as he used a brush (Plate VII).

The surprising thing about his Brown County canvases is their variety of subjects, or more correctly, their variety of compositions (Figs. 44–61). One would naturally expect this variety in his work between 1885 and 1907 because he visited so many places. But there is certainly a limitation of pictorial material in Brown County, however scenic it might appear to the average visitor.

Generally speaking his late pictures do not include people or animals, suggesting that Steele was striving toward the making of "pure" landscapes. He must have felt that the elimination of anything that bordered on the anecdotal would allow the technical elements to stand out stronger, elements which he termed the quality of a picture's tone, the music of its color. The introduction of people or animals into his compositions as points of interest seems to have almost ceased after 1914 (Figs. 49–50).

Returning to Indianapolis in winter must have given Steele a great deal of pleasure. However delightful the Brown County home was, it was isolated and he and his wife were alone most of the time. The hustle and bustle of the city, the art activities and exhibitions, could not help but be stimulating. He even changed his routine of painting landscapes by trying street scenes once in a while.

From the fourth floor of the Circle Building, where he had his studio for a few years, he could look down on the Soldiers' and Sailors' Monument and Christ Church in all kinds of weather, and he found the architectural forms and street traffic sufficiently fascinating to paint the subjects several times (Plate VIII and Fig. 56).

While he made a few compositions based on city views, he probably spent most of the time in his studio bringing to satisfactory completion many unfinished canvases, having some of them framed, preparing pictures for exhibi-

PLATE IX

House of the Singing Winds, 1922, 30 by 46 ins.
Private Collection

tions, and visiting with fellow artists, friends, and clients. It is easy to imagine that T. C. Steele's room in the Circle Building became, each winter, the favorite meeting place of the local Bohemians and their comrades. In fact, the Indianapolis *Star* reported on December 20, 1919: "It is a pleasure to Mr. Steele's many friends to know that he has returned to the city in greatly improved health—a fact testified by the freshness and vigor of his work. He is not planning for much painting while in the city but he will be at home to visitors each day in the studio, a plan offering a pleasant opportunity in the way of an all winter exhibition."

As mentioned above, beginning with 1922 Theodore and Selma Steele spent their winters in Bloomington. He was asked by President William Lowe Bryan to paint and work on the University campus to help advance the appreciation of art, and give the students an opportunity to see a professional painter at work. A studio was provided on the third floor of the library building, which was kept open to students at certain hours. He was not expected to give any instruction in art, but on occasion he gave informal art talks.

A professor of English on the Indiana University faculty, F. C. Senour, believing that many students would be happier if they knew something about how to look at pictures, wrote a series of what-to-do articles for the *Daily Student.* These were later published in a small pamphlet, with an introduction by President Bryan, which began with the sentence, "I believe that we need beauty as much as we need truth."

To what extent the guidebook stimulated the interest of the students in what painter Steele was doing we cannot say, but the author's chatty style probably made the young people less embarrassed when they met him and less reluctant to approach him to enter his studio. For instance, under the heading "What Not To Do" the following suggestion is made: "If you visit the studio do not go with a paralyzing reverence nor with a flippant nonchalance. If looking at pictures is a new behavior, do not trust too much to the judgment with which you buy clothes or sell eggs. Admit you have something to learn and then put yourself in the way of learning."

Prior to this advice he told why Steele was there: "Now the plain fact is that Mr. Steele is not here to teach, or to lecture, except by the grace of good nature, but is here to bring a benefit to us all by merely being present and practicing his art where we can see it."

Other chapter titles in the booklet are "A Typical Picture," "The Studio," "Lines," "Mass," "Texture," "Composition," "Color," and so forth.

Steele continued as honorary professor at Indiana University until his death in 1926.

What is our evaluation of Steele's canvases today? Some will appraise them more highly than others. Some will regard his attempts at poetical interpretation overly sentimental. Others will find the landscapes something of a spiritual refuge from a rather hectic world.

Putting it negatively, it appears from our point of observation that there is very little about his work that is commonplace or trite. His painting is strong without being coarse, sensitive without being sentimental. And certainly, no other Indiana artist has left behind so rich and varied a group of canvases for the pleasure of his fellow men.

INDEX

INDEX

Adams, Henry C., 22.
Adams, J. Ottis, 38, 40, 42, 44, 45, 111n, 134, 184, 188; sketch of, 65n; studies in Munich, 16, 25; buys Hermitage, 46, 65, 189.
Adams, Wayman, 159.
Adams, Winifred Brady (Mrs. J. Ottis), 65n.
Albright, Adam Emory, 131.
Alexander, John White, 144.
Armstrong, Mary (c. 1715–1792), 4.
Art Association of Indianapolis, organized, 33, 184–85; buys Tinker house, 50; builds museum, 51–52, 184; exhibitions, 35, 40, 183–84, 185. *See also* John Herron Art Institute.
Atlanta (Ga.), 42.
Ayres, L. S., 44.

Ballantine, Elisha, 152n, 194.
Bates, Dewey, 14.
Battle Creek (Mich.), 8–10, 176–77.
Baumann, Gustave, 67, 139.
Baus, Simon P., 154n, 156, 159.
Belmont (Ind.), 61, 63.
Benczur, Gyula (Julius), 17, 181.
Ben Greet, Sir Philip, 77.
Bergson, Henri, 145.
Beveridge, Albert J., 150, 195.
"Bloom of the Grape," 40, 50, 187, 188, 196, Plate IV.
Bloomington (Ind.), 61.
"The Boatman," 28, 30–31, 35, 39, 183, 188, Fig. 10.
Boston (Mass.), 143–44.
Boston Art Club, 36, 143, 194.
Bracken Hill, 64.
Bratten, Miss –, 12.
Brayton, Dr. Alembert, 83–84n, 118, 139.
Brooklyn (N. Y.) Museum, 192.
Brooks, Alfred Mansfield, 73–74, 160–61; on Steele's murals for City Hospital, 146–47n; on Indiana University exhi-bition, 150–51; on House of the Singing Winds, 159.
Brookville (Ind.), 46, 51, 189.
Brown, Charles F., 185.
Brown County, roads, 61–62, 63–64, 114–15, 159; backwardness of, 70, 98–100, 100–1, 103, 119–20; attracts artists, 131; exhibitions of Steele paintings from, 106, 110–11, 130 ff.; estimate of Steele canvases done in, 197–98. *See also* House of the Singing Winds.
Brush, John T., 15.
Bryan, William Lowe, president of Indiana University, 68n, 139, 151–52, 160, 199; portrait, 68, 71–79 *passim*, 194, Fig. 43.
Buehr, Karl Albert, 147.
Buenos Aires, International Exhibition, 138, 192.
Butler, John M., 22.
Butler, William W., 46, 195.

California, 50–51, 189.
Campbell, John Lyle, 194.
Carnegie Galleries, Pittsburgh, 188.
Carter, Frank H., 15n.
Central Art Association, 40, 185.
Chase, Ira J., 149, 194.
Chase, William, 16, 20, 28, 41, 65n, 181, 190.
Chicago (Ill.), 8, 44, 176, 185; Art Institute, 40, 43, 142, 147; World's Columbian Exposition, 39, 109, 186, 188.
Chicago Society of Artists, 188.
Christ Church, Indianapolis, 156, 198, Plate VIII.
Churchman, Francis M., 15, 22, 26.
Cincinnati (Ohio), 8, 44, 147, 176; Art Museum, 41, 188.
Cleveland (Ohio), 44.
Coffin, Charles E., 22.
Coffin family, 36.

203